INVENTIONS

INVENTIONS

*Writing, Textuality, and Understanding
in Literary History*

GERALD L. BRUNS

YALE UNIVERSITY PRESS   NEW HAVEN AND LONDON

Published with assistance from the Louis Stern Memorial Fund.

Designed by Nancy Ovedovitz and set in ITC Garamond type by P & M Typesetters.
Printed in the United States of America by Halliday Lithograph, West Hanover, Mass.

Library of Congress Cataloging in Publication Data
Bruns, Gerald L.
  Inventions.

  Includes index.
  1. Hermeneutics.   I. Title.
PN81.B78   801′.95   82-1992
ISBN 0-300-02786-9   AACR2

10   9   8   7   6   5   4   3   2   1

For Hans-Georg Gadamer

CONTENTS

PREFACE

I began this book in 1975, with time—and the chance to think twice—provided by a Guggenheim fellowship. It isn't the book I thought I was going to write. In the fall of 1975 I published an essay on "The Formal Nature of Victorian Thinking," which I had written as a pilot study for a larger work that would try to understand the Victorians, not by studying what they said, but by explaining how their minds worked. This seemed to me at the time the normal way for the study of a literary period to proceed. I could even appeal to powerful philosophical authority (Ernst Cassirer) for the distinction between the diverse products of mental life and the formal, unifying activities of the spirit that make such life intelligible in spite of its bewildering heterogeneity. To understand the Victorians on this model would have been to describe various features of this formal intelligibility of Victorian consciousness, and then, on the basis of this description, to sort out the ideas and attitudes, projects and illusions, secret fears and desires that make up the content of Victorian writing.

Even after I had begun reading Foucault rather than Cassirer—indeed, all the more so because of Foucault—it seemed to me that my project was a good idea. This perhaps helps to explain why my inclination now is to fault my project for the same reason I would fault most of what goes on in literary study today, particularly in that branch of it (literary theory) that has attracted the most talented people in the profession. Most of the major theoretical movements in recent literary study—structuralist analysis, semiotics, deconstruction, varieties of readerly analysis, Marxist analyses, not to mention archeologies of discourse—seem to me to rest upon a common procedure: in order to define their topics of study they must first characterize them as epistemological problems. Thus, local causes and intentions notwithstanding, the motive of each of these movements becomes (again) the desire to describe how the mind works—how it functions or operates, and also why it does not always, and perhaps does not ever, do what we think it does. My poor project of several years ago was only a naive schoolroom version of what is now carried on with astonishing methodological power: but the point remains that to understand anything is said to be to understand what goes on—what *really* goes on—when the mind is working. The horizon of study is defined repeatedly by whatever pertains to mental functioning, and this holds true whether one desires to uphold the norms of objectivity and plain sense or whether one wants to call these norms into question.

Of course, the movements that I have just listed are mainly variations on what has been called (by Paul Ricoeur, for example) the "hermeneutics of suspicion." What appears to go on, whether in a mind or in any of its cognates (a text, language, society, and so on), is taken to be a problematic that needs to be penetrated by analysis in order to lay bare the structures or dynamic principles, the forces or illusions, the ideologies or systematic dispositions of desire that form the content of what *really* goes on. In certain advanced forms of this hermeneutics we arrive at an epistemological skepticism where it is said to be impossible to decide whether anything really goes on in any sort of mental process or activity—the making of statements, for example, or the reading of a text. My guess is that skepticism of this sort is the final outcome (perhaps only a major outcome) of the traditional Cartesian need to know how knowledge is possible—or, much to the same point, how art or poetry or any sort of discourse is possible: in short, how human productivity as such is possible. The authorizing assumption in every case is that conditions of possibility (or, as it may be, impossibility) are mental, and that they can be uncovered by analyses of this or that activity, structure, process, or systematic assembly of constraints. Hence the proliferation of theories of consciousness, language, grammar, meaning, power, ideology, desire, and so on, including the various critical and ironical modes of reflecting on these theories in turn. Curiosity and the hope of certainty may have given way to suspicion and the Heisenberg principle, but the mind remains the metaphysical centrum of our concerns.

For example, people are now passionate concerning the subject of reading, and they have become very good at constructing models of the reading process that will enable one to say (more or less once for all) what goes on in the mind of the reader, or between mind and text, or between the mind of one reader and other minds as in a vast structure of intersubjective response. That people respond differently on different occasions and for different reasons still seems to many a defect that requires to be corrected by recourse to logic, method, or vigorous polemic; or, conversely, others suspect that all acts of reading are already regulated in some secret way, such that differences of response are illusory, or easy to efface by interested parties. Even those who plead for openness, or who wish to overcome the habit of dividing reading into normal and abnormal varieties, remain bound to the idea of a working mind authorized by a method—freeplay, for example, which is a sort of irregular regulation of reading designed to confound what passes as reasonable or familiar. This mind may be structured as a system rather than as a self—it may be more subjected than subjective—but it remains the center of interest all the same.

Suppose, however, that you were to characterize reading—or, better, interpretation—not as any sort of mental act but as a social practice? Suppose that you were to say that understanding is not something that goes on in anyone's mind—it is not a mode of consciousness, nor a product of unconscious manipulations—but is rather something that goes on in certain situations? Obviously, one has to be conscious in order to interpret anything, and without much doubt understanding can be shown to be problematical on any number of counts, but the question here is not what interpretation or understanding is as such but what happens when you characterize it in a certain way. The point is that the way you characterize a given phenomenon determines the way in which you will go on to study it. If, for example, you characterize interpretation as a mental act, you will be constrained to practice a form of epistemology, whether by constructing a theory of interpretation on the model of a theory of knowledge (thus to describe the *logic* of interpretation), or by practicing epistemological skepticism (thus to argue that interpretation is always *alogical*). If, however, you characterize interpretation as something that goes on in the world—that is, something that human beings regularly do under a variety of complicated circumstances and to accomplish certain things that need to get done—then you will be constrained to study the *history* of such goings-on. Interpretation will thus make its appearance, not as a mental process, but as a traditional practice that can be studied as one would study, say, a social custom. A custom, of course, can be described formally and analytically (and even suspiciously) as the product of a certain grammar of behavior; but it is also possible to regard a custom as something that occurs in particular human situations, that is, something that requires to be learned and practiced in order to have any reality at all—something that belongs to the historical and contingent domain of practical knowledge. A semiotics of custom would be indispensable to the understanding of custom as such; it happens, however, that no custom ever makes its appearance as such, that is, no custom ever emerges as an idea but only as a practice—something governed not by an inner logic but by prevailing cultural norms.

My concern, in other words, is not with what interpretation is but with the ways in which it makes its appearance and, therefore, with the ways in which it is to be studied. Obviously it makes a good bit of difference whether one studies allegorical interpretation, for example, as a mental act or as a social practice. As a mental act (which is roughly how we have been regarding it since the Enlightenment) allegorical interpretation seems like a logical aberration—a way of reading one's own thoughts into another's mind, or a way of obliterating an original intention or intrinsic meaning. As a social practice, however, allegory was in the ancient world a normal way of taking non-philosophical texts philosophically, or of normalizing them according to current philosophical teachings. For Philo of Alexandria, the allegorizing of the Law was not an aberration of reason but an achievement of it, a way of bringing the Law into the open or of making it philosophically plain, as when he recognized in the Cain and Abel story the universal opposition between two principles, self-love and the love of God. (He also read it as the story of the antagonism between rhetoric and philosophy!) One could say that, from Philo's standpoint, allegorical interpretation is consistent with a Platonistic epistemology of memory and recognition, not with an epistemology of subjects and objects and methods for verifying their correspondence. Epistemology, however, is not at issue—except to the extent that the conflict of these two epistemologies stands in the way of our understanding of Philo's hermeneutical practices. Our natural inclination is to resolve this conflict in our favor and against Philo, that is, in favor of one sort of interpretation (objectivist) as against another (allegorical). My own view, however, is that the difference between the objective and the allegorical is social rather than mental: it is a conflict between two traditions of understanding, one modern and one ancient. It is not a conflict between the logical and the illogical, or between knowledge and edification, but between two customary ways of talking about what is written, one familiar to us and one strange—but both equally rational, because norms of rationality are social: they are rooted in ways of life rather than in processes of knowledge. From this point of view, the conflict of interpretations does not exist for us to resolve; rather, we should adopt a historical attitude toward it and attempt to understand its meaning, or its emergence within the history of interpretation.

For me, the history of interpretation is the history of writing, textuality, and understanding, which I take to be practices that make their appearance within traditions, not mental acts or constructions to be analyzed according to timeless models. On this view, the history of interpretation is not reducible to the story of various normal and abnormal relationships between authors and readers, nor can one map onto it the model of subjects and objects, reading minds and readable (or not-so-readable) texts, analytical attitudes vying with superstitions for the possession of intelligible forms. I think that such a model would only serve to produce a picture of the history of interpretation as a history of error, or the history of mental failure or the failure of knowledge, or the history of delusion and the tyranny of fictions. Such a picture is, I think, what most people have when they say they have a sense of history, and it confirms for them the difference between traditional and enlightened mentalities, or between credulity and suspicion, or between them and us. It is no wonder that the history of interpretation is almost never studied: to do so could only be an exercise in nostalgia, or a sort of anthropology, or simply so much historical research—backgrounding against which we can showcase our more immediate and crucial concerns.

The book that follows, however, is not a history of interpretation. This history cannot be written; it can only be studied. It is too vast for any one scholar to comprehend it—it can never be turned into an object of knowledge—and anyhow we are all a part of it, which is no doubt why it seems such a strange subject. At all events this is why my own way of study (which I characterize in the introduction) is rhetorical rather than analytical, topical rather than comprehensive, speculative rather than descriptive. The important thing to be said about the book is that it is about the historicity of its topics. It does not propose theories about these things—does not propose to turn them into concepts—but seeks to study them (with all respect to the limits of invention) under the conditions of their occurrence. The assumption of such an undertaking is that to know what textuality is, for example, is just to know its history; it is not to have an idea of textuality, still less is it to have a method for reading and analyzing texts in order to find out how they are made and how they work and what other sorts of texts have gone into them. The question of how one knows the history of anything, or how one knows that one can know such a thing, seems to me needless and uninteresting. For me, it is enough to get on with it by saying that the practice of literary study seems to enable people to find things to say about the history of such things as writing, textuality, and understanding. Anyhow the practice of it has enabled me to get this book written. If you asked me how I did it, I wouldn't be able to say.

A more interesting speculation is that to know the history of anything is to know the truth of it, since it is only in its history that the truth of anything begins to emerge. It is admittedly strange to speak of knowing the truth of anything—truth is not often a subject that comes up in literary study, unless as an object of suspicion. For us truth is simply the utopian state of being certain that we aren't deceived. I once knew a physicist who glimpsed this truth from across a muddy pond, into which he disappeared. Yet knowing the truth is not impossible, even though it is true that such knowledge can never be objective, that is, it can never be the analytically rigorous possession of objects, because history always withholds from us great portions of what it is that we seek to know, principally by allowing us to know a thing only in its versions. As Heidegger says, the truth of anything occurs only in the midst of something else. These versions that we know are not representations of anything hidden behind or beneath history, or at history's end. They are just whatever makes its appearance in time, which is all, I believe, that anything ever does. For this speculation I am indebted to the beautiful man to whom this book is dedicated.

Portions of the book, in versions now revised, have appeared in the *Iowa Review, New Literary History, Renascence, Comparative Literature,* and *Boundary 2.* I am grateful to the editors of these journals for permission to use this material. I am particularly thankful to David Hamilton, editor of the *Iowa Review,* for knowing exactly what needed to be written, and for showing me how to do it. My debt to Donald G. Marshall, who arranged for Hans-Georg Gadamer's seminar and lectures at Iowa, is absolutely unpayable. The counsel of my road companions, David Morris and Marvin Bell, enabled me to work my way out of many bad ideas. A good deal of this book originated in courses that I have taught over the last several years with Oliver Steele and Jay Holstein, who will observe in many places that I still have not got things right. As always, Sherman Paul showed me his wisdom and kindness, while James Kincaid brought me to my knees with his objections and ridicule, thus helping to prolong needlessly the writing of this book. My special indebtedness is to the Morrells and the Kelleys. The Graduate School of the University of Iowa provided funds to help defray the cost of making a copy of the typescript. The John Simon Guggenheim Foundation gave me a fellowship at exactly the right time.

Introduction:
Criticism as Invention

In this book I want to give an example of a criticism that has no greater ambition than to discover what can be said in any given case. Such a criticism may be called rhetorical, because it is more concerned with finding than with proving, is more speculative than analytical, more heuristic than polemical, the more so as it requires a discourse that proceeds thoughtfully, even copiously, but not necessarily with great method or system. Indeed, one could say that from a rhetorical point of view method in criticism is what we take recourse to when our learning fails us: it is an alternative to invention. Method tries to reduce rather than to amplify, for it wants always to determine what *cannot* be said in this or that case, and so by closure or the natural exclusiveness of its design it forbids all statements but those it can account for. As Descartes knew, method is a good way to reduce one's inventory of unnecessary ideas. My opinion is that most literary criticism is rhetorical, but it has got deep philosophical desires. Regularly you will hear a critic ask, "What is the meaning of this text?" Often he will ask it with a philosophical wince or knowing smile to ornament the question with a show of suspicion. By contrast the mere rhetorician will ask, "What can we say about it?" The first question is, to be sure, the more serious one, but seriousness may be only a sign of single-mindedness. Most critics are fortunately single-minded chiefly in theory. The second question is plainly frivolous, for it appears to have no purpose or limits. Given a text (or a topic), there is almost nothing that cannot be said—within the limits of invention and decorum. We may (for the sake of emphasis) define invention in a rhetorical rather than Romantic way by saying that it is simply the art of finding things to say, and saying them, for whatever purpose. As for decorum: the saying of anything is always occasional, and occasions are disciplinary, for they are shadowed by various traditions of understanding and governed in turn by rubbery and half-heard rules that do not absolutely prevent you from saying whatever pops into your head but which ought not to be ignored in any imperious way—ought not to be ignored, for example, in front of an audience, which is normally so constituted as to expect you to speak to some matter at hand, and to some persuasive and substantial effect, as well as, if possible, delightfully. It is, of course, difficult to speak before an audience who wants its criticism in the form of methodological combat.

If it seems to you that there is something disreputable about such criticism as a rhetorician will practice, you are certainly right. It will appear to many that such criticism fails by desiring no results, only talk, when results are what we need, for they are the index of our proceedings and the assurance we are getting somewhere. But the rhetorician does not desire to get anywhere: this is a primary meaning of his disregard of method. He does not, for example, seek to solve problems. A problem, he will say, is only a manner of speaking, and it is one on which we have come to rely with more habit than passion; in fact, many can no longer think without it: very little else comes to mind. Is there anything in literary study that has not been called problematical? Certainly, not to have a fine ear for the problematical is to be, well, provincial, or at any rate complacent, which is a condition that rhetoric seems always to induce. The rhetorician seems never to be looking in the right direction when disillusionment occurs. He is a poor audience for philosophers, because he takes no alarm at the skepticism in which it is easy to implicate him. Is not skepticism, after all, the philosophical equivalent of a rhetorical habit of mind? The histories of philosophy insist on this point with greater piety than certainty—but no matter.

The philosopher is naturally defined by a position, the rhetorician by an occasion, which is why the rhetorician seems naturally evasive, and never more so than when it comes to asking, on whatever subject, "What is the nature of the case?" The desire to reduce things to their natures, or to remove their contingencies and local identities, is a philosophical desire, nor is anything more admirable than to yield to philosophy, thus perhaps to arrive at a conclusion or to render a judgment, as on the best textual evidence, or according to an undeceptious method. For the rhetorician, however, nothing textual is ever evidentiary, and nothing methodical is very eloquent. What is evidentiary and what is methodical are often alike in being censorious. Thus the rhetorician will always transform natures into topics and problems into meanings, not so much to assert the truth of things as, quite often, merely to know how things sound, or what it means to understand them. The rhetorician is a public meditator. Consider the old question of the poet's relation to the beautiful young man in Shakespeare's sonnets. From a rhetorical point of view you could not ask a worse question than, "What is the nature of this relationship?" Except when mad with single-mindedness most critics who ask this question learn very quickly to be rhetorical, for they quickly find themselves saying (in defiance of contradiction) that this relationship has many natures. It is, after all, a relationship, not an object, and therefore it is naturally susceptible to contradiction, or the multiplication of local identities: and so are we all, especially as we try to glimpse a human reality through the broken composition of a sonnet sequence. Thus the famous relationship appears to be equally erotic, aesthetic, virtuous, etc.—virtuous, no doubt, of necessity, nevertheless more passionate than rational, yet somehow platonic all the same, because nature has made a sexual relationship between two men impossible, or anyhow unnatural, but not inconceivable—nor, from a philosophical point of view, disadvantageous. My favorite commentary has it that the relationship is based on .a system of exchange that one recognizes from fairy tales: love me, the poet says, and I will immortalize you. What else but immortality does a common, middle-aged, and evidently impoverished poet have to offer the young courtier who has everything? Magically, the poet has the young man in his power (can render him eternally beautiful, etc.), and vice versa: he has his power only in and by virtue of the young man, whose beauty is the inspiration of eternalizing poetry—and so on, until invention wanes, as inevitably it must.

The end of rhetoric is to lend meaning to usage by indulging in it with an inconsistent regard for philosophy. Of course, a good rhetorician would never put it quite this way—would never openly antagonize a philosopher. He would speak complaisantly, thus perhaps to say that one function of literary criticism is to give meaning to the words we use when we talk about poetry or literature or writing of whatever sort. As we know from such things as the names of genres, this meaning is never very stable. From a philosophical point of view the instability of meaning makes one want to get rid of it altogether, put it down simply as one more illusion, but from a rhetorical point of view it is a situation that could hardly be improved upon, because it enables us to go on talking. Meanings in literary criticism (as in daily life) need to be replenished, not fixed. If words meant the same thing every time we used them, we would very shortly run out of things to say, not to mention reasons for saying them. We would be rich in certitude, but mute; we would know a true and almost heavenly complacence. But the motive of speech is the perpetual difficulty of making sense. Indeed, the plenum of discourse rests upon the impossibility of a philosophical language. It is always great good sport when philosophers hit upon this truth, and so turn to mathematics, or to poetry, sometimes even to rhetoric (rarely, alas, to silence)—only, of course, to begin dreaming again of propositions implacable in their rigor.

Somewhere someone is no doubt thinking advanced thoughts about a theory of criticism raised on the principle of an open and complaisant delight in the discovery of things to say, but for my part I hope it never happens. No one (I admit it) takes greater pleasure than I do in theories of criticism and the philosophical truculence they produce, nor can we have too many theories, and the more truculent they are the better; but a theory of the kind of criticism I have called rhetorical would be a vain expense of the spirit, especially since such a criticism would naturally hope to flourish—and would prevail in any case—outside or between the systematic constraints that normally hold the mind fast to theoretical positions or to linear and developing programs of thinking. To journey outside any sort of system is, of course, by turns dangerous and impossible, but it has always seemed to me that literary study remains virtuous in rough proportion as it is unassuming and unconfined. It is true that literary study without theory would lack romance, and some say it would lack nourishment, but the rhetorician is defined in part by his knowledge that theories eat as well as nourish, and one should have them or have at them but always leave a window or a door ajar. The world of literary study divides unevenly in two: there are those for whom a theoretical position is a mode of self-justification, the critical equivalent of the examined life, recourse against taste or tradition, and so on, whence criticism is capable of a discourse weighted with moral urgency and cultural interest; and then there are those who may admire this sort of thing or who may find it a bit too strenuously sublime, but who observe in either case a striking secondary phenomenon, that a theoretical position is not something one merely occupies but something that is liable to take possession of the mind of its occupant, simultaneously filling it with uncommon grandeur and emptying it of things to say. The rhetorician is full of contrasting (if somewhat adventitious) virtue: in an age when criticism is a regular agency of vanity and self-promotion, he pursues as a matter of course the separation of ego and idea. His major deceit, no doubt his major failing, is that he is never implicated in his words. Theories, he will say, are meant to be learned, not espoused; they are to be made part of one's inventory of understanding and to be consulted as the occasion demands. They are topics, not causes.

Criticism is an art of speaking to an occasion, as when one is called upon to address the meanings of words. Here is an example—nothing more than a schoolmasterly meditation on words: in this case two old and highly pleasurable words, *allegory* and *satire*. No doubt the first meaning of "theoretical" is to have a discourse on words such as these, but it will be clear directly that I am far from proposing a theory of allegory or satire or of the two together. I wish merely to reflect on certain of their commonplace or schoolroom meanings, and how these meanings behave (how they grow unstable, for example) when placed in various relations to one another. Their instability in relation to one another is manifest: one can only connect them by means of a third term—for example, *language,* or *figurative speech,* or the "veil of words." The way I wish to begin is by considering allegory and satire as figures for two different attitudes toward the veil of words, or for two different ways of evaluating it.

Allegory is the name of a figure whose emphasis is concealment, and so it is the preëminent figure of the veil of words, the more so when it becomes clear that concealment is not quite the right word for the kind of hiddenness that the veil achieves. We may figure allegory as the curtain that conceals (in order to be made radiant by) a sanctuary. The curtain mediates the light of what is hidden—*mediates,* because the light would blind us if we were able to look at it directly. Without the curtain we would be unable to see anything at all: it would be as if nothing were there. Allegory is an instance of darkening by means of words. It preserves us from annihilating vision, yet does not leave us so entirely in the dark that we cannot work things out on our own, adjacently or by means of interpretation. We cannot assimilate the light, only dissimulate it, or enlighten ourselves as to what is present by darkening it or turning it into a meaning (something we can understand).

No doubt this is what is meant when it is said that language makes things humanly accessible by turning them into names. An unnamed object would so transport or take possession of us that by comparison whatever is named would pale or grow abstract and seem no longer worth our attention. The named world would be obliterated by a world of outright objects. Language exists to protect us from what is unnamed. It protects us by seeming to contain on its own all that is, such that we can imagine nothing that is not named, which is why we exalt certain things or profess their sacredness by refusing to name them or by forbidding the utterance of their names, or by forbidding any utterance whatsoever in their presence. Nor is it exactly that what is transcendent is made immanent by language. Such immanence would be too humanly exacting, as in an incarnation or hierophany that would be its own sort of utterance, something quite unspeakable in its way or, more accurately, in ours, requiring from us something more faithful or desperate than words. For us, there is nothing anywhere else to be found except in language.

Yet so radiant is this veil of words that one is denied transcendence but not the pleasure of it. This is the pleasure of allegory and pleasure of a kind for the understanding, but a pleasure not easy to understand. As in the allegory of the theologians we are given to understand something but not to possess it as though it were simply an object of knowledge: what we are given to understand is that which recedes into a cloud of unknowing. Meaning is always a compensation for the inaccessible. Heaven is quite meaningless by virtue of its plenitude. No doubt it is the job of understanding to penetrate the veil of words and to disclose what is hidden, but in fact the understanding cannot accomplish this task quite in this way. He who understands something is usually less knowledgeable than resourceful: he is able to regard what is hidden by constructing a version of it or by construing a meaning of what is not evident—but throughout all his artfulness the veil remains intact. It could not be otherwise, for except the veil is present there is nothing to be construed. Hence the interpreter's reverence for concealment, for he knows that in this case concealment is not deceit or blank obscurity but an enabling condition, that which draws us near. He knows that to tear down or pull aside the veil is to remove at the same time any hope of understanding. Remove the hidden and you are left with a blank stare on your face. This is why for the allegorist language is a lustrous glass on which to paint one's figures: to darken the glass is to adorn it with figures that shape the light into signs we can understand. Imagine a world or a text that darkens and is radiant and you have allegory: a darkening radiance.

And for this short discourse on allegory the satirist is instinctively grateful, for it gives him just occasion (justification) to rise and be heard. At the word *transcendence* he reaches for his pen. By nature he would regard the term *darkening radiance* as a portentous deceit. Concealment is deception: it is as simple as that. Whatever is veiled can be sure to have ample designs and little substance: somewhere power is being put into play. Behind every veil of words there are only more words, frauds and donkeys, inanity, connivance, worms of consciousness. The satirist's transcendence is on his side of the veil, and in its light he has power to analyze and to judge. For him the veil is likely to be more radiant with odor than with light. The veil needs to be stripped away so that light and air may disperse what offends and confounds thee. Likewise figuration is distortion and error, more object than sign, or a sign from which the interest of meaning is turned aside, or a sign of a sign that points back at us in our own interest. We may confirm this opposition between satire and allegory by observing how they correspond to the two ways of remarking appearances. An appearance is that which does not stand comparison with reality, or that which may seem to be the case but, saving the appearances, can be given no countenance. And yet an appearance is also an event, as when a thing is said to make its appearance, or to appear as if by magic. (Curious how it is easier to say this of persons than of things.) To appear is to become present, to be there before us whereas before it was the theme of our imagining: an appearance in lieu of absence. The allegorist will claim that allegory is a certain way sacred things have of appearing, and some will acknowledge that dissimulating is the natural mode of every supernatural presence, including the Real Presence, which appears in an allegory of the Meal. (Divine wit always leaves us hesitating.) The difference between appearance and illusion always has to be worked out in words, which is why it is a difference more often accessible to testimony than to evidence or, as the satirist would say, more susceptible to ridicule than to proof. The satirist never hesitates. He is the agent of demystifying desire, scourge of appearances, connoisseur of absence, our Nietzsche and our perfect man.

Most critics write as if they had nothing to fear from the satirist, who is, after all, a figure of clear-headed sanity. Satire is Roman and therefore a civic or civilized or civilizing (if not always civil) mode of utterance. Yet is it so certain that the clear-headedness of satire puts us in touch with a superior reality or a finer array of values? What if such clear-headedness were a sort of intransitive or neutral clarity that reason might press into service but which is not intrinsically sane? No doubt this is a small and even perverse speculation. Surely it would be difficult to maintain (as part of a comprehensive theory, were such a thing possible) that satire is not intrinsically rational, or at least not intrinsically ethical or normative. Satire is famous in its instances of concerned discourse. Consider, for example, satire in relation to history: it appears to share with allegory (and, for that matter, with all poetry) a desire to be more philosophical than history. From a satirical point of view history is a deviation from the normative. To be in history is to be limited, contingent, earthly, fallen, duplicitous or divided or at odds with one's protests—and therefore deeply vulnerable to satire. Satire is the premier adversary of history, which it is always trying to correct, or which it deforms or reforms by subjecting it to ridicule and by purging it of its humorous inflections. Hence the schoolboy formula of ought/is by which satire is routinely defined: like allegory, satire depends for its authority upon a state of affairs to which history rarely attains. If we think of the veil of words as history and not simply as language, the veil is once more that which is to be transcended, but this time (that is, in the case of satire) by a moral rather than interpretive effort, or by an effort to see things not as they are (not as they are veiled) but as they (or we) are corrected, as when we are made aware of folly and deceit even when we can never hope to be innocent of them. If we are (being historical creatures) fallen, we can begin our redemption by our subjection to satire, which helps us to discover and measure our fallenness or our concupiscence. The aggressiveness of satire serves especially to make us feel our original or historical weakness as a kind of moral pain, an awakening in the middle of the night. It fills us with a brutally actual grace. It describes the warp of our virtue.

It is, however, never easy simply to confirm an orthodoxy. (Or, more accurately, it is never easy for the rhetorician simply to consider one side of any issue.) To speak concerning the virtue of satire intensifies the need to consider a contrary idea: namely, that satire is simply an empty form that can be filled by a variable content. In this case satire would not be intrinsically rational but would only be a certain way of speaking to be adopted by any ideology or whatever. The compelling question is thus whether satire can be trusted by its users, much less by its interpreters. What energies crisscross the emptiness of this form? One clue lies in the uncontrollable tendency of criticism to allegorize satirical texts, that is, to look beneath or in some fashion to get around the "characteristic" irony of satire in order to grasp satire's true or deeper concern. It is as though satire had to be disarmed in order to be understood. The victim of satire perhaps rarely understands what has happened to him. When reading satire one is always looking for a position to occupy (one is driven by satire to read it philosophically). Inevitably you will hear the critic say that satire moves us to laugh at ourselves, but not once has he been known to mean it. He will always read the text so as to be on the side of the satirist, that is, behind or on the right side of the veil of irony: somehow in the know—nestled among the laughing gods; and you will hear him complain from time to time that this or that satire fails because of its inscrutable or impenetrable irony. The terror of criticism is to be left in the dark as before an irradiant veil. Not to be privy to the irony of satire is to be made at once its victim. This may be one reason why scholars of the eighteenth century regularly adopt Augustan "views": they are not about to be outwitted by what they study. Satiric discourse compels us to allegorize as a basic recourse of self-defense. One has got to know what is going on behind the veil. What is therefore most interesting is that many satirical texts frustrate these allegorical impulses even as they incite them: the locus classicus in this regard is book 4 of *Gulliver's Travels*, on which it is supremely difficult to take a concerned stand, because the text maneuvers concern of every sort into position as a target (if your position is nameable, it's vulnerable). No one can confidently summarize the normative ground on which book 4 is written: I mean that no one can read book 4 without experiencing the sensation of vanishing positions, or of losing the guidance of a stable and homogeneous concern. There is always the sinking feeling that you may have missed the point. To get on the other side of irony is to get the feeling that someone is now staring at you from behind.

The textbooks try to tell you that the moral norms of satire are always accessible and usually clear, but this is not always what satire teaches, the more so because satire seems at times more quick to punish than to teach, more earnest to destroy than to correct. Here I would like to speculate that the true satirist is sometimes difficult to identify because he is not always a righteous character. Sometimes he doubles as minister and scourge, and the critic as Polonius is likely to get caught lurking in the dark: a classic case of being on the wrong side of the veil. If I were allowed (heuristically) to allegorize *Hamlet,* I would describe Hamlet as a satirist of complicated colors and stripes: he tries to be more philosophical than history, thus to moralize in order to correct, but he cannot help punishing history and, indeed, cannot help destroying it in the sense that he ends up killing what he meant only to ridicule or to expose. What I mean is that he is one sort of satirist in relation to Gertrude—"O Hamlet, speak no more:/Thou turn'st mine eyes into my very soul"—but quite another in relation to Polonius, whom he slays (in somewhat figurative fashion, mistaking the old man for another). Curious that the veiling of the old man is what leads to his skewering. Perhaps in this second case one could call Hamlet a repressed satirist whose deepest wish erupts into a true purgation, as it does more emphatically at the end when he rids the world of Claudius. Let me put this more boldly if I can: Hamlet satisfies (wittily yet unwittingly) the deepest wish of every satirist, which is not merely to correct but to kill, or to correct by killing. The Mousetrap, as Hamlet stages it, is a literary or figurative satire: it exposes villainy by holding a mirror up to an audience; it is satisfied by the mere catching of a conscience, while the villain slips away. But satire may also be real, as when the mirror is abandoned for the scourge, pen for the sword, and rapier wit yields to a true "envenom'd point."

More than one critic has satisfied himself that satire is a species of comedy, but it is also possible to imagine it as a species of tragedy as well, and it is equally possible to imagine it as generically unstable: something that is liable to break out at any moment, like an act of terrorism. In canto 32 of the *Inferno* (which Dante called the tragic portion of his *Comedy*) there is a truly appalling moment when Dante kicks one of the sinners in the head. No reader (no sane or civilized reader) can ever be quite prepared for this moment. The fellow (Bocca degli Abati) is frozen up to his neck in a river of ice—and Dante kicks him in the head! Dante tries to alleviate or confuse our horror by saying that he may or may not have kicked Bocca deliberately: it could have been an accident, he says, but then again it could have been willfully or fatefully done (*"se voler fu o destino, / non so"*).[1] Bocca, of course, knows very well that the kick was purposeful: he was fated to receive it: it was a new or improvised device of vengeance, at all events one torment the more. He understands the allegorical nature of the kick: nothing in hell (or in poetry) is without purpose, or without its deeper meaning, which in this case is the justice of divine abuse—and one of the major lessons Dante is required to learn on his journey. That is, he must unlearn human compassion, which in hell is a misplaced and blasphemous virtue. Better, in hell, to be vicious than to be kind: the absence of charity or mercy is what makes hell what it is: it is that which makes hell basically satirical. And we must in turn see hell for what it is, which is the point of Dante's kick. We must think no worse of Dante for kicking Bocca than of God for arranging a place for him. There is no thinking well or ill of either God or Dante. The kick is meaningless without its terrorism: we are meant to see Dante as minister and scourge, thereby to understand him—and to fear him. Nothing is more awful than the lucidity of God's justice.

This is a slippery point, to be sure. Knowing how to allegorize Dante's kick alleviates the horror of it. The general principle here is that allegory distances the terror of satire by generalizing its object, which is one reason why (as in Horace) it is satire's most conventional ally. Thus, for example, as Bocca personifies a certain economy of sin (the consequences of the treacherous life), so is he depersonified by the allegory in which he is figured. The allegory to which he lends the significance of his personal history robs him of that significance; it renders him sufficiently representative for us to acknowledge in heart as well as mind that Dante's kick is well meant and well placed. Perhaps not quite in heart as well as mind. It is often said that the effectiveness of satire is diminished in proportion as names are named—"Hold! for God's sake—you'll offend, / No names—be calm—learn prudence of a friend." That is, in proportion as satire becomes more historical than philosophical it becomes less obviously justifiable, more topical than principled, possibly malignant. Yet this idea has its opposite and inseparable point, which we may see in the meaning and value that Dante attaches to sheer literalness. Dante claimed for his allegory a theological authenticity, which is a large way of saying that he meant his poem to be read as one reads Scripture—allegorically, to be sure, but also with the understanding that the veil is not to be pushed aside: what is literally said possesses the truth of history. Bocca degli Abati enters Dante's poem bearing this truth in his name. And what is interesting is how this name serves as a pretext that is by turns satirical and allegorical. Bocca refuses to give his name when Dante asks for it, whence Dante tries to extract it by torture: in a rich amplification of abuse Dante pulls out tufts of Bocca's hair. The satirist punishes, the better to expose. Dante's intention is to turn Bocca's name against him by letting the world know how Bocca is numbered among the damned; it is to immortalize Bocca's earthly treachery. All poets immortal- ize, but the satirist is the progenitor of eternal infamy. Dante abuses Bocca, and also the memory of him, which henceforth is instinct with the idea of treason. Who now remembers Bocca degli Abati except by the sin for which God and Dante punish him? Or what is Bocca except a certain way of re- membering the issue of betrayal?

Of course, Bocca is more than any memory of him can sustain. Dante abuses a person, not an idea. To understand the meaning of this act we must know a little of its history and its mythology. Dante in canto 32 of the *Inferno* is a satirist in the line of Lucilius, father of Roman satire and the curse of his contemporaries—*"secuit Lucilius urbem, / te Lupe, te Muci, et genuinum fregit in illis"*:[2] Lucilius, father of Roman satire, whose progeny, however, enact a softening, or civilizing, whereby the satirist allegorizes his victims in order not to give pain. Lucilius is the authentic naming satirist. Even Juvenal, who lends his name to what is said to be satire of the fiercest kind—satire whose wit is drawn aside to disclose the desire for outrage— even Juvenal, though he speaks fiercely (*" 'cuius non audeo dicere no- men? / quid refert, dictis ignoscate Mucius an non?' "*), wants it understood that he is a moralist, not an abuser of persons.[3] This distinction lies at the heart of (and authorizes) civilized or literary or tolerable satire: allegorized satire as against renegade terrorism. Naming is a function granted to every poet, but not lightly to the satirist, whose naming remains too near the curse, the most feared of utterances: the word that kills. The satirist must be prevented from being too historical. To be named by a poet is to be brought back into being, brought to life or back to life as a poetic immortal (one with the gods). But to be named by a satirist is to be returned to the darkness, a figure featured in human memory as a creature of hell, whether the *Inferno's* Inferno or the *Dunciad's* Chaos and Old Night. Hence the fa- mous Roman law that allows the satirist to name only the dead: a law meant to civilize satire: a law by which Juvenal abides (still wary of the curse), and by which Dante abides as well, although with more attention to the letter than the spirit, since Bocca, dead to be sure when Dante wrote of him, had been Dante's contemporary, a treacherous Ghibelline and Dante's enemy. Juvenal named only the safely dead and already ignominious. Dante by his naming allegorizes historically as well as philosophically, ignominiously as well as sacredly, personifies ideas by recourse to the art of punishing ene- mies, and so mediates, as every poet should, between events and their meanings, between the veil of history and the truth we are given to understand.

Here is a good place to break off these reflections, for it is beyond my purpose or ability to get carried away by invention, which is often what happens, however, because invention is meditative rather than systematic: it proceeds topically rather than methodically, follows courses of learning rather than of logic, and thus it is apt simply to stop rather than to end. And this point bears upon the sort of relationships that obtain between such terms as *allegory* and *satire*. These are representative literary terms—indeed, they represent all words—precisely because of their power to enter into relationships that are more variable and contrary than necessary or fixable. That is, any relationship that one chooses to construct between them is bound to be more rhetorical than philosophical, because it is a relationship governed by traditions of meaning or usage rather than rules of logic or method. An apparently unrestrainable tendency of criticism is to believe that it is not a rhetorical enterprise; it is to imagine that its constructions are natural rather than verbal, accessible to analysis and demonstration and therefore superior to persuasion, and consequently meant to be organized hierarchically as into a theory rather than distributed topically in so many discourses. In a variation of this tendency some imagine that such constructions, because they are rhetorical, are not worth making, or are touchingly naive, or are worth making only in the belief that they are philosophically disreputable.

But criticism (like everything else) inhabits a doxological or doxographic world in which it is tolerable to have no fixed ideas: in which it is regularly the case that one's ideas, if they are any good at all, are open-ended and require perpetual revision: in which the fixing of thought is perhaps impossible except by constant recourse to geometry, or obstinacy. The value of rhetoric has always been its openness to the historicity of thinking, whence one thought is rarely the same thing twice but accrues the changes that thinking naturally rings upon any topic or theme because of the way occasions alter and new sources of understanding arise: thinking is always contingent upon learning, or the power of invention. This is why the rhetorician is inclined toward the view that the meaning of a word exists, not in itself (not *in* the word, nor as any sort of entity whether in mind or in language), but only in its versions, which belong to time, history, and the occasions of use. Someone more thoughtful might say (in the manner of Socrates) that nothing makes its appearance except in its versions, among which resemblances may be found to come and go, as most things do. It is, of course, not always congenial and rarely convenient to belong to this world (the rhetorical world of probability and resemblance), which many seek to escape as with a sense of moral duty or philosophical fortitude. Yet a good case could be made that one does not choose or refuse the rhetorical world; one is in it in any case, and only by the intervention of method or system can one make bold to get out of it, and even then one is never wholly free, quite for the same reason that no system is without the infiltrations of history or the contingencies of its making. Certainly rules and methods make possible momentary havens of every sort where one may experience simultaneities of meaning, but of such havens the soul of man seems to grow naturally tired or suspicious, thus to learn strategies of doubt and abuse and in general to spend itself pounding the great doors of system, not so much to break them down as to open them onto the secrets of deceit that surely lie within—which brings us part way back to allegory, and such ideas as philosophy is made of, namely, constructions (versions) of what lies just out of view: "views," which are less of things seen than of things to look for, and sometimes of things to say.

PART ONE
WRITING AND INTERPRETATION
AMONG THE ANCIENTS

1
Secrecy and Understanding

"The art of recovering the hidden meaning of a text": this schoolroom definition of interpretation is also the most fruitful, because it acknowledges the fundamental problem of secrecy. I should say at once, however, that my purpose in this chapter is not to figure secrecy as a problem but to reflect on its ancient character as a condition (a native companion) of understanding. It is true that for moderns like ourselves secrecy is simply one theme, and certainly a minor and dispensable theme, in a "problematics" of language, textuality, and knowledge. Within the context of a hermeneutics of suspicion secrecy is nothing less than the object of suspicion itself. It is the condition, not of understanding, but of disguise or deceit; it is precisely that to which recourse is taken when there is something to hide, or when knowledge cannot be allowed to occur. Secrecy presupposes someone to be kept in the dark; it is a category of power rather than of thought. When one desires enlightenment, secrecy is that which is to be dispelled like mist or darkness: it is a general term for any of the figures or formations that obstacles to enlightenment happen to take. It is the starting point for analyses of superstition and subterfuge. In Marxist and Freudian thinking secrecy possesses a short and disreputable life on the surface of what requires to be exposed. In the Nietzschean tradition the secret is somewhat more interesting: it is that across which language throws its figurative resources. It is not something to be penetrated or opened up but, on the contrary, it is what everyone (even without knowing it) manages to keep hidden—a sort of unspeakable danger like the lie that threatens to turn into the truth. More interesting still is the preëminence of secrecy in a text like Heidegger's "The Origin of the Work of Art," in which reserve and dissembling are figured as forms of concealment that belong to the nature of truth as *aletheia* or unconcealedness.[1] As such they are not reducible to the character of problems that can be solved or unknowns that proper methods of explanation will dispel; rather, the nature of reserve or withholding or secrecy is such that it cannot be comprehended systematically according to this or that method of thinking but becomes (inscrutably) that which thinking is called upon to preserve.

It is precisely this paradox of secrecy that the ancients understood very well. Frank Kermode's lectures on this subject remind us what biblical scholars seem to take for granted, namely that secrecy is a quintessential feature of the sacredness of sacred writings (that which is sacred, after all, is that which is set aside or apart: consecrated).[2] Indeed, it is the case that secrecy is an indispensable category of ancient biblical thinking: it is a way of figuring Scripture as a book of revelations which nevertheless (for reasons of its own, or for divine or providential reasons) withholds a good portion of itself—withholds perhaps its most sacred or vital portion. It withholds from man that which man desires most to have revealed: it withholds at any rate its most philosophical dimension, or that which answers to the name of wisdom—answers, but only in a manner of speaking (without giving itself away). Here is Origen's version of the *topos* of scriptural secrecy: "That there are certain mystical revelations made known through the divine scriptures is believed by all, even by the simplest of those who are adherents of the word; but what these revelations are, fair-minded and humble men confess that they know not."[3] The concept of secrecy is perhaps the principal way in which the ancients responded to the primary hermeneutical question: What do you do when the text you are studying doesn't make sense? Answer: you are now in the presence of the book's most sacred portion: you have come upon one of its secrets, and must now begin to ponder in earnest—to search the scriptures. The concept of secrecy was also a way of engaging a second question: Who can say what Scripture says? (Who, in other words, is privy to the mind of God?)

Secrecy thus pertains to the metaphysical disparity of the divine and the human. God's word will always resemble a secret because of the natural limitations of human understanding. God's word can only be expressed in the form of a secret, or only by means of a veiling that serves the double function of revelation and protection, as in the story of the radiant curtain: it is the hiding of the light that enables us to know its presence. A variation on this idea would stress the impossibility of plain speaking. The language of the scriptures is a language of double meanings, gramma and pneuma, and necessarily so: God speaks, but human authors write, which means that those who read must search between the lines of what is written in order to understand what is said. For who can say what is written? We must learn a special literacy (divination), whereby we understand one thing (the divine) in the language of another (the human). Only God can understand himself plainly and directly, but before man he is always hidden or disguised. Of special importance in this regard is the Islamic tradition, in which the categories of writing and speaking differently obtain: the Qur'ān is said to be, not a book exactly, but (as the name says) a recitation from a book, the *umm al-kitāb,* which exists nowhere but in heaven and which is, therefore, the most perfectly hidden or secret of books, and no doubt for that reason the most sacred: God has not allowed it to fall into human hands. No one but God can read the umm al-kitāb: no one but God can say what is written—no one save he and those to whom he reads or recites his book.[4] God did not so much speak to Muhammad as read aloud to him— according to tradition Muhammad could neither read nor write. The Qur'ān is that which God recited to the Prophet and which the Prophet recited in turn to his followers, or Companions, who were subsequently faced with the task of transcribing what had been heard and memorized (and, on occasion, taken down on the flat surfaces of stones and the shoulder blades of camels and sheep).[5]

There are two points here that are jostling against each other. The first concerns the duplicity of speech as such. To say anything at all is to endow it with a separate and hidden life: words are natural hiding places. There is no such thing as a meaning which is not hidden, except in the mind of God, where all things are hidden. To understand anything is necessarily to enter into a secret, or anyhow into the special reserve of natural languages. Scientists and philosophers prefer mathematics—Pythagoras, Galileo, and Descartes, for example, believed mathematics to be the language of God. By studying mathematics and by studying with it you can know what God knows and, more important, part of what you know will be the certainty of his understanding. The languages of men, by contrast, are very difficult to use; indeed, the history of usage shows clearly how they darken as by a natural inherence of figure and susceptibility to art. Heidegger would say that this is so because these languages possess an earthly as well as worldly character, that is, they are self-secluding and struggle to close themselves up before every effort of discourse and understanding.[6] What is at issue here, however, is not the weakness of natural languages but, on the contrary, the strength of their self-regard, their power to withhold themselves from whoever would speak in them. The history of usage testifies to the astonishing reserve of human tongues: despite our endless or relentless talk they show no sign of being used up. To be sure, this or that word will become disfigured and whole languages will grow opaque and unspeakable, but these disappearances are only the return of the languages to earth, their withdrawal from the world, that is, from consciousness and use. Languages are like time: there is an endless supply of them, and we can never know where they come form. As Heidegger suggests, languages do not die, they only grow more secretive and, therefore, less accessible to what we have in mind.

The second point embellishes the first. The lesson of the Qur'ān (which lets us in on the secret, namely the umm al-kitāb) is that revelation belongs to speech, or requires proclamation, whereas that which is written is hidden in the nature of the case, whence the understanding of it must await the fulness of time. What is it that happens when something gets written? In our time this question has won great acclaim, but it may be that the ancients knew the estrangement of writing more intimately than we, perhaps because they were more apt to think of writing as transcription, that is, as a taking down or documentation, rather than as literary expression or original inscription. To write something is to turn it into an enigma, or into that which needs to be unriddled. Putting something into words presupposes a scribal state of affairs, as when the giving of one's word requires not only someone to take it but someone to take it down. Such an act is secretive as well as expressive: when one gives one's word one does so for safekeeping, until the fulness of time or whenever something falls due. Ancient speech-writers (Lysias and others) no doubt produced original compositions, but they appear to have figured writing as a writing-down-beforehand, a pre-transcription performed on the principle that one could do better in writing what heretofore had been left to the inspiration of the moment. To deliver a prepared speech is, of course, to perform (secretly) a recitation: what is written remains hidden, a sort of umm al-kitāb, which preempts speech without, for the very reason of secrecy, displacing it. It is worth knowing that the ancient Greek word for "to write" was, not *graphein,* but *suggraphein,* literally "to write down" (as against speaking up, or rising spontaneously to say).[7] From the *Phaedrus* (275d) we learn that for Socrates writing is an act whose secrecy is essentially irreversible, that is, there is no recovering from writing that which gets put into it (not to mention what gets left out, or unsaid). He wondered what would happen if written words fell into dull or uncomprehending hands—which is, it turns out, what ancient writers sometimes counted on. Maimonides knew that it was the primary fate of writing to fall into the wrong hands, and so he composed his *Guide of the Perplexed* in Arabic, using, however, Hebrew characters, thus doubling the lock. The *Guide* is a work of scriptural exegesis: it proposes to teach "the secrets of the Law"—without destroying their nature as secrets.[8] It is a work of secret teaching which exploits the capacity of the written word to hide its message and, in this instance, to lead readers into a perplexity from which only one, perhaps two, will ever emerge. Maimonides took every precaution to ensure that his readers would understand his book as he understood it himself, or not at all. Accordingly at the outset he identifies the seven ways in which a writer may contradict himself, then advises his reader that his treatise will contradict itself according to the fifth and seventh modes.[9] On this procedure every misunderstanding is potentially the sign or result of how something is to be understood, and vice versa: literacy requires that you know a contradiction when you see one. It follows that a work of exegesis, insofar as its desire is to make plain that which is obscure, is a transgression against secrecy, except in the hands of a master *hermeneus* who understands the nature of writing, which does not transcribe or even imitate speech but, on the contrary, circumvents it: writing can safely put into words that which one dare not express, or speak aloud, namely "the secrets of the Law," as well as, for that matter, transgressions against such laws as forbid the teaching of the Law. Most of us err by the routine assumption that our writing is only a version of our speaking: Maimonides never made this mistake. His dates are 1135–1204, but already he is an adept of *l'écriture*. He chose each word of the *Guide* with Joycean care and placed it on the page with manifold design, sometimes hiding crucial words in unexpected places—hence his warning that the reader should aspire to understand not only the whole of each chapter but also each word in it, and even (or, indeed, especially) those words which seem not to have anything to do with the subject at hand. As in *Ulysses,* that which is most important to understand could turn out to be that which never gets mentioned.

The example of Maimonides is a reminder that for the ancients the secret is the form in which meaning makes its appearance: it is a word for meaning or, more exactly, it is a way of figuring meaning in the absence of the thing itself, or even a word for it. The secret is a circumlocution: it is a way of saying what cannot be said, namely, what it is that a text says or, more accurately, teaches: in the ancient world texts do not so much speak or mean as teach. The idea here is not easy to put into words because it is by no means clear that the ancients had a notion of meaning in our sense of the word. (What, by the way, *is* our sense of the word?) Aristotle thinks in terms of thoughts, things, and *onoma* or signifying sounds (*phonè semantikè*), but he does not say what this signifying produces, a point observed by the Stoics, who produced the word *lektòn* as a logical intermediary between thought and thing.[10] The Stoics knew that a word need not actually refer to anything in order to make sense, and that the sense it does make is likely to be determined by the occasions of its use. Generally, of course, meaning is naming, which is a conception that required the construction of etymologies on the one hand and of categories (substance, relation, genus, species, etc.) on the other.[11] What is this sense that gets made in the writing or deciphering of anything? The Latin *sens* is to be understood chiefly in terms of the rhetorical formula of *res et verba,* in which *res* doubles as thing (an object in the world) and thing (subject matter of a sentence or discourse). Thus Augustine divides his treatise on exegesis, *On Christian Doctrine,* into a discourse on things, or what Scripture teaches, and a discourse on signs, that is, the words of Scripture, which are divided into the plain, the obscure, and the figurative.[12] The "secrecy" of Scripture is thus treated as essentially a grammatical problem of designation (in order to understand Scripture you must know what it teaches, namely Charity) and a rhetorical problem of figuration, which is the way Augustine addresses the question of what to do when Scripture does not make sense: you figure it as a work of rhetoric, in which one thing is said in terms of another; or, again, you figure it in such a way as to make sense of it according to the rule of faith, or doctrine of Charity.[13]

It is interesting that for Augustine, and for the ancients generally, texts are plain or obscure or figurative but never meaningless. As if to avoid the thought of meaninglessness the figure of the secret (or of darkness or veiling) is brought into play as a way of designating that which has been set apart or out of the way of understanding, or that which remains to be said or understood. Our word "secret" derives from the Latin *secernere,* to set apart, separate, or distinguish. In this connection the natural opposite of the secret would be the commonplace, which belongs to orality by way of rhetoric and is, indeed, that which schoolboys routinely acquire and orators possess in copious supply. The commonplace is native to the discourse of civil men, the staple of public if not private confidence, marrow of the commonweal. It is the wisdom of everyday life. A commonplace is stored in memory and kept ready for use, nor does it ever need explaining to anyone (a proverb that needs to be explained is not a proverb but a dark saying or enigma); whereas the secret is that which results expressly from the separation of discourse from speech into writing, where what is meant (or taught, or proclaimed) is soon misremembered or forgotten and therefore susceptible to hermeneutics: hence the Rosetta Stone, which was once no secret at all but a special decree transformed into a secret by time and the superior durability of inscriptions. A commonplace is worth remembering but not worth writing down, although once it is written it will (like all texts) undergo a proliferation of senses. Time will relentlessly multiply and disclose its secrets; it will be found to be a reservoir of unheard or unheard-of wisdom. For the true secret is a reservation of sense as well as a preservation of it, the more so as it is a meaning that reserves a substantial portion of itself to itself, as in a deferred revelation or a revelation withheld until the appointed or providential hour. This is how St. Paul came to understand the letter of the Law, following Jesus, who proclaimed himself the secret of the Law, now made plain: "If you really believed Moses, you would believe me, for it was about me that he wrote" (John 5 : 46–47). Meaning here is not simply recorded in a special way (although writing turns out to be the only way it could have been recorded) but is said to be withheld or held back for special dispensations of understanding, as to those whose eyes are opened suddenly or for the first time (Luke 24 : 45–46), or, again, to those who are set aside or kept in reserve for special hermeneutical tasks—the *diastoles,* for example, or "men of separation and memory," seventy-two of whom (according to the famous legend) were summoned by Ptolemy II Philadelphus (285–46 B.C.) to Alexandria to translate the Pentateuch into Greek.[14] The seventy-two (known subsequently as the "Seventy") labored for seventy-two days to produce a text (the LXX, or Septuagint) that corresponded word for word with its Chaldean or Hebrew original. Nor did these men of the secret merely produce a letter-perfect translation; they produced a true Bible—a text whose every verse could bear seventy translations, one for every human language.[15]

The legend of the Septuagint is filled with hidden meanings, which means that it is not simply a legend but can be read for its teachings, that is, for the lessons that can be drawn from it concerning (among other things) ancient traditions of textuality and understanding. Philo's version of the legend, preserved in *De Vita Mosis* (first century B.C.) is something like a parable of secrecy. The translators, Philo says, had been set apart for their task, reposing to the island of Pharos, whereupon

they became as it were possessed and, under inspiration, wrote, not each several scribe something different, but the same word for word, as though dictated to each by an invisible prompter. Yet who does not know that every language, and Greek especially, abounds in terms, and that the same thought can be put in many shapes by changing single words and whole phrases and suiting the expression to the occasion? This was not the case, we are told, with this Law of ours, but the Greek words used corresponded literally with the Chaldean [i.e., the Hebrew], exactly suited to the things they indicated. For, just as in geometry and logic, so it seems to be, the sense indicated does not admit of variety in the expression which remains unchanged in its original form, so these writers, as it clearly appears, arrived at a wording which corresponded with the matter, and alone, or better than any other, would bring out clearly what was meant. The clearest proof of this is that, if Chaldeans have learned Greek, or Greeks Chaldean, and read both versions, the Chaldean and the translation, they regard them with awe and reverence them as sisters, or rather as one and the same, both in matter and words, and speak of their authors not as translators but as prophets and priests of these mysteries, whose sincerity and singleness of thought has enabled them to concur with the purest of spirits, the spirit of Moses.[16]

Here once more the guiding question is: What do you do when the text you are studying doesn't make sense? One answer is that you must alter the text in a way that will enable you to make sense of it. Revision has a hermeneutical dimension: it is designed to bring out what is hidden beneath an unknown or obscure or garbled expression. In the case of the Septuagint, scribal or grammatical emendation took the form of a wholesale transformation, that is, the turning of one text into the language of another. The question in this event is not whether it is possible to transfer a text from one language to another but whether it is possible to transfer the authority as well as the sense of what is written. The problem is scriptural rather than, strictly speaking, textual; it is hermeneutical rather than technical. Anyhow it is a problem of authority.

The production of the Septuagint, Philo says, took place in secret, with each scribe working alone or separately, yet the whole was the work of an unseen hand, or rather a voice ("an invisible prompter") dictating to each scribe, that is, reciting the original but this time in a new tongue. The scribes were as one possessed, which means that the true alteration took place in the spirit rather than in the letter. The translation required beforehand the transport or turning of each scribe into the original author, that is, a transformation of scribe into prophet, or a transfusion of the original prophetic spirit into each of the Seventy—at any rate it was in the spirit of Moses that the whole rewriting into Greek was undertaken and performed. The scribes wrote, not as scribes, but as Moses would have written had he done so originally in Greek. The concurrence or fusion of author and scribe underlies and, in effect, authorizes Philo's insistence on the literal as well as spiritual correspondence of Greek and Hebrew texts, which are said to speak in one voice: the voice of Moses and of God, spoken in the manner of geometry and logic, or as the result of an ideality of meaning that makes possible the portability of expressions. Geometry, analogous to Moses in the purity of its spirit, is the same in every language.

Portability, however, is double-edged. It accommodates the relations of letter and spirit only to vex them, for it exposes their contingency: letter and spirit are tied together by lines of authority that belong to history rather than to logic, whence it becomes the need of every scribal tradition to regulate history by devising and following rules of textual transmission. From both Philo and the *Letter of Aristeas* (100 B.C.), which preserves another version of the Septuagint legend, we learn that the very success of the Seventy required the elevation of secrecy from a natural condition (the inevitable feature of unknown tongues) into a code that would prohibit not only further revisions of the text but even quotations from it, as if the text were a text (that is, fixed) in two senses: its letters can no longer be altered, and neither can they be carried elsewhere or transported to another text (taken out of context).[17] In the *Letter of Aristeas* the force of this code is illustrated by two cautionary tales— (1) of Theopompous: "when he was on the point of introducing into his history certain matter which had been previously translated from the Law ..., he suffered a derangement of the mind for more than thirty days"; and (2) of Theodectes, "the tragic poet," who was afflicted suddenly with cataracts when he tried to insert something from the Law into one of his plays. The topos of the eyes that are suddenly opened, or of scales that miraculously fall from the eyes, is neatly reversed by the cataracts of Theodectes, who was privy once to that which is now withheld from him. The lesson is that whatever is no longer a secret in consequence of time and the confusion of tongues can be made so by divine intervention or (what amounts to the same thing) interdiction of the law. "Interdiction" is a telling word in this connection: originally it meant a decree that forbids entry into that which has been set apart as sacred (the mysteries), yet it was a word meant not so much to keep people out as to remove them once they had got in, that is, after they had already been initiated or separated from the ignorant and unwashed. It is a word of excommunication that is voiced or fixed between the word and those who can no longer lawfully hear it. It restores the word to secrecy. The Septuagint itself eventually fell under interdiction (as if between word and text) by falling into the wrong hands, as it did when it became the authorized Christian version of the Old Testament. In Christian Ginzburg's words, the *sopherim* or Jewish scribes— "custodians of the sacred text"—anathematized the Septuagint in the first Christian century by declaring that "it was not made by the seventy-two elders, but by five, and that the day on which it was made was as calamitous to Israel as the day on which the golden calf was substituted for the true God, because the Torah cannot adequately be reproduced in a translation."[18] The Septuagint is a colossal forgery.

In fact, the story of the Septuagint conceals a sobering truth, which is that Scripture is not to be found anywhere except in a revisionary and proliferating state. Scripture as such is, like the umm al-kitāb, inaccessible to human hands; it is an ideal or transcendental text. We speak of it, of course, in just this wise, as if it were a single work of authorship that reposes in unitary satisfaction on our shelves, but in truth it did not come into being all at once nor has it ever stopped changing. In an essay on "The Old Testament in the Making," Peter Ackroyd says that "it is only rarely that we can point to individuals as authors—the author of Job, the author of Ecclesiastes perhaps, and a few more; more often we can point to compilers, single figures or schools—Deuteronomists, the Priestly Writers, and the Chronicler whose work has undergone some substantial amplification in the same spirit." The Seventy, whoever they were (Hellenic Jewish scholars of the third century B.C.), belong to this category of authorship. "Again," Ackroyd continues, "we may point to great men whose personality and vision lie behind collections—and above all here the figures of the great prophets and other leaders around whom tradition has gathered. The Old Testament is not, on the whole, greatly concerned about authorship: it is more concerned about authority."[19] One should say perhaps that as a "work" Scripture is authored by tradition whose authority is characterized by the name "Moses." Better, however, to speak of Scripture not as a work but as a complicated network of textual traditions in which those who write do so as scribes, that is, not by any authority of their own but in the name of someone else—in the name of God, or of Moses, in the name of the Father, Son, etc. One scribe whose name we know, of course, is Ezra, scribe of scribes, who had to write the Torah over again after it was destroyed in a fire, and who therefore is sometimes called "the second Moses"; yet even Ezra composed only in virtue of the one who put words in his mouth, namely the Spirit who instructed him as follows: "Go, gather the people together, and tell them not to look for you for forty days. But you must prepare for yourself many writing tablets, and take with you Seraiah, Dabria, Shelemiah, Elkanah, and Asiel, who are able to write swiftly." The writing of the scriptures requires the concealment of the writers, as if to write were in the first place to go into hiding (hence perhaps the long association of writing and exile, as against speech and public life)—nor is all that gets written to be brought out again or published to the world, which is a point on which God takes special care to be explicit: "And you are to come here, and I will light the lamp of understanding in your heart, and it will not be put out until the things you are to write are finished. And when you have finished, some things you shall publish and some you shall hand down secretly to the wise. At this hour tomorrow you shall begin to write" (2 Esdras 14 : 23–26).

Scripture is something that is always turning into new versions of itself. This was obviously the case prior to the period of canonization (400 B.C.– 100 A.D.), that is, before there was any notion of a text as something to be fixed in an unalterable form. As it happens we know very little about the way texts were conceived in this precanonical period, and only a little more about how they were transmitted—and what we do know is mainly negative: we cannot suppose that the rules and categories of transmission bear any resemblance to what we are able to imagine today.[20] Thus we ought to speak of the transmission of teachings rather than of texts, and we should understand that the boundaries that separate the oral and the written, memory and manuscript, were defined only gradually and without great rigor.

We do know that these boundaries remained open even into the period of the great rabbinical scholars, of whom the greatest of all was Rabbi b. Akiba (c. 57–135 A.D.), who said: "If you wish to be strangled, be hanged on a large tree, and when you teach your son, teach him from a corrected scroll"—to which Rabbi Mesharsheya is said to have added: "A new one [i.e., a new scroll], for once an error had entered, it remains."[21] Rabbi Mesharsheya's point is that it is not easy to know an error when you see one, for once made they are likely to hide forever, disguised as (or at all events indistinguishable from) true readings. After all, what are the conditions that make it possible to recognize a textual error, as against an error of teaching that anyone might spot? One indispensable condition would be a stabilized text and a corresponding ability to accommodate or dispense with (as the occasion requires) variant readings. The *Letter of Aristeas* appears to testify to the formation of just this state of affairs: hidden in the story of the translation of the scriptures is the story of the stabilization of the scriptures, or their coalescence into textuality. We may read the *Letter of Aristeas*, for example, as a prohibition of what had once been routine, namely the rewriting of texts as a way of keeping them intelligible or consistent with current practices and teachings, for what is written, if it is to speak at all, must always speak to the situation at hand, the more so if what is written requires to be applied or fulfilled, like law or prophecy. By contrast, the revisions of the rabbis, like the legendary translations of the Seventy, were designed to produce, not simply a correct or error-free text, but a *finished* text, a text that possesses finality and, therefore, the authority of a text that speaks for all time (a truly prophetic text, able to foresee every contingency): a text that can serve as a fixed center in the determination of variants and against which copies can be made and corrected—in short, an original.[22] Most important, such a text would have the power of turning variants into deviations, thus to make possible the concept of the textual error as such. In a sense, a system which makes possible the existence of errors (that is, unacceptable readings or variants) must be established before their eradication can occur. The rabbis produced such a system, some part of whose operation is illustrated in the famous anecdote concerning the Scrolls of the Temple Court:

> Three scrolls were found in the Temple Court: the scroll *m'on*, the scroll *za'tute*, and the scroll *hi'*. In one scroll they found written *m'on* (Deut. 33 : 27), in the other two *m'ona*; the sages [sopherim] discarded the reading of the one and adopted the reading of the two. In one they found written *za'tute*, in the other two *na're* (Ex. 24 : 5); they discarded the reading of the one and adopted the reading of the two. In one they found nine occurrences of *hi'* [spelled *hy'*], in the other two eleven [spelled *hi'*]; they discarded the reading of the one and adopted the reading of the other two.[23]

Errors systematically obtained are, of course, highly formalist in character: they have no status as errors except within the system that defines them—and the same is true for the "correct" readings thus produced. This is why variants ought never to be erased or forgotten, or why some provision should be made for them in the margins or at the bottom of the page. The rabbis (whose genius for textual criticism matched our own, although we somewhat exceed them in method) knew this very well, and so they developed a number of subsidiary systems for revising a text without actually altering any of its letters. There was, for example, the tradition of the *Kethîb-Qerê* ("written-spoken"), which allowed the rabbi to correct the text orally during a liturgical reading of it: thus in certain instances (1) a word missing from the text could be inserted into the recitation; (2) a word present in the text could be dropped from the recitation; (3) a word written in the text could be modified or exchanged for another.[24] A similar tradition is the *tikkûnê sôpherîm* ("scribal emendations"), which is a formal list of corrections (numbering from eleven to eighteen in various sources) to be applied during the reading of the text in order to remove unwanted (but not in fact erroneous) meanings, as when the word "bless" is allowed to be substituted for the word "curse" in Job 2 : 9 ("Curse God and die") on the grounds that the cursing of God, while not absolutely unthinkable, is liturgically unspeakable.[25] A related phenomenon is the Targum, or the translation of the Hebrew text into an Aramaic recitation. The *Pesikta Rabbati*, a collection of homiletic material for special liturgical occasions, contains this interesting turn:

> Let our master instruct us: [At a service,] When Scripture is being read aloud, may the translator look at a written text as [translating the Hebrew, verse by verse, into Aramaic] he follows the reader?
> Our Masters taught as follows: He who translates orally must not look at a written text [of the translation]; as for the reader of Scripture, he must not, lifting his eyes away from the text of the Scroll, recite from memory, for the To-

rah was given solely in the form of a written text, as is said, *The Lord said: . . . I will write upon the tables* [Ex. 34 : 1]; on the other hand, he who translates orally must not turn his eyes upon the text of the Scroll. These injunctions . . . are clearly indicated by *The Lord said unto Moses: "Write thou these words"* [Ex. 34 : 27], which refer to the text given in writing; and by *For these words are by mouth* [ibid.], which refer to the translation that must be given by word of mouth.[26]

The Torah ("given solely in the form of a written text") is fixed, but it is permissible and, indeed, necessary to unfix it orally, for otherwise who will understand it? It is worth remarking that here the oral is ancillary to the written, not its source but its supplement, but it is also true that, strictly speaking, the Torah is not reducible to the form of a text. It is rather to be spoken of as a composition of textual and oral traditions—the written Torah, and the Mishnah, Talmud, and Midrash, which taken together are figured as the "Oral Torah," whose basic hermeneutical task is to soften the rigidity of the letter without, however, violating its sacredness (whence not a jot nor a tittle will be allowed to pass away).

For the point is certainly that the fixity of the letter does not produce a corresponding fixity of meaning; on the contrary, the hermeneutical function of the Oral Torah is precisely to maintain the openness of what is written to that which is unforeseen or which is yet to come—new situations of human life and new sources of understanding which will require what is written to be fulfilled in ways that cannot be accounted for by the letter alone. This is so not only of those portions of the oral tradition that possess specific legal and procedural concerns *(halakah)*, but it is true in a special way of Midrash, or midrashic *haggadah*—the extraordinary rabbinical tradition of scriptural interpretation. In this tradition it is not possible to imagine that the letter, being fixed, is dead; rather, Midrash speaks directly to the endless reserve of the letter, its power to put new words into the interpreter's mouth and to address itself to whatever is suddenly at hand, to enlarge upon itself and to suggest in turn that there is always more that remains to be said. Midrash is concerned not merely to preserve the understanding of what is written but to expand it, often in breathtaking ways, as in the case of the *Sefer ha-Yashar*, an eleventh-century life of Abraham that represents more than a thousand years of midrashic or haggadic development, and which Geza Vermes calls "one of the latest examples of the rewritten Bible."[27]

The concept of rewriting is crucial to an understanding of biblical textuality, but it does only small justice to the phenomenon of Midrash. According to its textbook definition the word *midrash* refers to the activity of interpretation as well as to its results and, in turn, to the whole hermeneutic institution which thereby obtains, and which comes down to us as a vast assembly of exegetical, homiletic, and narrative commentaries on scriptural texts. In fact, however, these commentaries are almost impossible to describe in a shorthand way. Take, for example, the midrash preserved in the *Midrash Rabbah* on Exodus 6 : 3, "I am the Lord; I appeared to Abraham, Issac, and Jacob as God almighty, but did not make myself known to them by my name Yahweh"—an interesting text for the way in which it figures God as the one who withholds his name. What is doubly interesting, however, is that the midrash addresses this verse only by indirection, or secretly, by commenting instead on Ecclesiastes 2 : 12, "So I turned again to look upon wisdom, madness, and folly; for what can the man do who comes after the king?" This verse, we are told, refers to Solomon and Moses—Solomon? "How," the midrash asks, "does it refer to Solomon?" The question turns out to be, among other things, a pretext for the following story about Solomon and the letters of the Torah:

> Our Sages said: At that time the *yod* [a character of the Hebrew alphabet] of the word *yarbeh* went up on high and prostrated itself before God and said: "Master of the Universe! Hast thou not said that no letter shall ever be abolished from the Torah? Behold, Solomon has now arisen and abolished one. Who knows? To-day he has abolished one letter, to-morrow he will abolish another until the whole Torah will be nullified."

To which God responds, " 'Solomon and a thousand like him will pass away, but the smallest tittle,' " etc. God himself, as it happens, has had a hand in cleaning up some scribal errors, yet his procedure, the midrash assures us, is to move the letters around within the text, not to cancel them: the *yod* he erases from one text will find itself restored in another.[28]

Solomon is a midrashic figure of considerable interest: in most contexts he is not the enemy of Torah at all but the one who searched its words and for the first time rendered it accessible to understanding. Indeed, so far from erasing the Torah, Solomon (in perfect midrashic fashion) *adds to it*, as we learn from a midrash for the Song of Songs: " 'Thou didst seek out words of Torah,' " God says to Solomon. " 'I swear that I will not withhold thy reward. Behold I cause the holy spirit to rest on thee.' Forthwith the holy spirit rested on him and he composed these three books, Proverbs, Ecclesiastes, and the Song of Songs." It is important to notice that these writings are figured as works of interpretation, although in a complicated way: their relation to the Pentateuch is midrashic, yet they possess the authority of original compositions. They are called "handles to the Torah" and, more exactly, parables that convey us to the innermost places of what is written (and, in the bargain, enable us to find our way out again). The passage in question here is worth quoting in full, because it illustrates perfectly the amplifying or embellishing character of midrashic thinking:

[Solomon] pondered the words of the Torah and investigated the words of the Torah. He made handles to the Torah. You find that till Solomon came there was no parable. R. Nahman gave two illustrations. Said R. Nahman: Imagine a large palace with many doors, so that whoever entered could not find his way back to the door, till one clever person came and took a coil of string and hung it up on the way to the door, so that all went in and out by means of the coil. So till Solomon arose no one was able to understand properly the words of the Torah, but as soon as Solomon arose all began to comprehend the Torah. R. Nahman gave another illustration, from a thicket of reeds which no one could penetrate, till one clever man came and took a scythe and cut some down, and then all began to enter through the cutting. So did Solomon. R. Jose said: Imagine a big basket full of produce without any handle, so that it could not be lifted, till one clever man came and made handles to it, and then it began to be carried by the handles. So till Solomon arose no one could properly understand the words of the Torah, but when Solomon arose, all began to comprehend the Torah. R. Shila said: Imagine a jug full of water with no handle by which it could be carried, until someone came and made it a handle, so that it began to be carried by its handle. R. Hanina said: Imagine a deep well full of water, cold, sweet, and wholesome water, but no one was able to get a drink of it, until one man came and joining rope to rope and cord to cord, drew from it and drank and then all began to draw and drink. So proceeding from one thing to another, from one parable to another, Solomon penetrated to the innermost meaning of the Torah, as it is written, *The proverbs of Solomon son of David king of Israel: to know wisdom and instruction,* etc.: through the proverbs of Solomon he mastered the words of the Torah. Our Rabbis say: Let not the parable be lightly esteemed in your eyes, since by means of the parable a man can master the words of the Torah. If a king loses gold from his house or a precious pearl, does he not find it by means of a wick worth a farthing [i.e., an *assarius*, a small Roman coin]? So the parable should not be lightly esteemed in your eyes, since by means of the parable a man arrives at the true meaning of the words of the Torah. Here is a proof that it is so; for Solomon by means of the parable penetrated to the finest nuances of the Torah. R. Judah said . . . [29]

And so on. The passage is essentially a litany of parables giving the theory of the parable as a hermeneutic rather than (as we would figure it) a literary form: the parable is a vehicle of instruction in the meaning of Scripture—but notice that it is a vehicle of a special kind. It does not convey a meaning to an audience, rather it conveys the audience to the meaning. The meaning of the Torah is, after all, a hidden meaning and is meant to remain so: it is not to be carried out of the Torah, that is, its hiddenness is not to be dispelled by understanding but requires to be preserved, for hiddenness is an essential part of that which is to be understood.

The lesson here is that the rabbi must teach the secrets of the Law without transgressing the secrecy of the Law—and this is so even when he teaches, as Solomon did, in public, for it is not that the secrets are to be opened up to the public but rather that the people are to enter into the secret. Here we encounter the mystery of Israel as a nation set apart—literally a secret nation, as in Numbers 23 : 9:

> For from the top of the rocks I see them,
> From the hills I behold them—
> Lo, a people living by themselves,
> Not accounting themselves as one of the nations.

Here is a midrash on this verse:

> *Lo* [*ben*: a character of the Hebrew alphabet], *it is a people that shall dwell alone.* What is the meaning of *ben*? All letters can be conjoined except these two. Thus *aleph* plus *teth* is ten, *beth* plus *heth* is ten, *gimmel* plus *zayin* is ten, *daleth* plus *waw* is ten; only the *ben* is left to itself. Similarly, the letter *nun* has no partner; for the *yod* plus *zadde* is a hundred, the *kaf* plus *pe* is a hundred, the *lammed* plus *ayyin* is a hundred, the *mem* plus the *samek* is a hundred, only the *nun* is left to itself. God said: "Just as these two letters cannot be combined with the others but stand apart, so cannot Israel be joined with the idolaters of antiquity but must keep themselves apart."[30]

And so on. This passage, like the long sequence on parables quoted earlier, does not come to an end, for Midrash is a hermeneutic discourse that possesses its own progress or history. It is a continuing discourse that alters its direction as new commentators enter and make themselves a part of it, but one does not (and, indeed, cannot) enter it in order to bring it to a close. One enters it rather as one enters into a secret or, again, as one enters into the understanding of the scriptures themselves. There is no question here of grasping a fixed meaning or of fixing a meaning that forecloses future understanding; instead, one is taken up into what is written—in the manner of Solomon, who became a part of that which he understood. He becomes, one might say, part of the secret. For if we may think of the Midrash, and of the Oral Law generally, as a way of keeping the written Torah open, or of keeping it tacitly unfinished, we must at the same time understand its profoundly secretive function: "God gave the Israelites two Laws, the Written Law and the Oral Law. He gave them the Written Law with its 613 ordinances, to fill them with commandments, and to cause them to become virtuous. . . . And He gave them the Oral Law to make them distinguished from the other nations. It was not given in writing so that the nations should not falsify it, as they have done with the Written Law, and say that they are the true Israel."[31] Only those who possess the oral have access to the written;

or, again, it is precisely by their possession of the Oral Law that Israel is set apart as a secret nation, or the nation which alone is privy to the secrets of the Law.

It is as if the Oral Law were a response, not to the fixity and reserve of what is written, but to its portable and, indeed, fugitive character. For the point is, again, that it is not really possible to speak of Scripture as a text; call it rather a superabundance of texts, or of heterogeneous and heterodox versions of a Sacred Book. Here, for example, is a short inventory of scriptural versions: various Hebrew recensions; Aramaic Targums; the Samaritan Pentateuch (and its Greek version, called the Samariticon); Syriac Peshitta; Massoretic texts; the Septuagint; Origen's Hexapla; the Quinta, Sexta, and Septima Greek versions; the Vetus Latina or Old Latin version of the Septuagint; the Itala (and a staggering array of local Latin texts); Jerome's Latin Bible, later called the Vulgate (together with its numerous types, mixtures, corrections, and recensions, some of which are still appearing); the Philoxenian, Harklean, Palestinean Syriac, and Coptic versions of the New Testament, whose Gospel is itself versional in character; the Novum Instrumentum of Erasmus (who, to everyone's horror, substituted *sermo* for *logos*); and the Complutensian Polyglot, a magnificent printed object as utterly useless as it is remarkable (it gave you the Vulgate Old Testament flanked by a Hebrew Text and a version of the Septuagint). No need to list the various revised and authorized vernacular versions emanating unto the present day.

Origen's Hexapla (c. 230–40 A.D.) is regrettably lost. It is estimated to have exceeded 6,500 pages and probably never existed all at once, although, for that matter, the Bible in the ancient world almost never took the form of a single volume but traveled piecemeal in rolls and codices. The Hexapla, however, gave you six versions of the Old Testament side by side. Column 1: a Hebrew text in Hebrew characters; column 2: a Hebrew text in Greek characters, showing you how to pronounce the text in column one, which was a consonantal text with no diacritical marks;[32] column 3: a Greek translation of a Hebrew text, or perhaps a revision of the Septuagint, by Aquila (c. 76–138 A.D.), so literal as to be virtually unintelligible to someone ignorant of Hebrew; column 4: a Greek translation by Symmachus (c. 170 A.D.) which attempted to accommodate the Hebrew to the norms of Greek eloquence; column 5: the Septuagint as emended by Origen, who believed that even scribal errors and obvious mistranslations contain hidden meanings, but who wanted to have all the textual facts at hand in his disputes with the rabbis;[33] column 6: Theodotion's revision (c. 180 A.D.) of an unidentified Greek version. No copy was ever made of the Hexapla, but the Septuagint column, known as the Hexaplaric Recension, was widely reproduced, with disastrous results. Origen had marked his emendations, or anyhow some of them, with asterisks and obeli to show what, in his view, should be added to the Septuagint, and what should be canceled, in comparison with the Hebrew text. Unfortunately, copyists routinely ignored these sigla, and eventually the Hexaplaric Recension circulated without them, making, at times, no sense at all.

The Hexapla illustrates nicely the problem of the scriptures: you cannot enter into an understanding of them until you know that you have actually got them in front of you, but it is difficult to say when you have actually got them.[34] Scripture is a text whose versions are replicas, not of an original text, but of one another, as in a family wherein there are resemblances countermanded by disagreements brought on by tangled lines of descent. Storytelling, that is, textual legends of the kind preserved in Philo and in the *Letter of Aristeas*, is simply a practical way of sorting out lines of authority. This was the recourse of Augustine, who was thrown into alarm by Jerome's Latin translation of the Old Testament. Jerome had finessed the Septuagint (which he had tried, unsuccessfully, to revise into a coherent text) by translating directly from the Hebrew, whence Augustine wrote to him, wishing Jerome had not done such a thing:

> For my part, I would much rather that you would furnish us with a translation of the Greek version of the canonical scriptures known as the work of the Seventy translators. For if your translation begins to be more generally read in many churches, it will be a grievous thing that, in the reading of Scripture, differences must arise between the Latin Churches and the Greek Churches, especially seeing that the discrepancy is easily condemned in a Latin version by the production of the original in Greek, which is a language very widely known; whereas, if any one has been disturbed by the occurrence of something to which he was not accustomed in the translation taken from the Hebrew, and alleges that the new translation is wrong, it will be found difficult, if not impossible, to get at the Hebrew documents by which the version to which exception is taken may be defended. And when they are obtained, who will submit to have so many Latin and Greek authorities pronounced to be in the wrong?

Augustine saw directly that by depriving the Septuagint of its legendary status as an original—that is, the status which it had so long held in the Christian churches as a base text for subsequent Latin versions—Jerome had undone its authority. Jerome had not, of course, explicitly undone anything, but by his translation he had made the old formula *Hebraica veritas* a logical, tangible, and productive scriptural rule. This was a damnable thing to do, for who knows Hebrew? (No one, it turned out, but Jerome, who had made himself privy to a secret tongue.) The Hebrew Bible is for the Greek-

and Latin-speaking faithful a secret text, and even when accessible it is alien: who could be expected to submit to its authority? Augustine refused to submit. He repeated and upheld the legend of the Septuagint to the end, but he knew that the Septuagint would now have to answer for its divergences from Jerome's version (which is to say, by extension, its divergences from the "new" original)—and this answer, in the end, is the one he wanted most urgently from Jerome: "I wish you would have the kindness," he writes in this same letter, "to open up to me what you think to be the reason of the frequent discrepancies between the text supported by the Hebrew codices and the Greek Septuagint version."[35]

Jerome (shrewdest and most rhetorical of the Fathers) had a rich inventory of answers to this question, most of them designed to confound two widely circulating charges: (1) that he had filled his "Hebrew" translation with countless forgeries, and (2) that he had intended his translation as "a censure of the Seventy."[36] The Septuagint, Jerome would say, had been corrupted, not only by lazy or foolish copyists, but by Origen, who had altered it in his Hexapla on the basis of faulty competing Greek versions, and who had doctored the text besides with his own crazy ideas; but most important the Seventy, in making their original translation, had not been wholly forthcoming, but on the contrary had found it prudent to keep the best parts of the original revelation secret: "since their work was undertaken for King Ptolemy of Alexandria, [they] did not choose to bring to light all the mysteries which the sacred writings contain, and especially those which give the promise of the advent of Christ, for fear that he who held the Jews in esteem because they were believed to worship one God, would come to think that they worshipped a second."[37]

Augustine, for his part, went somewhat further by inferring from variant texts correspondingly variant revelations, and so, in effect, revised the Septuagint legend as follows:

> The truth is that there shone out from the Seventy so tremendous a miracle of divine intervention that anyone [namely Jerome] translating the Scriptures into any other language will, if he is a faithful translator, agree with the Septuagint; if not, we must still believe that there is some deep revealed meaning in the Septuagint. For, the same Spirit who inspired the original Prophets as they wrote was no less present to the Seventy as they translated what the Prophets had written. And this Spirit, with divine authority, could say, through the translators, something different from what he had said through the original Prophets. . . .

"So much," Augustine goes on to say, "for additions and omissions": what we have here is a case of divine revision, whence we are to "conclude, in the case of something in the Hebrew which is missing in the Septuagint, that the Spirit elected to say this by the lips of the original Prophets and not by the lips of their translators. Conversely, in the case of something present in the Septuagint and missing in the original, we will conclude that the Spirit chose to say this particular thing by the lips of the Seventy rather than by the lips of the original Prophets. . . ."[38] The Septuagint, in other words, is not a version of the Hebrew Bible; it is a version of Revelation—a second (or new) revelation which alters and thereby dispenses with the first. As Jerome had finessed the Septuagint by translating directly from the Hebrew, so Augustine finesses Jerome by embellishing the Septuagint, turning the Greek Bible from a translation based merely on words into an original expression of the Spirit.

After all, what do words matter? Revelation is pre-textual, or perhaps post-textual; anyhow it is a secret which the text conceals even from its author—which is how Augustine figures it in the *Confessions*:

> Now, as with burning heart I confess these things to you, my God, light of my eyes in secret, what harm does it do me if different meanings, which are nevertheless all true, can be gathered from these words? What harm can it do me if my view of what Moses meant is different from someone else's view? Certainly all of us who read are endeavoring to find out and to grasp what the man whom we are reading meant to say, and when we believe that he is a man who tells the truth we dare not imagine that he said anything which we ourselves know or believe to be false. So while we are all trying in our reading of the Holy Scriptures to grasp what it was that the author of them meant to say, what harm can it do if a man grasps hold of something which you, who are the light of all truthful minds, show him is true, even if the author whom he is reading did not grasp this truth—although of course the author did express a truth, but a different one?[39]

"What harm can it do me?" The question is characteristically the first step in rationalizing a transgression. In this case Augustine seeks divine permission to transgress the letter of the Law and to read an original truth as the medium of a belated one. God would surely stay his foot were it dangerous to proceed, as proceed he must since he is caught up in a conflict of interpretations produced by the unstable textual history of the scriptures. One might say that it is not Augustine who transgresses the letter but time: Augustine gathers from the text, as any Christian would, a sense hidden from its author, for the sense in question is temporal rather than textual, and belongs to the text only insofar as the text belongs to history. The sense of what is written is hidden in time and circumstance, inscribed in history: it is a sense unveiled only in the fulness of time. As Origen said, history turns idle words into prophecies.[40]

What matters, in other words, is not what is written, but what is read.

"But in finding the meaning," Augustine says in the *Confessions*, "there are so many truths which occur to us from these words, according to whether we understand them in one way or another. Is there any one of us who can say: 'This is what Moses thought,' 'This is what he meant us to understand in that passage,' with the same confidence as he would say, 'This is true' or 'That is true,' whether Moses meant it or not?"[41] The intention of Moses is inaccessible, and also dispensable, not because Moses desired to say anything false, nor because we do not wish to know what he had in mind, but because there remains more to be said, or more to be learned, than Moses thought. This is the theme of the Christian appropriation of the Hebraica veritas. The center of this appropriation is the figure of Christ the hermeneus, as in Origen's *Homily on Joshua*:

> When we hear the books of Moses read, by the Lord's grace the veil of the letter is lifted and we begin to understand that the Law is something spiritual. ... [And] if we are capable of interpreting the Law like that and realizing that it is something spiritual, as St. Paul says, the reason is ... that the person reading the Law to us is the Lord Jesus Christ himself. He it is who reads it for all people to hear. ... Jesus reads us the Law when he reveals to us the secrets of the Law. We do not despise the Law of Moses because we belong to the Church; we still accept it, provided that Jesus reads it to us. If Jesus reads it to us we can take it in its proper sense; when he reads it we grasp its spiritual meaning. The Disciples who said: "Were not our hearts burning within us as he spoke to us on the road and when he made the Scriptures plain to us?" [Luke 24 : 32] had understood the spiritual meaning of the Law. You will agree, I think, that it was because Jesus had explained it to them when he read it all to them and made plain to them what had been written about him, from Moses to the prophets.[42]

In a sense, Christ performs upon the scriptures the most audacious midrash of all: he rewrites the Bible in his own name—or, rather, he reads the scriptures in his own name by reading himself into them, making himself the secret of the Law, now revealed or made plain "for all the people to hear." The Law is read, not as Law, that is, not as Moses would read it (or Solomon or Akiba), but as Prophecy, or according to a hermeneutical structure of promise and fulfillment. Prophecy is the secret or hidden meaning of the Law. It is, in this context, a category of interpretation, not a category of authorship or visionary epistemology.

The lesson here is that the scriptures proliferate vertically as well as horizontally. They exist, not in themselves, but in versions of one another distributed historically from an inaccessible beginning to an end not yet in sight; but they also exist midrashically as different *kinds* of text, or as texts distributed metaphorically, as Augustine says, "according as we understand them one way or another." Figure it this way: the scriptures are different kinds of writings, one concealed *within* the other as Christian prophecy is concealed within Mosaic Law; or they are different versions of the same Sacred Book, one concealed by another as the Hebraica veritas is concealed by the Septuagint or by the Vulgate or by a whole history of vernacular turnings. These two modes of scriptural existence cannot, of course, be considered in isolation from one another; on the contrary, their importance is precisely that they coincide at the moment when the scriptures are opened and read—or, to speak more accurately, they are joined at that moment *before* a text is to be read and interpreted, because they bear upon and, indeed, give shape and substance to the *foreunderstanding* of the scriptural work. Here the question is not what the scriptures are empirically but what they are figured to be beforehand by the one who is called upon to say what it is that is written. We may imagine that Augustine's characterizations of the scriptural text are naive or uncritical, but it is crucial for us to know what sort of book he thought he was reading when he wondered, for example, what harm it would do to understand the scriptures differently from the way Moses meant them to be taken. He certainly did not imagine that he was reading a Hebrew Bible, nor even a translation of one, which is why he took alarm at what Jerome had done: it was not that Jerome's translation had disrupted Augustine's textual attachment to the Septuagint; rather, the translation had disrupted Augustine's foreunderstanding of the scriptures as a one, whole, and Christian work, in which the Old Testament is to be figured, not as a Hebrew "document," but as a secretly Christian text, that is, a book whose hidden or secret teaching is the doctrine of Charity brought to light in the New Testament. The Old Testament, in other words, is a secret version of the New: this, anyhow, is the pretext under which it is to be read.

On roughly this same point the whole hermeneutical tradition of allegory is supported in giddy balance. What do you do when the text you are studying doesn't make sense? The sense it would make is inseparable from the reason why you are studying it in the first place (what is it that you wish to know?). This question may be asked in a different way: What would this text have to become in order for you to make sense of it? Or, again: What sense are you inclined to make of it? Most readers in the ancient world were philosophically inclined, or desired their scriptures (whether the Bible or the Qur'ān) to make philosophical sense. Thus the Law made sense to Philo chiefly by becoming moral philosophy, as when the story of Cain and Abel turns into a treatise on the conflict between two elemental principles of the spirit ("There are two opposite and contending views of life, one which ascribes all things to the mind as our master . . . . the other which follows

God, whose handiwork it believes itself to be. The first of these views is figured by Cain who is called Possession, because he thinks he possesses all things, the other by Abel, who name means 'one who refers [all things] to God' ").[43] Averroës, in "The Decisive Treatise Determining the Nature of the Connection between Religion and Philosophy" *(Fasl al-Magāl)*, gives the traditional philosopher's view of allegory as that which mediates between the authority of Tradition and the authority of Reason in the determination of what is written. The starting point for Averroës is that "Philosophy Contains Nothing Opposed to Islam," even though the two appear to contradict one another at every turn. Better to say, however, that nothing in Islam is contrary to Reason. For Averroës, Reason is simply that which is hidden in the Qur'ān: it is that to which men of understanding, or what Averroës calls "the demonstrative class," are privy, or which they know how to obtain, for only they know the secret signs by which Reason has inscribed itself within the plain sense of what is written. And what are these signs? They are what every man of reason recognizes at a glance, but which the unlearned pass by without a second thought, not knowing they are signs: they are logical contradictions, violations of Reason and Nature, abuses of sense. Contradictions form a special scriptural language which only the learned can read and understand, and what they understand is that there is more to what is written than the unschooled eye can see: every contradiction is the sign of a hidden meaning.[44]

It is as if every sacred text concealed within itself another text more sacred still, which in turn concealed a still more sacred text, and so on—into the mind of God as in a ratio of increasing holiness and reserve. As Averroës figures it, there is a category of sense for every category of reader (or listener). The Qur'ān is a book which is accessible to everyone and to no one, to the many and the few alike, but it is never quite the same book in every case, for in one instance it is a book of images, so many representations of the miraculous, whereas in another it is a book of recondite teachings. Or, again, there are texts of Scripture, Averroës says, which must be taken in their plain sense, even by men of understanding, and then there are those which must be interpreted allegorically, that is, made consistent with the conclusions of demonstrative reason; but the greatest number are those texts which can be taken plainly or allegorically: texts, as it happens, on which men of understanding hold divergent opinions—because, as the Qur'ān says, "no one knows the interpretation thereof except God" (Sūra III. 7). What God knows, after all, is what matters, and this in turn is what matters to men of understanding, who seek agreement, not with one another ("it is not possible for general unanimity to be established about allegorical interpretations"), but with God, who accommodates all men "according to the level of each one's knowledge of demonstration" (298–99). The Qur'ān is, among other things, a summons to learn what God knows, even as it is a summons to allegory, which is a certain way of knowing what God knows: the "apparent contradictions" of the Qur'ān, Averroës says, "are meant to stimulate the learned to deeper study" (p. 293). To interpret a text allegorically is to search beneath the plain sense for what is contained, not (exactly) in the text, but in the mind of God. To allegorize a text is not to expose what is hidden in it; rather, it is to be conducted into the recesses of wisdom, or taken into God's confidence. Allegory in this case is not so much decipherment as it is meditation upon what is written, or a learning from what is said. There is, in any event, no question here of bringing anything out into the open; on the contrary, the whole orientation of the interpretive task is toward the preservation of secrecy, or what amounts to the same thing, namely the preservation of the boundaries of understanding, which are not to be transgressed: "The unlearned classes," Averroës says, "must take such texts in their apparent meaning. It is unbelief [i.e., an act of infidelity] for the learned to set down allegorical interpretations in popular writings."[45]

Here we come round to the final point that needs to be made concerning secrecy, namely that it is essentially philosophical in nature, or alien to rhetoric and to any rhetorical conception of writing and textuality. In relation to Scripture, Averroës says, people fall into three classes, and the first of these is composed of those "who are not people of interpretation at all: these are the rhetorical class" (302)—the multitude, the unlearned, those who must be spoken to, or who must listen in order to understand. From Socrates to Derrida the philosophers have always defined themselves by their opposition to what can be put publicly into words. Philosophy is secretive, whereas rhetoric is full of public exclamation. Rhetoric, to be sure, is the art of concealing motives, designs, or ulterior purposes—but not doctrines or meanings; rather one should say that rhetoric uses meanings for the concealment of practical objectives, whereas philosophy is secretive precisely in respect of what it knows (or what it seeks), as was Socrates, who made it part of his self-definition, part of the whole justification of his life, that he never spoke in public, and who left the world ignorant of what it was that came to him in those periods of philosophical enchantment when he would stand for hours motionless and alone (*Symposium*, 220c–220d).

In this way one can begin to account for the historically anomalous character of sacred writing, which occupies an unstable position between philosophy and rhetoric, for it appears to belong now to the one realm, now to the other, depending on whether one's attention is fixed on a Maimonides, for whom Scripture is a secretly philosophical work whose "truths [are to] be glimpsed and then concealed again,"[46] or a Luther, who said that "Philosophy knows naught of divine matters,"[47] and who believed that allegory is valuable chiefly for rhetorical reasons, or to the extent that it comforts the consciences of men.[48] You can see Origen's uncertainty on this point in the *contra Celsum*, in which he first makes a show of defending Christianity against the charge that it is a cultic system, or system of secret knowledge, but then abruptly concedes the charge, since there is nothing very remarkable in it: "to speak of the Christian doctrine as a secret system is altogether absurd," Origen says. "But that there should be certain doctrines, not made known to the multitude, which are revealed after the exoteric ones have been taught, is not a peculiarity of Christianity alone, but also of philosophic systems, in which certain truths are exoteric and others esoteric."[49] The ancients routinely (without a second thought) divided the world into exoteric and esoteric realms: these are basic categories of definition, like nature and culture. The illustrious antagonism of philosophy and rhetoric is rooted in (and nourished by) this division, nor is it any wonder that sacred writing should find itself divided accordingly: it is a universal proclamation—the Word which fills the world, every nook and cranny of it, transgressing all boundaries and addressing itself to every manner of audience (giving scandal to the wise); yet it is also a proclamation which opens inwardly upon reserves of unspeakable wisdom and so turns out to be, upon reflection or study, a book of all that cannot be said. The cruel and saintly Cardinal Ximenes de Cisneros, scholar and Inquisitor, who supervised the production of the Complutensian Polyglot (1514–17; published 1522), figured the text this way:

> Certainly since there can be no word, no combination of letters, from which there does not arise, and as it were spring forth, the most concealed senses of the heavenly wisdom; and since the most learned interpreter cannot explain more than one of these, it is unavoidable that after translation Scripture yet remains pregnant and filled with both various and sublime insights which cannot become known from any other sources than from the very fountain of the original language.[50]

Scripture is not a fully interpretable or fully translatable text, and this is by reason of its polysemous nature: to interpret or to translate is to bring forth a meaning, but in Scripture's case something is always left behind in the original, which "remains pregnant and filled with both various and sublime insights"—a cornucopia of meanings. For Luther, however, Scripture con-

founds interpretation (and is, in its way, confounded by it in turn) by reason
of its plainness: "The Holy Spirit," he says, "is the simplest writer and ad-
viser in heaven and on earth. That is why his words could have no more
than the one simplest meaning which we call the written one, or the literal
meaning of the tongue. But [written] words and [spoken] language cease to
have meaning when the things which have a simple meaning through interpretation by a simple word are given further meanings and thus become
different things so that one thing takes on the meaning of another."[51] Or,
again: "Scripture is its own interpreter [*sui ipsius interpres*]"[52]—a self-
authorizing, self-disclosing text: a book with nothing to hide because there
is nothing that is hidden, save what the mind confounds by compounding
the sense of what it reads. For Cardinal Ximenes, Scripture is hardly reducible to a textual existence: it cannot be comprehended alone in any one of
its versions—rather the Vulgate and the Septuagint must be read back into
the fathomless and copious Hebrew original, but even then Scripture remains more than any one interpreter can read and understand. It is not systematically intelligible; it is not simultaneously comprehensible in each of
its parts. It is like a story which cannot be told all at once but requires to
be endlessly repeated or turned repeatedly into new renditions, each one
offering a unique glimpse of that which each rendition is meant to disclose,
namely the unspeakable thing itself.

Luther's thinking on this subject, however, more nearly resembles our
own textual imagination, which is systematic rather than versional. Scripture
for Luther is fulfilled once for all in its letter: "Why should I add any glosses
to it?"[53] he asks, alluding to the great medieval Christian equivalent of Jewish Midrash, the *Glossa Ordinaria*, in which a text of Scripture is surrounded on every side (and between its lines) by centuries of anonymous
notation, commentary, instruction—and diverse revisionary matter.[54] The
Glossa Ordinaria may be characterized as the product of an essentially midrashic habit of mind—a mind which is neither Jewish nor, indeed, Oriental
but ancient, and therefore Christian and Islamic as well: a mind which imagines reading to be more than the simple deciphering of words and phrases:
more than a grammatical literacy. Reading is a speaking to the occasion of
the text and, therefore, is a real addition to it, or rather may be legitimately
(authoritatively) made part of the original. The nature of this addition is not
easy for the modern mind to understand, but one can figure it by analogy
with adornment, which is not merely an extraneous and superfluous ornamentation but is an essentially hermeneutical activity that brings what is hidden into the open by adding lustre to that which conceals it.[55] Luther imagined, however, an originally plain text obscured by secondary constructions,

as when Origen, Jerome, and Augustine devised allegories in order to make the text weighty with "philosophical ideas."[56] The text for Luther does not divide into letter and spirit, no more than it divides into polysemic arrangements of any sort: nowhere does it exhibit the fourfold sense of the schools. The text is made of letters, which any schoolboy knows how to read. What is called the spirit is not concealed in the letter but is "inscribed only in the heart, and it is a living writing of the Holy Spirit."[57] In such writing as this there is nothing that anyone cannot understand.

Imagine, therefore, two conceptions of the scriptural text: one ancient and one modern. On the one hand, the text is imagined to contain all that can be said, and a good deal more besides, since it recedes into the unspeakable source of all that can be put into words. Scripture contains that which no one has thought it possible to say. One cannot speak the truth save that one has been anticipated by Scripture, which contains the whole of it. On the other hand, however, the text is imagined to be univocal and, therefore, requires only to be read by anyone knowing the method of it. The text withholds nothing of itself, for what is there that requires secrecy? Luther speaks for the whole of the modern world by his categorical rejection of secrecy, which becomes now a textual aberration—or, more accurately, it is something to be assimilated into the category of misreading or misunderstanding: a pretext (like allegory) for reading into the text that which the text has no reason or desire to receive.

2

The Originality of Texts in a Manuscript Culture

Perhaps this chapter will make better sense if I say beforehand that it is secretly controlled by a distinction between two kinds of text: the closed text of a print culture and the open text of a manuscript culture. I use the word "kinds," but really my subject has to do with the ways in which textuality is imagined and, therefore, with the ways in which this imagining bears upon the art or practice of writing—and not the art of writing only but also, in turn, all of the things one may do to writing once it gets written. Our natural or, at least, modern instinct is to think of texts as objects—stable, durable, self-possessed entities—and this is certainly one way of taking them, but it is also true that texts are historical creatures (they are temporal as well as structural), and their historicity complicates and sometimes confounds their objectivity in ways that we may not be able to see. As Plato knew, things exist more as versions than as objects, not that they are less in existence for all that, but their existence in this state of affairs tends to be open, fluid, and subject to odd problems of interpretation. I want to say that this is particularly true of whatever gets written, and that it is even more visibly and interestingly the case with texts that make their appearance in a culture of manuscripts rather than of printed books.

By a closed text, in other words, I mean simply the results of an act of writing that has reached a final form. What form this finality will take is variable in nearly every respect that one can imagine, but in our experience there is this noticeable feature: a text is most often thought to be closed when it succeeds into print, whereupon it is sometimes called a "work." Print closes off the act of writing and authorizes or, in a technological way, canonizes its results. The text, once enclosed in print, cannot be altered—except at considerable cost and under circumstances watched over by virtually everyone: readers, critics, the book industry, the legal profession, posterities of every stripe. There are numberless complicated forces of closure in a print culture, although one hardly notices them because they are so rarely challenged. One has to imagine odd cases, such as that of the serial novelist who naturally produces a heterogeneous or unsystematic text to the extent that he cannot, once an episode has been published, revise it in behalf of continuity and wholeness, or the clean interrelationship of parts. Publication closes him off from his work and poses in turn dramatic obstacles to invention. What is printed cannot be altered—except, of course, to produce a revised version or edition, which is the result of a reopening that introduces into the text new or different matter, or removes from it whatever has been affronted by history. The world of revisions is richly complicated and is a famous source of exasperation and delight among literary critics, especially those who must contend with writers who can leave nothing unrewritten and whose canon thus contains many different published versions of single poems. Think of Robert Lowell's work, and the uncertain complaint that he ruined many poems by changing them. What does it mean to rewrite (or to have different versions of) a finished poem? In what does the singleness (or finish) of any poem consist?

A culture of printed books makes it a bit cumbersome to address these questions because of the way it tends to disguise (under semblances of fixity, or by its power of reproducing identical versions) the temporality or natural contingency of what is written. Here I wish simply to reflect on some of the ways in which texts remain open in a manuscript culture—and what I wish to address are certain topics having to do with the finality of authorship: originality, imitation, translation, and plagiarism.

One way to engage these topics is to conceive them as events that record the gradual loss of authority, or (if we reverse the sequence) that describe an ascent from apprenticeship to mastery. At one pole we may imagine an act of creation *ex nihilo,* or the primordial Saying of Heidegger's poet, or simply a rhetorical genesis that results in a "new" work; at the other we may imagine an act of bogus authorship, the scribal despair that Borges dramatizes in "The Library of Babel," for example, or the youthful poet's characteristic idolatry. "He is so much in love with Vergil's charms," Petrarch says of his apprentice, "that he often inserts bits of Vergil into his own work."[1] Imitation and translation for their part are functions of learning that replicate or appeal to the authority of a prior text or model; yet they are also acts that disturb such priorities, often without intending to. Quintilian observes "that it is often easier to achieve more than to achieve the same; an exact replica is very difficult." Originality is a sort of happy accident that disrupts imitation. What Quintilian means is that individuality is luckily difficult to suppress. In principle, he says, "every imitation is a mere artifact, accommodated to someone else's scheme"; but in reality—in the domain of "nature and real vitality"—imitation always produces a difference, because it comprises virtues that cannot be taught or borrowed: "Talent, facility of discovery, force, fluency, everything that art cannot supply—

these things," Quintilian says, "are not imitable." As the saying goes, eloquence is an art of nature as well as of the school. Moreover, as invention is the lesson of learning, so improvement becomes the motive of imitation, as in the poet's desire to transform a brazen world into a golden, or when a certain writer is said to have stimulated the envy of his originals: "No art," says Quintilian, "is as it was when it was discovered, or has confined itself to its starting-place."[2] Similarly, a translation may seem, as Don Quixote said, like the reverse side of a tapestry, but it may also recover a lost (or achieve a new) efficacy, as in the King James or "Authorized Version" of Scripture, which competes, in the absence of the original, against various antecedent translations, and prevails, where it can, by dint of royal decision and by the special way it graces or adorns the vernacular. It also bends divine authority to Jacobean purpose, and so God's Word is doubly forged. To complete this thought: between imitation and translation other categories intervene: parody, adaptation, collaboration, quotation, allusion, diverse forms of attribution ("as myn auctor seyde, so sey I"), the utterance of commonplace matter, mnemonic storytelling (who could not extend this inventory?). Concerning stories and commonplaces we may wonder what happens when an oral tradition is subsumed or overlaid by a manuscript culture, such that the authority of the tradition is altered or diverted by the authority of bookish learning that textual traditions strive to maintain. (One thing that happens is that authors come into being as ways of figuring the presence or dominion of an authority that has literally been silenced, as when the authority of the oral tradition is translated into the eponymous authority of Homer, Moses, Aristotle, and so on.) Precisely what sort of authority, however, does a text possess in a manuscript culture? What I mean especially to ask: What sort of finality does a manuscript possess, particularly in relation to the rights, privileges, and conventional arrogations of a "later hand"?

Here I want simply to recall three well-known features of writing in a manuscript culture: (1) the grammarian's art of embellishment; (2) the desire to produce a vernacular text; and (3) the clerical as opposed to vatic or Orphic conception of *poiesis,* which constrains writing in ways that we have forgotten, in part because such writing remains innocent of any implicit or corollary claim to creativity. (Not until the eighteenth century was writing considered to be the result of a "creative" act; until then a writer was likely to desire fecundity and to think of creativity as an attribute of God or a power of the king, at whose word peers of the realm are brought into being.) In each of these cases—grammatical embellishment, vernacular writing, clerical making—the terms "originality," "imitation," "translation," and "plagiarism" are not at all what we may mean them to be: they come into play chiefly as variations on the ancient theme of authority.

Consider, for example, Chaucer in relation to Boccaccio's *Il Filostrato:* What did Chaucer really do to this antecedent text when (evidently with the help of a French intermediary) he conjured from it his *Troilus and Criseyde*? Chaucer's narrator, who claims merely to be relating his literal or faithful translation of a Latin text, does not speak with authority on this point; or, rather, he speaks with a fictional authority that has been carefully constructed (and sharply restricted) by the author, who chooses to conceal his originality, which is to say the faithlessness of his translation, the diversions and elaborations of his imitation, his own talent, facility of discovery, and so on. (Plagiarism is evidently not at issue; no one is certain why it isn't.) Certainly, one reason for this deferral of authority becomes apparent in the Envoy:

> But litel book, no makyng thow n'envie,
> But subgit be to alle poesye;
> And kis the steppes, where as thow seest pace
> Virgile, Ovide, Omer, Lucan, and Stace.
> [V. 1789–92][3]

These lines recall the tradition of the *sermo humilis,* the humble or lowly style which is, however, "secretly sublime,"[4] for its purpose is to render lofty themes (tragedy, love, Christian doctrine) accessible to every manner of audience. To circulate the tragedy of Troilus and Criseyde through a clerkly, plainspoken, loveless but warm- and openhearted narrator is to execute this style with unexceptionable decorum. It is in the self-effacing spirit of the sermo humilis that Chaucer commends his book to the "moral Gower" and the "philosophical Strode" (V. 1856–57)—commends it wholly and without reserve, granting to them the authorial privilege of correcting his book wherever they might think it necessary. This humility, moreover, is doubly conventional, for it coincides with what we might call the grammarian's "ethos," which enjoins the subordination of authorial will to the ideal of a correct text—a text correct, not in the sense that it reproduces an original, but in its words and usage, in the handling or rendering of its matter, and above all in its doctrine. "For myne wordes, heere and every part," the narrator says of his own (admitted) enlargements upon Lollius, "I speke hem alle under correccioun," and accordingly he confers upon his audience ("yow that felyng han in loves art") the right to emend his text in turn—"to encresse or maken dymynucioun / Of my language" (III. 1331–36).

A second example will help to illustrate the distinction implicit here between authorial and editorial corrections, that is, between corrections which alter an original (as if the original were always open to second thoughts) and those which seek to restore a text to its original or pristine state. Consider Petrarch's Latin translation of Boccaccio's tale of Griselda (*Decameron,* X. 10). Petrarch wrote to Boccaccio about this, explicitly to méntion Horace's precept that translators should not try to render their originals word for word. Accordingly, Petrarch says, "I have told your tale in my own language, in some places changing or even adding a few words, for I felt you would not only permit, but would approve, such alterations."⁵ The alterations, of course, are considerable, the more so because what Petrarch calls his "language" entails a theory of what is required to write in that language. Petrarch translates Boccaccio's story not only laterally into a different tongue but upwardly into a more noble style (*stilo nunc alto*), and this noble style stipulates in turn large amplifications of matter. Or, again, Petrarch transposes the story from the locality of the vernacular to the universality of Latin, which is a way of finishing the story and publishing it to the world. The vernacular text becomes a learned text. It may be that we can most accurately describe what Petrarch thought he was doing by saying that he translated Boccaccio's story into Literature: a story that does not make its way into Latin is a story that goes to waste, because it acquires no institutional reality. At all events Petrarch's translation confers upon the vernacular story the authority of a Latin text, and thus we may think of the translation as a way of enshrining the story or finding for it a permanent authoritative place. From this follows the important point that Petrarch's presumption is not an insult but a tribute: it is a way of honoring Boccaccio, Boccaccio's story, *and* the language in which the story was originally composed. A final point is that Petrarch's presumption is not presumption of any sort; his translation is not unauthorized but is sanctioned by the grammarian's ethos.

Even so late or modern a writer as Dryden understood this ethos very well. In his Preface to *Fables, Ancient and Modern*—a miscellany of his translations, "to which," he says, "I have added some Original Papers of my own"⁶—Dryden remarks of Chaucer's *Troilus* that it had already been "written by a Lombard Author; but much amplified by our English Translatour, as well as beautified; the Genius of our Countrymen in general being rather to improve an invention, than to invent themselves" (101–02). Nor did Dryden, in translating Chaucer into "modern *English,*" scruple to improve upon his original—did not hesitate to add, as he says, "somewhat of my own where I thought my Author was deficient, and had not given his Thoughts their true Lustre, for want of Words in the Beginning of our Language. And to this I was the more embolden'd, because (if I may be permitted to say it of myself) I found that I had a Soul congenial to his, and that I had been conversant in the same Studies. Another Poet, in another Age, may take the same liberty with my Writings; if at least they live long enough to deserve Correction" (111).

> Our Sons their Fathers' failing *Language* see,
> And such as *Chaucer* is, shall Dryden be.

An interesting sidenote is that in his Preface Dryden describes translations as a "transfusion" (pp. 112–13), by which he means the transfusion of new life into an old text, or of new efficacy into an archaic or obsolete utterance; but he also means the reincarnation of the original author in a new writer: "Spenser more than once insinuates, that the Soul of Chaucer was transfused into his Body" (95)—one recalls the way Ennius thought himself the reincarnation of Homer. Dryden possesses, he says, "a Soul congenial" to Chaucer's, such that he translates as if by becoming Chaucer, not as Chaucer was, of course, but as he would have been had he lived in the seventeenth century, when (among other ripenings) the English vernacular had sufficiently matured to become capable of a Latin or literary "correctness." Chaucer lived, Dryden says, "in the infancy of our Poetry, and . . . nothing is brought to Perfection at the first. We must be Children before we grow Men" (105).

Transfusion, however, is a rich and variable metaphor. In *MacFlecknoe* Dryden uses it as a synonym for plagiarism:

> When did his Muse from *Fletcher* scenes purloin,
> As thou whole *Eth'rdig* dost transfuse to thine?
> But so transfus'd as Oyl on waters flow,
> His always floats above, thine sinks below.[7]

In Shadwell's case, of course, it is as though old life had been transfused into new deadness, without effect: the best parts of Shadwell's plays remain the plays of Etherege. But this raises an interesting question: Had Shadwell other than a genius for sinking—had he a "Soul congenial" to Etherege's— would these transfusions constitute a plagiarism? They would, no doubt, but remember that in *Of Dramatick Poesy* Crites says of Ben Jonson (by way of praising him as "the greatest man of the last age") that "he was not only a professed Imitator of Horace, but a learned Plagiary of all the others; you track him every where in their Snow" (p. 15). To which Neander later adds:

> He was deeply conversant in the Ancients, both Greek and Latine, and he borrowed boldly from them: there is scarce a Poet or Historian among the Roman Authors of those times whom he has not translated in *Sejanus* and *Catiline*.

But he has done his Robberies so openly, that one may see he fears not to be taxed by any Law. He invades Authors like a Monarch, and what would be theft in other Poets is onely victory in him. With the spoils of these Writers he so represents *old Rome* to us, in its Rites, Ceremonies, and Customs, that if one of their Poets had written either of his Tragedies, we had seen less of it then in him. If there was any Fault in his Language, 'twas that he weaved it too closely and laboriously, in his serious Plays: perhaps too, he did a little too much Romanize our Tongue, leaving the Words which he translated almost as much Latin as he found them. [50]

So well, it seems, did Jonson plagiarize that he verged upon originality; or, again, so "conversant" was he in the Ancients that he mastered them and assumed their authority.

Jonson's authority derives in fact from the tradition of the *translatio studii,* the transference of the dominion of learning from the empire of the Ancients (Athens, "old Rome") to that of the Moderns: Paris, the "new Rome" of Christianity, and even London. Dryden's point is that Jonson is the true translator: he did not misuse this dominion—did not destroy it as a barbarian like Shadwell might have done—but was so "conversant" in Ancient learning that he became its legitimate heir and ruler. Jonson in this respect rules under the title of Grammarian-Poet (not the Philosopher-Poet, which is another, more remote lineage, with its own requisites of authority, such as the Vergilian power of ascending to the sublime or lofty style: vide Milton). The grammarian has always presided over the dominion of learning—has done so, with propriety and proprietorship, ever since that inaugural (if apocryphal) moment when Peisistratus, who ruled Athens from 560 to 527 B.C., gathered together Homer's fugitive texts and, recending them, inserted into the *Odyssey* (XI. 631) a line of his own devising.[8]

As codified by the Romans, grammar is said to consist of the *"recte loquendi scientiam et poetarum enarrationem"* (Quintilian), the recitation and interpretation of the poets. Strict grammatical interpretation, like Priscian's famous analysis of the first twelve lines of the *Aeneid,* entailed no more than the study of case, gender, number, and so on; elsewhere it included commentary on an author's prosody and particularly his use of the figures, but in the Middle Ages it was not uncommon for such commentary to become an exegesis carried on under the sanction of embellishment, whereby the grammarian would add to a text a construction of his own— his own sense, thoughts, wisdom, and occasionally even evidence of his own skill in storytelling. Moreover, the medieval grammarian might literally add to the text, for such embellishment customarily took the form of marginal and (more interesting still) interlinear commentary.[9] And it is at this point that differences between originality and imitation, invention and interpretation, translation and poiesis, one text and another, become hard to define. In his book *The Rise of Romance,* for example, Eugene Vinaver regards interlinear commentary as the formal nexus of grammar and romance writing. He observes that both Gottfried von Strassburg and Marie de France describe the romance writer's task explicitly as a form of secondary writing on the model of grammatical exegesis. In the Prologue to the *Lais* of Marie, for example, we are told that "it was the custom of the ancients, as witnessed by Priscian, to speak obscurely in the books they wrote so that those who came later and studied those books might construe the text and add their own thoughts."[10] Accordingly, "what a good romance writer is expected to do," Vinaver says, "is to reveal the *meaning* of the story . . . adding to it such embellishing thoughts as he considers appropriate; by doing this he would raise his work to a level of distinction which no straightforward narration could ever reach" (17). As we know, medieval vernacular narratives are seldom straightforward. Auerbach, comparing Vergil's treatment of Camilla in the *Aeneid* (VII. 8–0–17) with its twelfth-century counterpart in the Old French *Enéas,* writes as follows:

> It is . . . evident that though the Norman poet deals with the same incident as Vergil, he does so in an entirely different way. The main difference, from which all the others follow, is that he destroys the happening by continually interrupting it. In Vergil the references to Camilla's person are brief and so selected as to fit into the flowing movement. In Vergil, Camilla comes into view and rides past; not for a moment do we lose sight of this happening. The French poet interrupts it in the second line (3968); goes back to it almost fifty lines later (line 4008: *Vers l'ost chevalche la meschine*), but very briefly; and finally completes it, after a further interlude of almost eighty lines, in lines 4085–4106, without further interruption but with a leisurely garrulousness that contrasts sharply with Vergil's pace. The interstices are filled in with moralizing descriptions, and it is to these that the poet obviously attaches the greatest importance. Most modern critics find them overlong, inappropriate, and somewhat ridiculous.[11]

The interstices are filled in with moralizing descriptions: in other words, the *Enéas* is written virtually between Vergil's lines, and for Auerbach this amounts to a defacement of the original text, because for Auerbach the original text is closed. To open it for embellishment is not to honor it but to "destroy" it. The rewriting of Vergil is an obliteration of him. But the point here concerns medieval rather than modern principles. Contrary to our textbook definition of medieval romance as a chivalric tale, romance writing consists in what is *done* to such a tale. In the Proem to *Erec et Enide,* for example, Chrétien de Troyes speaks of himself as one who adds to "a story of adventure a pleasing argument"—"Et tret d'un conte d'avanture /

Une mout bele conjointure"[12]—who fashions a more perfectly connected work, a more correct work, by which Chrétien means, however, not only a more carefully designed but also a more *sententious* work: a work of learning. For Chrétien, the story itself is only a point of departure for copious invention: it is the matter to be imitated, but this imitation can only be made whole—can, indeed, only become authoritative—by what amounts to an interlinear expression of learning. Thus, in *Cligés,* the eyes of Alesaundre and Soredamours meet, but this event is for Chrétien an opening, as though between the lines of his original, for an analysis of love—a discourse of learning that "fills in" the book that he has before him (or, conceivably, in his memory) as he writes. To be sure, this discourse takes the form of two extended interior monologues, but the monologues are not instances of mimesis or characterization; they are enunciations of so many topics in the doctrine of love—imitations, if you like, of clerkly instructions: treatises. As Vinaver says, "Chrétien lets the characters enact a line of argument that happens to interest him, no matter what kind of characterization, real or unreal, may emerge from the result."[13]

For Chrétien, imitation is not of nature, nor is it strictly the imitation of a text. It is imitation without representation. It is an imitation of antique authority: it is imitation that incarnates rather than replicates. In the Proem to *Cligés* Chrétien is explicit on this point. He observes (rehearsing the topos of the translatio studii) that "chivalry" originated in Greece, then "passed to Rome, together with that highest learning which has now come to France," where, he prays, it will, with his help, flourish anew. For the fame of the Greeks and Romans is heard no longer: "Their glowing ash," he says, "is dead."[14] Their disappearance opens the way for Chrétien, whose writing will not merely be a duplication of what has already been written but a continuation of it as of an ongoing discourse—a discourse that requires Chrétien's intervention if it is not to go the way of its original authors.

Let me embellish this conception of writing as textual intervention with a note on the grammarian's mythology, which is full of rich and contrary themes. One theme is that the letters of the alphabet contain the universal range of words, and these in turn harbor or conceal all that can be said about all that God has created. To write is to penetrate this system of letters and to disclose some portion of the truth that lies hidden therein as though behind a great veil of words or within a Great Book of the kind imagined by the alchemists. Writing is thus always in some sense hermeneutic, which means that it is never an original activity but is always mediated by the texts that provide access to the system. To write is to intervene in what has already been written; it is to work "between the lines" of antecedent texts, there to gloss, to embellish, to build invention upon invention. All writing is essentially amplification of discourse; it consists in doing something to (or with) other texts. Currently, Northrop Frye and Jacques Derrida are the most illustrious exponents of this mythology of the letter, and so, in a residual sort of way, is Harold Bloom.

We will misunderstand this mythology of the letter, however, if we do not consider it simultaneously with its counterpart or antithesis, namely the figure of the unschooled poet, whose utterances are original by their very nature, because the unschooled poet exists outside the system of letters at the Source or Origin of poetry, as in the story of Orpheus. This figure is as durable as the letter itself—has existed from Homer and Hesiod to Heidegger as a sort of explanatory myth of poetry (why, after all, is there such a thing as poetry? Why not silence or, at the very least, mundane utterance?). Variants of this figure recur in Plato's *Ion* and in the *Peri hupsos* of "Longinus"; in the story of Caedmon and in countless legends of the blind bard; in the pastoral myth, with its figure of the poet as unlearned swain (whose constant recourse is to the "learned Sisters," or Muses, who are the primary agents of his song); in the Renaissance sonnet cycles, whose authors claim to be erring and artless (thus the introspective Astrophil and Shakespeare's "unletter'd Clerk"); in Romantic poetry and poetics and, indeed, in all theories of poetry that privilege voice over script, poetic experience over the poetic work, vision over craft, nature over art. The poet in Wolfram von Eschenbach's *Parzival* asks us not to think of his text as a book. "I don't know a single letter of the alphabet," he says at the end of book 2: *"Ine kan decheinen buochstap."* Wolfram is an aggressive antigrammarian: "Plenty of people get their material that way, but this adventure steers without books. Rather than have anybody think it is a book, I would sit naked without a towel, the way I would sit in a bath": unadorned, unembellished.[15] Of Shakespeare Dryden's Neander says that "all the Images of Nature were still present to him, and he drew them, not laboriously, but luckily: when he describes any thing, you more than see it, you feel it too. Those who accuse him to have wanted learning, give him the greater Commendation: he was naturally learn'd: he needed not the spectacles of Books to read Nature; he look'd inwards, and found her there" (48).

Just so, inwardness is made the source of poetic authority, concerning which history has devised countless theories—theories of genius, imagination, creativity, vision, transcendence, individuality, experience, the Self. In *Poetic Individuality in the Middle Ages* (Oxford, 1970), Peter Dronke relies heavily on these value-laden terms in an effort to assert the primary, untraditional, experimental, and therefore original and "ungrammatical" character of certain medieval texts—the *Ruodlieb, Semiramis,* the *Ordo Virtutum* of Hildegard of Bingen. No need to romanticize the ancients—but it is true that the position of the medieval vernacular poet is unstable: he exists, so to speak, on the periphery of letters and strives to attain the privileged center where Vergil dwells; that is, he is in transit from orality to script, from nature to culture, from the outside to the inside, from anonymity to authority. Yet having once attained the center, he acquires (as perhaps only a grammarian can) the dream of an original utterance, or of speech that originates from within the writer himself rather than from his encounter with other texts. This point contains many issues, some of which are present in one of Petrarch's letters to Boccaccio:

> I grant that I like to embellish my life by quoting others' words and admonitions, but I do not so adopt them in my writing. I quote the authors with credit, or I transform them honorably, as bees imitate by making a single honey from many nectars. I much prefer that my style be my own, rude and unrefined, perhaps, but made to the measure of my mind, like a well-cut gown, rather than to use someone else's style, more elegant, ambitious, and ornamented than mine—a style that keeps slipping off, unfitted to the modest proportions of my mind. An actor can wear any kind of garment; but a writer cannot adopt any kind of style. He should form his own and keep it, for fear we should laugh at him, dressed grotesquely in others' clothes, or plucked, like the crows, by other birds that assemble to reclaim their stolen feathers. Certainly each of us has naturally something individual and his own in his utterance and language as in his face and gesture. It is better and more rewarding for us to develop and train this quality than to change it.
>
> [*Letters from Petrarch,* 183]

The statement that "a writer cannot adopt any kind of style" is a schooled way of defying the school traditions of grammar and rhetoric—and, indeed, perhaps the most important thing to say about Petrarch's assertion of individuality is that it is composed almost entirely of commonplaces. Hence it is traditional to assert one's individuality or originality, not explicitly, but by disingenuously confessing the plainness or lowliness of one's style, even as (by contrast) one asserts one's authority by claiming kinship with the antique authors, which is the message of the translatio studii topos, and which is what Dante is careful to portray in Canto IV of the *Inferno.* The sermo humilis would in this view be the natural language of original authorship, although it is not so for Dante, who, as part of his project to overcome the opposition between authority and originality, claims that the vernacular is both natural *and* illustrious.

Petrarch adds to his forbearing texts, not his words, but himself: he does not write between antecedent lines; rather he incorporates these lines into his life or, indeed, into himself, for they become part of that of which he is made, and therefore part of his self-expression. He does not embellish others; they embellish him, and he, in turn, is self-embellishing, adorned (however rudely) according to a principle of decorum peculiar to himself. In a fine essay on "Petrarch and the Humanist Hermeneutic," Thomas M. Greene cites this letter of Petrarch's. It is, he says, an instance of humanist composition, which is self-assertive writing that, nevertheless, bears within itself "the latent presence of an ancient author"[16]—as if ancient had been transfused into modern. For Greene, the humanist text is not one text but two: it harbors an ancient subtext or an array of such subtexts, which means that the interpretation of the humanist text requires an act of subreading that can catch the encounter of humanist and antiquity. This encounter entails but is not reducible to exchanges of matter or doctrine because it is, as Petrarch makes clear in the quoted letter, above all a stylistic exchange. As Greene explains, "The interplay between the surface text and the antecedent or sub-text involves subtle interpenetrations, an interflowing and a tingeing, an exchange of minute gradations, that cannot be measured wholly or formulated. . . . Reading and sub-reading it means dealing with the implicit, the incipient, the virtual, and the inexpressible—'ut intelligi simile queat potius quam dici' " ["The quality is to be felt rather than defined"] (p. 213). This felt, ghostly, or unspoken otherness defines for Greene the openness of the humanist text, which unfolds inwardly upon a whole civilization of authorship—to which it now adds itself as a distinctive yet authoritative utterance.

Similarly, we may speak of a text that opens outwardly as well as inwardly, in the sense that it seems to a later hand to invite or require collaboration, amplification, embellishment, illustration to disclose the hidden or the as-yet-unthought-of. A useful notion in this connection is the figure of translatio, or turning, which is more than the turning of a text into another language because it implicates the general notion of metaphorical turning as well.[17] My argument would be that in a manuscript culture the text is not reducible to the letter; that is, a text always contains more than it says, or more than what its letters contain, which is why we are privileged to read between the lines, and not to read between them only but to write between them as well, because the text is simply not complete—not fully what it could be, as in the case of the dark story that requires an illuminated retelling (that is, by one who understands). This is why it is important to remember that the grammarian's embellishment is an art of disclosure as well as an art of amplification. Or, rather, amplification is not merely supplementation but also interpretation: the act of adding to a text is also the act of eliciting from it that which remains unspoken. Embellishment adds lustre, but this addition illuminates what is hidden in the original, which is to say again that a text is never reducible to the letters of which it is composed but is always capable of becoming more than it is. The text is, in any case, tacitly unfinished: it is never fully present but is always available for a later hand to bring it more completely into the open.

But what precisely is this "open"—this space between the lines where the grammarian embellisher intervenes? The modern mind would figure it as absence, the ancient as plenitude. In an appendix to his *Truth and Method* Hans-Georg Gadamer says that "it is part of the reality of a work of art that around its real theme it leaves an area that is indefinite"—an indeterminate area that waits to be filled or fulfilled with a meaning. "To leave an enormous amount open," Gadamer says, "seems to belong to the essence of a fruitful fable and to myth. Precisely thanks to this open indeterminacy, myth is able to produce constant new inventions from within itself, with the thematic horizon continuously shifting out in different directions."[18] Gadamer gives us here another instance in which it is not easy to distinguish between originality and belatedness, interpretation and invention, imitation and discovery. Such distinctions are always difficult to make (and perhaps impossible to sustain) when one is concerned with rhetorical rather than Romantic invention—that is, invention conceived as the art of finding what it is that can be said in any given case, not invention as "creative" and unprecedented origination. The grammarian embellisher as I have constructed him is rhetorically rather than Romantically inventive: he is the writer who dwells among texts and who is always discovering in them more things to say. He is, as Gadamer might say, alive to their empty spaces, their areas of indefiniteness—regions, however, that are not reducible to absences but are rather like horizons that continually open onto new landscapes. Hence for the grammarian there is nothing that cannot be rewritten or enriched by further writing, because no text is closed to him, not even (as we have seen) Vergil's. He dwells, it is important to remember, *among* texts, not over and against them, and accordingly he is without anxiety, because his antecedents are great inventories that produce in him the copious mind, which is a mind capable of endless invention—invention which is, however, textual rather than natural, insofar as its point of departure is always prior writing, not worldly or mental experience. The library (or its mental equivalent: memory) is the grammarian's equivalent of Romantic imagination.

Yet to speak in this fashion about the grammarian and his texts is at once to wonder whether the word "text" is appropriate to the conception of writing and rewriting that is at work in a manuscript culture. The word "text" itself is worth consulting in this regard. Etymologically it refers to the way words are put together in a piece of writing, their weave or texture in a written discourse, or their (more or less) formal order, pattern, or sequence. Its early vernacular usage, however, is almost exclusively in reference to Scripture, that is, Revelation in its written character: there is only one "text," and that is the Bible, which is, however, not one text but an array of texts (and, in the Middle Ages, an array of texts and glosses). The metaphor of openness finds its complication here in the fact that the word "text" refers to something which (practices to the contrary notwithstanding) is not to be altered but which, on the contrary, must be adhered to—scribally, morally, doctrinally, spiritually, and so on. In general it appears that there can be no conception of "text" without a corresponding notion of fixity. Thus Chaucer is thinking of his work textually, that is, as authorized writing that must be reproduced word for word, when he admonishes his scribe:

> Adam scriveyn, if ever it thee bifalle
> Boece or Troylus for to wryten newe,
> Under thy long lokkes thou must have the scalle,
> By after my makying thou wryte more trewe;
> So ofte a-day I mot thy werk renewe,
> It to correcte and eek to rubbe and scrape;
> And al is thorugh thy negligence and rape.
> [*Works,* 534]

A text is simply fixed writing, and is therefore closed by definition. To speak of an open text thus makes no sense at all—until one remembers Chaucer in relation to *Il Filostrato*: Why did Chaucer not treat this text as a text (that is, as closed)? Why did he not adhere to it—or, more accurately, why is his adherence to it sometimes embarrassingly faithful (word for word, saving "oure tonges difference," I. 395) and sometimes marred beautifully by embellishments? The question is interesting in part because one of Chaucer's purposes was simply to produce a vernacular version of the more literary Italian: it was in effect to determine whether a poem like *Il Filostrato* could exist in English. It is doubly interesting, however, because Chaucer's narrator in the Troilus is nothing if not "textuel," which is the word Chaucer regularly uses to describe those who are clerkly or literary, who know texts word for word and are proud of their ability to adhere to or reproduce them exactly, literally, as with a strict scribal devotion to the fixed and the authorized. The Parson's Prologue has these lines:

But natheless, this meditacioun
I putte it ay under correccioun
Of clerkes, for I am nat textueel;
I take but the sentence, trusteth weel.
Therfore I make protestacioun
That I wol stonde to correccioun.
                    [lines 55–60]

The Parson is not a man of letters but a man of sentences. By contrast, the narrator of the *Troilus* insists everywhere that "Myn auctour shal I folwen, if I konne" (II. 49). He is more scribe than grammarian, which is to say of lesser authority than the grammarian, in the sense that he is not authorized to go beyond the letter of his original. What this means is that to be original is not to be "textuel," which in Chaucer's case means that one cannot imitate one's "auctores" simply by following their texts word by word; rather, to imitate an "auctor" requires that one take words into one's own hand, thus to weave them (or to reweave them) according to one's own design, wisdom, or grasp of the hiddenness of what is written. To imitate an "auctor" means precisely the imitation of authority rather than the imitation of a text. To be original in this sense is to transcend textuality (as indeed one is expected always to transcend the literalness of one's antecedent texts by finding in them openings for further invention). The grammarian embellisher, therefore, is not a textualist; rather, he aspires to the authority of his originals, and indeed may attain it—but with this difference, that his mode of aspiration or composition can no longer be the mode of original utterance or authorship, because it is necessarily an inter- rather than extralinear mode. The grammarian is preeminently the schooled writer, whose desire is to transcend the letters that limit and define him, or make him what he is.

The doubleness or even duplicity implicit in this desire is perfectly represented by *Troilus and Criseyde,* with its scribal narrator or man of letters whose profession of literalness conceals only to emphasize the richness of the grammarian-poet's embellishments. Another way to put this would be to say that the grammarian's originality is itself inter- rather than extralinear: it is textually derived by an act of rewriting that (contrary to Romantic poetics) does not seek to put aside or to destroy its forbearing text but rather seeks to assimilate that text into its own embellishing spirit and even to confer upon it thereby a presence it would not otherwise possess. Thus for many readers (most English-speaking readers, certainly) *Il Filostrato* is always more than itself because it exists inseparably from the *Troilus:* we might not come to it if translation and embellishment had not constituted for Chaucer a normal mode of composition—arguably *the* mode of vernacular poiesis. Our modern attachment to "creativity" inclines us (one should not hesitate to say "trains us") to resist this point, whose assimilation might be assisted, however, by a final thought: the text as I have been discussing it is still as much an utterance as an object; it exists as an adjunct to speech. It is an utterance in a form that one might write as well as read. Indeed, it is an utterance that bears repeating, which is as good a way as any of defining an authoritative utterance (the kind of utterance for which or of which texts are made). For Chaucer, at any rate, *Il Filostrato* was a text worth repeating, but grammatically rather than scribally so: the repetition of *Il Filostrato* provides the text in which the *Troilus* is to be found.

PART TWO
METHOD AND SYSTEM
AMONG THE MODERNS

3
A *Grammarian's Guide to*
the Discourse on Method

PREFACE

The starting point or beginning of Cartesian philosophy is, of course, the celebrated *cogito ergo sum*; or, rather, the *cogito* is Descartes's philosophical starting point, but it is not exactly the beginning of his philosophy, and still less is it the beginning of his philosophical experience, which is in many ways more interesting (and more instructive) than his philosophy. Part 4 of the *Discourse on Method* contains the formal beginning of the philosophy, and a new beginning in the histories of philosophy, because it inaugurates a new era of epistemological thinking, wherein everything is thought to be determined or made intelligible by the workings of the mind. In the *Discourse* we have only a sort of foreshadowing of this epistemological era. A more formal prospect is to be found in the *Meditations on First Philosophy* (1641), an explicitly inaugurating text, published four years after the *Discourse* and at least a dozen years after the composition of the posthumously published *Regulations for the Direction of the Mind,* which for its part originates in what we may think of as a desire for a grammar of thinking.

It is customary to call this desire a fundamentally modern phenomenon. It is at least true that the perception of a need for method in thinking is one that is shared by many modern writers, each of whom, however, conceives the nature of method differently (a natural state of affairs for which the world of thinking seems never able to prepare itself, and one reason why a grammar of thinking is thought to be necessary, grammar being perennially the logician's refuge against polysemic storms raised by words like "method"). In the second of the *Meditations* Descartes writes: "I am indeed amazed when I consider how weak my mind is and how prone to error. For although I can, dispensing with words, apprehend all this in myself, none the less words have a hampering hold on me, and accepted usages of ordinary speech tend to mislead me."[1] One recalls here the way Bacon implicated words in a double failure: they are (because of the way they are used) imprecise, equivocal, indeterminate; and they are incommensurate with things, and so form a screen or barrier between mind and world. For Descartes, however, words are not only a barrier but weights that cling to the mind even after one has done with them. He would (and does) dispense with words, yet even so they continue to "have a hampering hold" on him; they slow him or stop him in his tracks as he attempts the progress of self-inspection. Or they tend to divert him from his way: their meanings or "accepted usages" deceive him as to his course or direction. But apart from this difference in metaphorical description of words Descartes shares with Bacon (and with most of us) the conviction that one can no longer philosophize in the language of "ordinary speech." One needs a reconstructed language, that is, a reconstructed way of speaking (a *philosophical* language), which for Descartes means a mathematicized or systematized speech—speech or meditation (one's self-conversation or dialogue with oneself) that progresses according to the model of mathematical procedures. Mathematics (especially the best parts of geometry and algebra) is an ideal language, because it is pure: it is uncontaminated by a history of usage. It promises a new way of finding things to say and so implies a whole new theory of invention. And insofar as it is a language of relations rather than of things or of thinglike words, it is not encumbering. It is portable and transparent and allows one easy access to something one may call (philosophically) one's self. With Descartes *ego* replaces *bios* as the primary category of self-reflection.

The difficulty is, however, that not words only but whole libraries cling to the mind. In the *Regulations* Descartes says that intuition and deduction together constitute the mind's primary and natural way of proceeding; but this innate method is deformed by such things as school logic. Left to itself, the mind will not err, but the mind is never left to itself but is encumbered by schooling: received ideas, authorized knowledge, institutionalized modes and bodies of learning—in short, usage writ large and copiously and testifying to the sorry absence of method in the history of man's search for truth. Against this absence and against this history the *Discourse* proposes a new philosophy, that is, the construction of philosophy ex nihilo, as if no one had philosophized before. What the *Discourse* shows is that this radical theory of philosophical originality requires beforehand the construction of a new philosopher. The new philosophy is predicated upon the ability to dispense with the old, but this requires the philosopher's self-dispensation: he is required to play a New Adam who absents himself in order to rise, purified, once more to embark and this time not to go astray. Descartes constructs, not merely a new philosophy but, prior to this, and as a condition of its possibility, a new Descartes: new, because this Descartes has no history. The new Descartes is a mind that doubt or skepticism fashions for itself; it is a mind figured by skepticism as a pure act of thinking. It is pure, because it knows no usage, and it is doubly chaste because it is innocent of body, feeling, and imagination. And, finally, it is utterly self-possessed, because it possesses (and requires) nothing but its own native and inward way of proceeding, which in this case is a grammar purified of whatever accrues to it historically. For the first time invention without an inventory is possible.

Accordingly, it is both odd and necessary that the *Discourse* should take the form of an autobiography. It is odd, because its chief figure proves to be a mind without a history—a mind that obliterates its autobiographical portion; and it is necessary, because without autobiography no such mind would be up to its task, for it is a mind, after all, that has to be arrived at; it doesn't just happen. Or, again, Cartesian philosophy begins with what appears to be the Cartesian's inescapable experience of himself (or whatever doubt leaves behind): I think, therefore I am. This formulation is indeed the first principle whence all other principles are to be derived. Yet the philosophical "I" or the ego of the cogito would be somewhat ghostly or abstract, not something Descartes could call his own, without the "I" of autobiography to provide it with an occasion and a future: if the "I" of the cogito is therefore to exist, then by all means there must be something in which this existence can therefore occur, if only tacitly or, as if not to let skepticism know, in secret. The cogito, after all, retains the character of an event, whatever systematic desires it may need to fulfill. Still another way to put this would be to say that autobiography provides the material by which to construct a philosophical self, but only in the odd sense that it is not material which goes *into* the construction of the self but rather material which defines the construction by being kept out of it. Otherwise who could imagine the "I" of the cogito, this chaste and chastened being (or thing) whose whole essence is merely to think—who would see the need of it? But surely this is a complication in advance of itself. Let it simply stand that the thinking self must prepare a way for itself (and for us) by constructing its own history, that is, by showing its mental progress as its own precursor, who exists in order to disappear at precisely that inaugural moment when history ceases and philosophy begins.

COMMENTARY

. . . the ability to judge correctly, and to distinguish the true from the false— which is really what is meant by good sense or reason—is the same by nature in all men . . . [2; 2][2]

It is not really surprising, in view of the rhetorical nature of the *Discourse* (which is a sort of precursor text designed to make straight the way of troubling and perhaps forbidden ideas)—it is not really surprising that the *Discourse* should begin with a received idea, the staple of rhetorical culture. The topos concerning the equal distribution of reason is, among other things, the first authorization of the cogito as a first principle. It is also the guise under which Descartes (the "I" that shortly will go in search of itself) makes his first appearance: "As for myself," he says, "I have never supposed that my mind was above the ordinary" (2; 2). There is some abstract complication in this, because the topos deprives the "I" of the conventional sanctions of autobiography: namely, exemplary character, or (failing that) a telling uniqueness. Descartes, however, figures himself as typical rather than exemplary (an example is a normative, not a statistical phenomenon). Thus we may remark of Descartes's first appearance that it does not contain much interest, but that such interest as it may accrue depends upon the quality of good fortune that, happily, Descartes does not hesitate to claim for himself: namely, the stumbling, "in my youth, upon certain paths which led me to certain considerations and maxims from which I formed a method . . . " (2; 3).

Method: the word transports Descartes from the world of rhetorical commonplaces to the world of philosophical romance. It is the agency of the hero's fortune and of his identity as well: it transforms Descartes anyhow from a typical cipher (a nobody: just another man of good sense) into an example of the man of good sense in fortunate (because methodical) progress toward the truth. The word individualizes Descartes, identifies him by differentiating him, setting him up and apart from the ordinary run of good men who have not stumbled so fortunately as he—does all of this, however, without making him any the less ordinary. Thus he is careful not to claim for himself the authority of the philosopher, and he disavows the moral grace of the exemplar: "it is not my intention to present a method which everyone ought to follow in order to think well, but only to show how I have made the attempt myself. Those who counsel others must consider themselves superior to those whom they counsel" (3; 4)—and of course they must also show themselves superior by radiating the proper example. Descartes makes no such show. His *Discourse on Method* is not really a discourse on method; it is not really a philosophical text at all. On the contrary it is almost aggressively vernacular: an unschooled text. It is only the discourse of a man of good sense whose good luck is that he has a story to tell: "I only propose this writing as an autobiography [*histoire*], or, if you prefer, as a story in which you may possibly find some examples of conduct which you might see fit to imitate, as well as several others which you would have no reason to follow" (3; 4). How you take the text is up to you. Of course, we do not as yet know what it might mean to follow Descartes on the path he has found or formed for himself, and which he will (with strange diffidence) shortly disclose to us. One senses that it would mean less trouble for him if no one would take his example to heart and pursue it so seriously as he. In some worlds it is better not to have followers—is safer, at any rate, because followers form schools and grow contentious. But quite apart from this we can foresee that the very notion of follower mars the decorum of the cogito—depletes its romance—because the cogito is before everything else a first principle. It follows nothing, and therein lies its exemplary character. To follow the Cartesian path is to strike out on one's own, leaving received ideas behind.

From my childhood I lived in a world of books ... [3; 4]

There is no making one's way in a library, although there are many paths to follow, as in a labyrinth. As in a labyrinth, the paths are fixed, but one is often misled or mistaken as to what their ends are. Descartes began, he says, by following the lettered way, thus evidently to enter "the ranks of the learned" (3; 4), but instead he lost himself among their number: "I found myself saddled with so many doubts and errors that I seem to have gained nothing in trying to educate myself unless it was to discover more and more fully how ignorant I was" (3; 4). This is disingenuous to be sure: the discovery of one's own ignorance, followed by an increase in self-reliance, is the native theme of the moral education. The lettered nourish themselves on such themes. Thus Descartes is ordinary only on the face of it: "I had learned," he says, "everything that others learned," and again: "I was in no way judged inferior to my fellow students" (3; 5). For beneath the conventional encumbrances of learning that saddle or shape him, and indeed perhaps because of them, he forms a new relationship with himself (or forms a new attitude of self-assertion). He centers himself in his own age as it competes with the past by identifying himself as a Modern, and in relation to others and to the world of letters generally he becomes (in his own mind) exemplary or normative as with a vengeance: "it did not seem to me," he says, "that our own times were less flourishing or fertile than were any of the earlier periods. All this led me to conclude that I could judge others by myself, and to decide that there was no such wisdom in the world as I had previously hoped to find" (4; 5).

This centering of himself is also a displacement by which Descartes puts away the things of the child: books. One could call it a ritual separation from one's ancestry, that is, from the authority of antique, traditional, or institutional learning (although not quite from any external authority whatsoever). Descartes sets out on his own by putting his normative character into play: he sits in judgment upon "the disciplines of the schools" (4; 5), not so much to condemn them as to distance himself from them, or, more accurately, to show how they affect the distance between self and mind. Thus the study of antique learning is like traveling abroad: "It is good to know something of the customs of various peoples.... But when one spends too much time traveling, one becomes at last a stranger at home" (4; 6). By contrast, mathematics nurtures self-intimacy by opening the mind to the primary and superior experiences of "certainty and self-evidence" (5; 7). Interestingly, Descartes "deschools" poetry and eloquence, which belong to the domain of genius and thus are beyond the competence of an ordinary man of good sense: they are "gifts of nature rather than fruits of study" (5; 7). On this point they are curiously analogous to theology, from whose province Descartes carefully banishes himself. You will not find anywhere a finer example of vernacular irony than this: "I revered theology, and hoped as much as anyone else to get to heaven, but having learned on great authority that the road was just as open to the most ignorant as to the most learned, and that the truths of revelation which lead thereto are beyond our understanding, I would not have dared to submit them to the weakness of my reasonings. I thought that to succeed in their examination it would be necessary to have some extraordinary assistance from heaven, and to be more than a man" (5; 8).

I resolved to seek no other knowledge than that which I might find within myself or perhaps in the great book of nature ... [6; 9]

Traveling and building are the two regulative metaphors of the *Discourse.* Their figurations are sometimes literal, as when Descartes turns himself out of school: "I spent a few years of my adolescence traveling, seeing courts and armies, living with people of diverse types and stations of life, acquiring varied experience, testing myself in the episodes which fortune sent me, and, above all, thinking about the things around me so that I could derive some profit from them" (6; 9). This is a "book of nature" chiefly because one reads it by experience; it differs from Bacon's chiefly by containing little that is natural—better to call it a "book of culture." Actually, one is apt to associate it with such later texts as *The Persian Letters,* or with *Rasselas* ("I found nothing there to satisfy me," 7; 10), or with any number of real or imagined philosophical and sentimental journeys. Descartes's "book of nature" is at any event inconclusive yet diversifying: it acquaints him with the analogy of custom and opinion (both are local and arbitrary: mental encumbrances), and by its agency he is "gradually freed ... from many errors which could obscure the light of nature and make us less capable of correct reasoning" (7; 10). But these are negative results, and accordingly the book of nature goes the way of the library: "after spending years in thus studying the book of nature and acquiring experience, I eventually reached the decision to study my own self ... " (7; 10).

I remained all day alone in a warm room. [7; 11]

When Descartes studies his "own self," what does he see, or find, or know? For that matter, how does he proceed? A reader today is likely to be disappointed at the absence of resonant or romantic consciousness in Descartes, who thinks of the self rhetorically in terms of *pensées*. Pensées are the medium of reflection: the mind does not so much conceive as find and use them. They are inventions that help the mind to focus upon the truth of things. In moments of self-reflection one meditates not upon one's self but upon certain appropriate themes of self-reflection—themes designed to help one to discover the truth about one's life. One does not reflect upon one's self as a self reflected in a mirror, because one cannot see one's self face to face, or think of one's self (or soul) as an object of thought, no more than one can encounter God so. One can only engage oneself in the act of doing something else, as when one enters a warm room and discovers oneself at the center of a copious repository of received ideas. What one does there is as good a sign as any of what one is: not a psyche, not a person capable of self-scrutiny and self-discovery, but an individual thinking being, which means one who enters a *contemplum* and occupies its central place (the seat of reason), there to receive and consider those pensées which are summoned, or which otherwise occur, as in a sequence of meditative turnings or in the amplification of a theme. Descartes's self-study is in this tradition of rhetorical rather than romantic introspection. It is a conventional *examen de conscience,* which is a meditation upon the truth of things that takes the form of an inventory of the mind: "I remained all day alone in a warm room. There I had plenty of leisure to examine my ideas. One of the first that occurred to me was"—and here the truth of things is localized, the keynote sounded—"that frequently there is less perfection in a work produced by several persons than in one produced by a single hand" (7; 11).

A mind critical or analytical in its training might ask, "Is this idea true?" A mind schooled in rhetoric would ask, "How many ways are there of expressing this idea?" Descartes follows the way of rhetoric, builds upon his theme by finding analogies for it, and doing so he asserts the primacy of the individual thinker and, simultaneously, declares his allegiance to the *spirit of system*. For whether it is in the making of buildings, or in the development of a city, or in the formulation of a code of laws to govern a nation and make it whole—in whatever case, there can be no systematic construction which does not proceed from a single starting point, or which is not guided by a single authority, or which is contaminated by the intervention of other minds. What is perhaps most interesting here is the way self-study proceeds in a sequence of self-characterizations: as he meditates upon the analogies of construction, Descartes discovers the truth about himself, for he is figured in his representations of architect, city planner, and prudent legislator, in whose forms of progress things must be made to unfold from within, not allowed to accumulate randomly from without. This principle of systematic construction is, moreover, a principle of self-authorization, because it enables Descartes to affirm "the simple and natural reasonings of a man of good sense concerning the things which he experiences" over and against "the sciences found in books" (8; 12–13), that is, the empire of learning, which has been built up from the beginning by a process that knows neither order nor unity, neither certainty nor truth. Again: it is a principle of self-authorization, because what it authorizes is the freedom of the self or the man of good sense from the empire of learning.

We may think of this freedom (perhaps somewhat too romantically) as a self-exile that is also self-possession. What Descartes seeks is the restoration of the self to its original, unschooled condition. We have all of us, after all, been schooled, whence it is "impossible," Descartes says, "that our judgments should be as pure and firm as they would have been had we the whole use of our reason from the time of our birth and if we had never been under any other control" (9; 13). This condition of purity and solidity is, of course, irrecoverable and no doubt for all of that imaginary. Anyhow we cannot actually return to the unschooled state. Yet we can deschool ourselves artificially and reconstruct the original state of things, that is, the state prior to the establishment of the empire. And we may in turn construct a new empire, one that unfolds from within us according to systematic principles. Yet on this point we must remember that the man of good sense is not a homogeneous character; rather, he is by definition one who proceeds prudentially as well as systematically, because his progress, although private and even solitary, is not secret. The man of good sense is not merely a figure of inwardness; he is also a man of considered rhetorical principles, because, after all, he is a man of the world.

By this example I was convinced that a private individual should not seek to reform a nation by changing all its customs and destroying it to con-

struct it anew, nor to reform the body of knowledge or the system of education. [9; 13]

What is the relation of the man of good sense to other people? It is, of course, a negative relation, because the man of good sense begins his progress toward self-possession as the possession of another (as the apprentice is possessed by the master, or as one is demonized by antecedents); but it is also a positive relation, because the man of good sense, as he journeys toward self-possession, will not wish to alienate those whom he leaves behind. Hence the division of Cartesian character into public and private selves. One's relationship with one's self is logical, because (as Descartes is fond of remarking) one cannot have any reason to deceive oneself; one's relationship with others, however, is naturally rhetorical, and this is especially so: a major function of rhetoric is to maintain the order of things so that significant changes can take place. This is an essentially conservative notion, and it is Descartes's chief principle of composition in that part of the *Discourse* which proposes that private revolutions are without public consequences: when one chooses, one most certainly does *not* choose for all people. Descartes's intention is not so much to persuade as to reassure: it is not to move men to follow the Cartesian way (at least not directly) but to keep them from moving (as though in hot pursuit) once they discover that the Cartesian way turns upon a principle of subversion (the overthrow of learning and the ascendancy of system). This is what is meant when it is said that rhetoric is the art of disguising oneself in the act of disclosing one's principles. Descartes takes elaborate care to characterize himself as the disengaged and purely philosophical revolutionary. The rejection of received opinions, he insists (following Montaigne), does not imply any devaluation of the institutions that preserve and disseminate them. These institutions are plainly defective, yet their defects are not warrants to seek their reform: "present institutions are practically always more tolerable than would be a change in them; just as highways which twist and turn among the mountains become gradually so easy to travel, as a result of much use, that it is much better to follow them than to attempt to go more directly by climbing cliffs and descending to the bottom of the precipices" (9–10; 14).

This is plainly contradictory, and would remain so if we did not remember that we are confronting here Cartesian rather than romantic inwardness. The Descartes of the *Discourse* is not to be figured as an organic self whose expressions are continuous emanations from within. He is a rhetorical rather than romantic construction: his utterances tell us more about his audience than about himself. Inner and outer selves are versions rather than images of each other (a condition that contains perhaps the whole meaning of rhetoric, wherein things are outwardly determined rather than inwardly derived).

Having made this observation, however, it is necessary also to notice how Descartes wishes to seem unrhetorical, or at all events untendentious, as in the case of the poet who affects the plain or unlettered style. He has, he says, nothing but disdain for those "mischievous spirits" who are perpetually crying out for reform: "If I thought the slightest basis could be found in this *Discourse* for a suspicion that I was guilty of this folly, I would be loath to permit it to be published" (10; 15). His reasons for writing, insofar as they are rhetorical, are epideictic: "Never has my intention been more than to try to reform my own ideas, and rebuild them on foundations that would be wholly mine. If my building has pleased me sufficiently to display a model of it to the public, it is not because I advise anyone to copy it" (10; 15). The *Discourse*, whose theme is design, has designs upon no one; it is simply *there,* a text, construe it as you will: a construction to be admired or ignored. This rhetorical attitude—this seeming indifference: this deliberately anti-Galileovian posture of disregard—helps to explain the odd and almost dialectical alternation of the traveling and building metaphors. These metaphors are, to be sure, devices of exposition, but they are more: their most important (because most silent) function is to control the reader's perception of his relation to the Cartesian enterprise. Thus the one metaphor beckons us to follow; the other motions us to stand back. The one shapes us into disciples; the other maintains us as spectators.

Among the branches of philosophy, I had, when younger, studied logic, and among those of mathematics, geometrical analysis and algebra; three arts or sciences which should be able to contribute something to my design. [11; 17]

Descartes's interior journey is not a romantic quest for self but a search for "the true method" (11; 17); but it is not easy to say where self ends and method begins, because method is crucially affective, not perhaps in its nature, but in its operations and results. Method is that which enables you to know that you know, because it enables you to do so twice, or repeatedly, thus to convince you that you have not got it wrong. Method produces certainty, the natural companion of true knowledge (to be certain of something is, for Descartes, to know it). What Descartes seeks is a logic that is mathematical rather than propositional, which means not only that he seeks a more precise logic but also that he desires as a major fruit of reasoning the sort of intellectual repose that one experiences in mathematics. Hence the first "principal rule" of Cartesian method requires that nothing be accepted as true unless it presents itself "clearly and distinctly" to the mind (12; 18). And if you ask, "How do you know when something is present 'clearly and distinctly'?" the answer is that you do not know and will never know unless you have had beforehand the experience of mathematical certitude. This experience is normative, and so therefore are the procedures that unfailingly excite it. These procedures are enshrined in rules 2 and 3, which map the mind's itinerary as it aspires (1) to reduce a large difficulty into its component simplicities, and (2) to deduce from what is "simplest and easiest to understand" that which is more difficult, thus "gradually and by degrees reaching toward more complex knowledge" (12; 18).

The true end of such progress, however, is so not much complexity as completeness or totality, as we learn from rule 4, which asserts the powerful and, indeed, supreme principle of systematic wholeness: methodical thinking requires the integration of elements into increasingly larger units, eventually to form a hierarchy of relations from which nothing, "among all things knowable to men" (12; 19), has been omitted, and which is governed by the law of internal necessity. It is this law that holds systems together and makes them beautiful; it is the law of containment that literally "rules out" as unthinkable that which cannot be made part of the system. It is this law that secures for Descartes the certitude that he desires, for by its ordonnance a proposition, in order to be true, is not compelled to bear a relation to a real state of affairs: it is, so to speak, retrieved from history and, therefore, placed beyond suspicion. Truth in this event is a function of the interdependence of parts, whence it becomes proper to describe truth as relational rather than propositional: and this is nothing less than truth turned (modernly) on a mathematical model, such that a real state of affairs is no longer required to be otherwise than whatever it appears to be within the system that one has constructed, or which otherwise obtains (systems being, in a sense, self-constructing in the same way that method is self-operating).

Notice the decorum that obtains between the metaphor of building and the ideal of systematic thought, wherein progress toward completion becomes a matter of finding the right connections (or, as in a geodesic dome of truths, the right *mode* of connection). Thus once things have been set in motion, one needs only to stand back and allow progress to occur. A more important point is the way in which the model of "geometrical analysis and algebra" constrains Descartes to conceive progress toward completion as a problem-solving activity, according to which a real state of affairs ("all things knowable to men") becomes imaginable chiefly as a field of problems, solutions to which (when possessed or achieved) constitute the condition of true knowledge. Hence the risk and romance of method. To look on the world mathematically is to regard it problematically as a universe wherein to be insoluble (that is, resistant to systematic assimilation) is to be unthinkable, perhaps even mysterious, or full of mystification and deceit; but method conspires to reduce or resolve the insoluble, and to absolve the universe of our doubts about it, whence doubt may succeed (as Galileo knew) to the promise of knowing creation as God knows it: completely, perfectly, in all its complexity of term and relation—that is, as a closed system whose plenitude, although somewhat contrived, is at last without concealment. A system is almost by definition that which contains no secrets, because it allows nothing to be set apart. Thus God's knowledge is not set apart from man's in the same way that his mathematics could not be more perfect than what man could conceive—more advanced, perhaps, or more complete, but not more perfect. As Descartes discovers from his examination of geometry and algebra, "there is only one true solution to a given problem, and whoever finds it knows all that anyone can know about it" (14; 21). In such a principle a system of universal knowledge (a truly divine science) finds the condition of its possibility—to which Descartes now modestly turns, swelling not so much with power as with confidence, which is perhaps the psychological precursor of certitude: "What pleased me most about this method was that it enabled me to reason in all things, if not perfectly, at least as well as was in my power. In addition, I felt that in practicing it my mind was gradually becoming accustomed to conceive its objects more clearly and distinctly, and since I had not directed this method to any particular subject matter, I was in hopes of applying it just as usefully to the difficulties of other sciences as I had already to those of algebra" (14; 21). (Notice here that method does not produce clear and distinct ideas directly but only by a process of transforming the mind's power of conception. In our own day, the Age of Methodology, this notion of method as a disciplining of thought has given way to the notion of method as a substitute for thought. For us the virtue of method is that it is safe: it is chiefly instrumental insofar as it operates only on its objects, never on its user. Yet to use a method is to subject oneself to it. . . .)

In planning to rebuild one's house, it is not enough to draw up the plans for the new dwelling, tear down the old one, and provide materials and obtain workmen for the task. We must see that we are provided with a comfortable place to stay while the work of rebuilding is going on. [15; 22]

To the metaphor of building Descartes adds the metaphor of insulation, on the evident grounds that philosophy is one of the inconveniences of ordinary life; it infringes on man's life in the world and requires him to adjust himself both to other people and to himself in striking and complicated (and sometimes unphilosophical) ways. Such an adjustment is the famous "provisional code of morality" (15; 22) that Descartes now adopts in order "to live as happily as possible" during the construction of the system (15; 22). The code, it turns out, is "provisional" only in the abstract, for it contains elements that are not wisely or safely to be abandoned. Its function is to insulate the man of good sense from those effects of his reasoning that may be more logical than sensible. Thus the code sharpens and, indeed, seems to formalize the separation that we noticed earlier between mind and will, or between the thought of Descartes and his conduct. The first maxim of the code concerns allegiances of a communal nature: Descartes resolves "to obey the laws and customs of my country, constantly retaining the religion in which, by God's grace, I had been brought up since childhood, and in all other matters to follow the most moderate and least excessive opinions to be found in the practices of the more judicious part of the community in which I would live" (15; 23). Philosophy is useless to the man who renders himself an alien, or a nuisance, or who diverges from the norms of sensible behavior. We might be inclined now to regard philosophy as a method of alienation, but for Descartes it had to remain a function of citizenry, part of the whole life of man—part, but not metonymically so: the life of the mind is not meant to consume (or to engender) the whole life of man: ideas ought not to be allowed to spill carelessly into action and so disrupt the serenity that makes the having of ideas possible. Philosophy must be moderate in what it requires from life.

More than this, however, philosophy ought not to be purchased at the cost of moral isolation, wherein man is helpless to defend against himself. This is what appears most to concern Descartes, that he might be morally inadequate to the transformations that are taking place in his thinking, and so become his thinking's victim. Hence maxim 2 of the code, which seeks to preserve the active life from the consequences of doubt: Descartes—the statement should be read with great attention—Descartes resolves "to be as firm and determined in my actions as I could be, and not to act on the most doubtful decisions, once I had made them, any less resolutely than on the most certain" (16; 24). Certitude belongs to logic, not to life. To be irresolute in conduct is worse than to persist in philosophical error. "In this matter," Descartes adds, "I patterned my behavior on that of travelers, who, finding themselves lost in a forest, must not wander about, now turning this way, now that, and still less should remain in one place, but should go as straight as they can in the direction they first select and not change direction except for the strongest of reasons" (16; 24). The echo here is of the commonplace that skepticism ought to be avoided, not because it is without reason, but because it is without anything else, and is therefore morally debilitating because it deprives one of the ability or incentive to act. Poets and rhetoricians regularly fashion turns upon commonplaces of this sort. Descartes, for his part, disarms the commonplace by seeming to affirm it: the mind must be governed by reason, that is, by the principle of internal necessity, but it is sufficient for the will to be governed by probability—custom, tradition, the rhetorical domain of received ideas, king and country, the ancients, and "the more judicious part of the community in which I would live."

My third maxim was always to seek to conquer myself rather than fortune, to change my desires rather than the established order, and generally to believe that nothing except our thoughts is wholly under our control . . . [16; 25]

To be governed by probability is to be governed by fortune, or history (or rhetoric), against which philosophy offers the consolation of, well, philosophy figured as system, which frees the mind from the powerlessness of the will, whose natural subordination is not to the reason of internal necessity but to reason as it is expressed in the established order of men and things. *Nothing except our thoughts is wholly under our control.* This applies not only to fortune and feeling but to ethical and religious matters as well. We are not in a position to control our actions as we can control our thoughts, because action always involves us with other people and with the authority by which they are gathered into communal harmony. Self-possession is a figure of systematic thinking. It follows that we may describe the philosopher as one who submits to a double authority: that of method, and that which is institutionalized. (Later in the *Discourse* Descartes will speak of "people to whom I defer, and whose authority over my actions is hardly less than that of my own reason over my thoughts," 38–39; 60). To method Descartes subjects the life of his mind, transforming himself thereby into a philosophical subject prepared to array before himself a world of objects or, failing that, of systematic relationships. To the order of authorized conduct, however, he consigns René Descartes, the historical gentleman who lives, "in appearance, just like those who have nothing to do but to live a pleasant and innocent life and attempt to obtain the pleasures without the vices, to enjoy their leisure without ennui, and to occupy their time with all the respectable amusements available" (19; 30). We should not ignore the mild irony of this statement, and yet the point on which Descartes is careful to be explicit is that none of his duplicity is a mere charade; rather, it is a self-construction or self-division that makes doubt a habitable condition as well as a purgative by which to rid the mind "of all the errors that had previously accumulated" (18; 28–29).

This doubt is methodical, not personal or ethical; it does not touch the whole man, as does Pyrrhonism, because it does not stipulate a mode of conduct (for example, withdrawal into silence). Paradoxically, Descartes is free *to* doubt because he has made for himself a life free *from* doubt. He is a contemplative free from confinement, the philosopher abroad as a Citizen of the World. The life of his mind requires detachment, to be sure, but not seclusion. He is a most gregarious doubter: "And inasmuch as I hoped to obtain my end more readily by conversing with men than by remaining any longer in my warm retreat, where I had had all these thoughts, I proceeded on my way before winter was wholly passed. In the nine years that followed I wandered here and there throughout the world, trying everywhere to be spectator rather than actor in all the comedies that go on" (18; 28). There is nothing private about Cartesian subjectivity; if anything, Descartes is almost too gregarious. Nine years pass, and no thought is given actually to begin formal construction of the system—but there is plenty of talk. Descartes learns that his conversations have made him not only a public but a finished philosopher (the word is that he has "already completed" his system), and so he is compelled not merely to begin at last but to follow the creature of rumor that has preceded him: "I did not want to be taken for more than I was, and so I thought that I should try by all means to make myself worthy of my reputation" (20; 30–31). In the *Discourse* (1637) Descartes writes: "I should not have dared to start so soon . . . " (19; 30); in the first of the *Meditations* (1641) he says "I have delayed so long."[3] Whether too soon or too late, he does not so much follow as flee: "to enjoy all the comforts of life to be found in populous cities while living in as solitary and retired a fashion as though in the most remote of deserts" (20; 31).

I then examined closely what I was, and saw that I could imagine that I had no body, and that there was no world nor any place that I occupied, but that I could not imagine for a moment that I did not exist. [21; 32]

To doubt is very difficult. One must with considerable creative effort imagine that things are not what they seem. Indeed, the experience of Descartes suggests that imagination is the requisite of skepticism, as though the willing or methodical suspension of belief were as poetic as credulity or as credible as poetry. In the *Meditations* Descartes observes that merely abstract denial is useless; one must be *persuaded* that this or that sensation or opinion is not to be trusted—and what such persuasion requires is imagination's power to deceive. Concerning, therefore, certain compelling convictions that threaten to be unshakable, Descartes writes (in the first of the *Meditations*): "I think that I would not do badly if I deliberately . . . deceived myself in pretending that all these opinions are false and imaginary" (21). Skepticism is not so rational as it is willful. One must extirpate credulity by cultivating the power to hallucinate philosophically, as when one imagines what is neither merely hypothetical nor entirely believable: for example, that one is bodiless, or wordless, or a pure act of thinking. Madmen have thought less, although Descartes knows that only a lunatic would believe himself so ethereal and, let us say, so purely spaced: "how could I deny that these hands and this body are mine . . . ?" (*Meditations*, 18). Who is to say, however, that lunacy does not sometimes descend upon the man of good sense? The first law of enlightenment is that one should not presume upon one's reason ("I must remember that I am a man." *Meditations*, 18), and the second is that one should not despair of it, for the moment of lucidity will surely come, as it does for Descartes when imagination fails him clearly and distinctly: "I could not," he says, "imagine for a moment that I did not exist" (21; 32). And if we ask, What sort of imagination is it that tries to produce so many nothings? the answers are several and the same: a rationalizing and demystifying imagination, precursor and liberator of philosophy, the un-creating word: imagination provides the nothing that is not there in order that philosophy might occur—begin cleanly, free at last from the dogged-ness of prior and uncertain opinions (from rhetoric and its damnable and incoherent learning).

This does not mean exactly that the *cogito* will be free of presupposi-tions, only that those on which it depends are so many inversions of belief, as when Descartes conjures the marvelous trickster-god of the *Meditations* in order to doubt as conclusively, or with as much certainty, as he can: "I will therefore suppose that, not a true God, who is very good and who is the supreme source of truth, but a certain evil spirit, not less clever and deceitful than powerful, has bent all of his efforts to deceiving me. I will suppose that the sky, the air, the earth, colors, shapes, sounds, and all other objective things that we see are nothing but illusions and dreams that he has used to trick my credulity" (22). He who imagines this need imagine no more, but is made a philosopher, or a self-made (because self-certain) *res cogitans*. "I am something real and really existing," Descartes writes in the *Meditations*, "but what thing am I? I have already given the answer: a thing which thinks. And what more? I will stimulate my imagination to see if I am not something beyond this. I am not this assemblage of members which is called a human body; I am not a rarefied and penetrating air spread throughout all these members; I am not a wind, a flame, a breath, a vapor, or anything at all that I can imagine or picture to myself" (26). To be is to be unimaginable.

They are so accustomed never to think of anything without picturing it—a method of thinking suitable only for material objects—that everything which is not picturable seems unintelligible. [24; 37]

It is not exactly and conversely true, however, that to be picturable is therefore to be unintelligible, or to seem so; it is only that the existence of anything is doubtful until it is secured by thinking, which in one way is a kind of bodiless picturing that in turn works best when what is being pictured is also bodiless, like God. The decorum in this helps to undo a fine complication of metaphor, because Descartes's desire is to "see" clearly and distinctly, in the manner of an angelic visile. By the metaphor of seeing he means, of course, not the picturing of anything but the figuring of thinking on the model of unobstructed vision—thinking that occurs independently of a thinglike or intervening medium, that is, without words or images or the darkening glass of unreasoned ideas: thinking mediated not by any sort of matter but by method only. To "see" clearly and distinctly, however, is only one of the several operations that a thinking thing can perform (or processes it can undergo: better not to speak of "activities") in order to be certain of itself, for this thing is, as Descartes says in the *Meditations,* "a being which doubts, which understands, which conceives, which affirms, which denies, which wills, which rejects, which imagines also, and which perceives" (27). The term "thinking thing," in other words, is an operational category: it includes the mind at its widest angle and deduction at its narrowest. The mind is never altogether clear and distinct, nor does it need to be, but a deduction *must* be, if only in its time of culmination ("... I am"). Or, again, the mind is never altogether clear and distinct, but deductive thinking can make it so. A deduction is the mind methodized, as in the ontological argument that Descartes develops in the first flush of his self-certainty: If the trickster-god did in fact exist, there would be no *cogito ergo sum,* with its compelling and alleviating lucidity. Certitude in light of such divinity would be unthinkable, not merely one illusion the more but—nothing: One of those ideas that never occurs to anyone, an experience one could never have. Self-certainty dispels the god of doubt and gathers in his stead "a being more perfect than my own," a true God figured as the absolute absence of Descartes's defects: "I saw that doubt, inconstancy, sorrow and similar things could not be part of God's nature, since I would be happy to be without them myself" (23; 36). And as for the existence of this being, than whom none more perfect can be conceived, "it was clear, for example, that if we posit a triangle, its three angles must be equal to two right angles, but there was nothing in that to assure me that there was a single triangle in the world. When I turned back to my idea of a perfect Being, on the other hand, I discovered that existence was included in that idea in the same way that the idea of a triangle contains the equality of its angles to two right angles, or that the idea of the sphere includes the equidistance of all its parts from its center" (23–24; 36).

It is plainly so: the idea of a being absolute in all of its predicates but somewhat short of existence is, logically, a bad idea—badly made, finally inconceivable. God, in order to be a clear and distinct idea, must exist; otherwise one simply has an imperfect idea of God. Descartes wants to add that the idea of God's existence is even more surely true than any geometrical proof, but he draws back, sensing perhaps that method has begun to overheat: "it is at least as certain that God, who is this perfect Being, exists, as any theorem of geometry could possibly be"(24; 36). Good geometry; bad theology. Descartes's is a deduction that deduces very little, even though we have had the signal of certainty that the deducing apparatus has operated to satisfactory effect: ideas of some clear and distinct kind have interlocked to make a systematic declaration of God's existence. To be sure, the whole value of geometrical reasoning is contained in this self-sufficiency, whereby truth is the function of well-placed terms; but it is also true that the certainty thus obtained is a bit soft, because the knowledge of which one is certain has merely been removed from harm's way—brought indoors, so to speak. What is real, for example, is no longer what is known, but simply what must be the case. Knowledge is revaluated in terms of its systematic grace, or for the irresistibility of its internal development, as when it is said that what matters in philosophy is not the object but the kind, quality, or problem of knowledge. This revaluation (which is perhaps the major project of modern philosophy, with its great feeling for systems and its corresponding disdain for things) is required by the Cartesian collapse of being into the logically possible: the one is conceivable in virtue of the other, and is also dispensable thereby, like a cold desire (for which a dose of absence is the only remedy). The propriety of triangles is superior to their reality, and so it is with things, whose appearance in the mind is what busies the philosopher; the rest is God's affair. No longer is it one thing for the object to exist in the understanding, and another for the mind to understand that the object actually exists; rather, it is by consulting our minds that we will henceforth know what the world must be like, and what it must be like to know it. It may turn out, of course, that there can be no knowing what it is like—but no matter so long as methods conduct us toward this end.

I... have also discovered certain laws which God has so established in nature, and the notion of which he has so fixed in our minds, that after sufficient reflection we cannot doubt that they are exactly observed in all which exists or which happens in the world. [26–27; 41]

The Cartesian universe is not merely mechanical; it is also technological, in the sense that one understands it not by knowing what it is but by learning how it is made—how God did it, and by what rules and operations. To know something in this fashion is to know how to duplicate it—how to build it, for example, on a more abstract and modest scale, thus to show the principles (the grammar!) by which the original must have been obtained. The effect of such knowledge in the long run is to make the original seem obscure, phantomlike, or inaccessible beside its simulacrum—hardly worth knowing, certainly not worth quarreling about: as when people gave up the study of languages for the study of Language. The method of Cartesian physics at any rate is to study the world by abandoning it, together with its burden of controversies, and to construct a new one in its place, this time paying attention to the necessary connections. "I therefore resolved to leave this world for them to dispute about," Descartes says, "and to speak only of what would happen in a new one, if God should now create, somewhere in imaginary space, enough matter to make one; and if he agitated the various parts of this matter without order, making a chaos as confused as the poets could imagine, but afterward he did nothing but lend his usual support to nature, allowing it to behave according to the laws he established" (27; 42). (The image is almost Rabelaisian: God creates the world, scrambles it, then withdraws to watch, doubtless with simian delight, as it assembles itself once more automatically into a cosmos; a variant is that God bashes the world from time to time—earthquakes in Lisbon, that sort of thing—yet after each blow the world rights itself like some magnificent toy.

Note that God creates matter, not things. If, not having seen it, or not having believed what one has seen—if one were to picture matter, what would it look like? It would be geometrical matter, that is, neither matter as one senses it to be nor the prime matter of the schoolmen, but that which is accessible to both imagination and understanding: "a continuous body, or a space infinitely extended in length, breadth, and height or depth; divisible into various parts which can have different shapes and sizes and can be moved or transposed in any way" (23; 36)—three-dimensional extension, which possesses a graceful inability to sustain chaos. For God does not, on this hypothesis, merely create matter; he makes it rational—programs it to behave predictably (methodically), so predictably that Descartes can, as he did in his suppressed and "fabulous" essay on *The World; or, Treatise on Light* (1633), reproduce the original assembly of the world into a universe of bodies moving as to geometrical music: "I showed," he says in the *Discourse,* "what were the laws of nature, and . . . that nature is such that even if God had created several worlds, there would have been none where these laws were not observed. After that, I showed how the greater part of the matter in this chaos would, in consequence of these laws, become arranged in a manner which would make it similar to our skies; and how nevertheless some parts must compose an earth, and some planets and comets, and others a sun and fixed stars. And here, enlarging upon the topic of light, I explained at considerable length . . . "(28; 43)—and so on, until a plenum is reached that must be very like God's own, the only difference being that perhaps God *could* have created the world once for all as a universe of finished objects and relations, that he need not have proceeded according to a table of inferences, whereas the "imaginary" (or, rather, philosophical) universe of Descartes unfolds from within as though in mathematical evolution. This difference alters nothing concerning material objects; it is only, Descartes says, that their "nature is much easier to conceive when one pictures their gradual growth in this manner rather than considering them as produced in their completed state" (29; 45).

Those who are not well versed in anatomy will find difficulty in understanding what I am going to say if they will take the trouble, before reading this, to have the heart of some large animal cut open before them, for the heart of an animal with lungs is quite similar to that of man. [30; 47]

God not only creates matter; he moves it—or, rather, in the beginning he gave it a push, and since that time he has needed only to maintain the quantity of matter and motion in the universe as constant as himself. From the motion of matter all differences among individual objects derive: motion determines the distribution of particles, their forceful relations among one another, their changes of place and direction, form and quality; and thus matter is shaped and sized and ordered into regular patterns of behavior— but it is never brought to life. That bolting hare that you see, that magnificent bass, the malevolent turtle: they only seem to be alive. In fact, they are examples of the intricacies of mobile composition that are possible within the flow and collision of extended matter. The distinction between animate and inanimate nature is illusory; one should rather distinguish between the mobile and the inert.

In the *Discourse* the mysteries of motion are made to pass through the ventricles of the heart, and are dispelled thereby, along with the ghost of animism. As Descartes tries to show by means of a detailed anatomy, the heart is a machine and a good synecdoche of the "living world," because its motion "follows necessarily" from the disposition of its parts, "just as the motions of a clock follow from the weight, location, and configuration of its counterweights and wheels" (32; 50). The heart is merely the main piece in a hydraulic system that powers the body, much as the automated men, women, and beasts in the famous grottos of Saint-Germain-en-Laye are powered by cunning combinations of water, ropes, springs, levers, wheels, pulleys, and air.[4] If the brothers Francini, who designed these automata, could be so cunning, why not God? As Descartes wrote to Henry More in 1649, "it seems reasonable, since art copies nature, and man can make various automata which move without thought, that nature should produce its own automata, much more splendid than artificial ones. These natural automata are animals."[5] What is interesting about this demystification is that it is prompted less by a disbelief in vital spirits than by the exigencies of method, whereby things are to be made intelligible, not by adducing a new explanation for every new difficulty, but by depending on some few reasons already established. "Everything moves by pushing and pulling," Aristotle said. The Cartesian ideal is to be able to let it go at that, but Aristotle required that there be some alert agency by which this pushing and pulling gets put into play; hence it is necessary to postulate on behalf of the animal kingdom souls which are at the very least spontaneously appetitive. But the Cartesian reduction of the laws of nature to the rules of mechanics removes the need for animal agency by referring us back to the original agency of God, whence it becomes the case that the local movement of beasts, like the rolling of stones and the warming of passion, are so many variations within the perpetual motion of the universe. Later ages would fault Descartes for being insensitive to nature and oversensitive to God, but these complaints miss the point, which is to substitute method for Aristotle (technique for tradition) as a power of explanation. A further point (really, part of the same point) is that machines are things of great beauty, and that their beauty increases as their secrets vanish. A living thing would not be beautiful for the same reason that it would not be necessary.

And this proves not merely that animals have less reason than men, but that they have none at all, for we see that very little is needed in order to talk. [37; 58]

The crucial division occurs, therefore, not between the living and the ponderous, but between man and nature, or more accurately between mind and matter. Neither of these two regions, taken separately, is mysterious, nor is there any doubt that Descartes meant them to be taken separately: the second rule of the method demands it, and thus you have no one but yourself to blame if you are puzzled concerning their connection. Descartes, for his part, was puzzled not in the least, evidently because it seemed to him merely convenient, not necessary, to affirm any connection. He had, after all, already concluded that he was "a substance whose whole essence or nature was only to think, and which, to exist, has no need of space nor of any material thing." To be sure, man's extension into space is doubtful until proved, but in this case the only connection that method and system require is logical, not psychological or psychophysical. Accordingly, the *Discourse* (as are the *Meditations*) is innocent of any reference to the pineal gland, that great nexus of spirit and flesh on which Descartes so absurdly fashioned his passion for explanation.[6] We may regard the theory of the pineal gland as an example of the spontaneous overflow of thinking—and an abrogration of method.

To begin again: the crucial division occurs between mind and matter, not between animate and inanimate nature. The mind is spontaneous, not mechanical; it is capable of the free origination of its own acts. The sign of this spontaneity is language, or (there being no such thing as language) speech; or, more exactly still, it is the power of conversation—the ability not merely to speak but to answer as well. "It is conceivable," Descartes says, "that a machine could be so made that it would utter words, and even words appropriate to physical acts which would cause some change in its organs.... But it could never modify its phrases to reply to the sense of whatever was said in its presence, even as the most stupid of men can do" (36; 56–57). It is one thing to respond to a stimulus; it is another to respond to an objection. This is the major theme of Cartesian linguistics, yet it is an oddly misappointed and even reactionary theme, because the whole drama of Descartes's project lies in pursuit of regulated thinking. That which is spontaneous is also unreliable, especially in matters requiring the calculation of order, measure, and results. Spontaneity in calculation is a species of enthusiasm and as likely to be comic as any encroachment of the mechanical upon the living—as in the story of the mathematical genius who could produce unexpected sums. This is why it would one day seem (did already in the seventeenth century seem) preferable to have machines that would do man's thinking for him: and what are computers anyway but technological versions of the systems of language, culture, and ideology that secretly regulate the operations of the mind? Certitude requires the mechanical operations of one's spirit, because in order to be certain of one's conclusions one must be able to arrive at them even without wanting to, or at least without trying: simply by being turned on, or methodized.

The genius of the machine lies in its power of duplication, which is the

condition to which the philosopher, though not naturally mechanical, naturally aspires. This is the more true because the life of philosophy is a history of disputation, or a conflict of interpretations: its theme is the endless
and maddening proliferation of different versions of the truth. It is a mistake to suppose, therefore, that the machine, being predictable in its operations and results, is therefore dull. For Descartes what is no longer endur-
able is the spontaneous eruption into controversy of every philosophical
statement not able to be arrived at by anyone save its author. The difficulty
is that, whereas one can regulate one's thinking, one has no control over
the way in which other minds arrive at one's ideas. "I have often explained
some of my opinions to very intelligent people," Descartes says, "who
seemed to understand them very distinctly while I was speaking, nevertheless when they retold them I have noticed that they have always so changed
them that I could no longer accept them as my own" (44–45; 69). Thinking
will remain controversial until it can be made single-minded—which,
as it happens, is the whole point of turning ideas into systems. A system is,
in principle, incapable of existing in the form of versions: that is the whole
difference between a system and a story, which can only exist in the telling
of it, and which can never get told the same way twice. Systems presuppose
the operations of method, which is to say the power of duplication wherein
the production of a different version of anything is either an accident or an
error.

*I have always tried to remain indifferent to having or not having a repu-
tation, but since I could not avoid having some kind, I thought I should at
least do my best to avoid a bad one.* [48; 74]

One has no control over the way others arrive at one's ideas, but one has
rhetoric. It is well to remember that the *Discourse* is a public but not strictly
or conventionally a philosophical document. In it Descartes philosophizes
chiefly by allusion to what he has already thought. His true thinking has occurred, or one might say is hidden, elsewhere. The *Discourse* is the work
of the philosopher's public, rhetorical, and therefore unphilosophical or un-
constructed self. Three years are allowed to pass, however, between the *Discourse* and its publication. Descartes says that the delay is owing to prudence: the unfortunate case of Galileo has shown that one should naturally
prefer one's own censure to that of people who have authority over one's
actions. "This occurrence," Descartes says, "was enough to make me change
my resolution to publish the treatise, for although the reasons for making
it were very strong, my inclinations were always much opposed to writing
books and I was quick to find other reasons to excuse myself for not pub-

lishing" (39; 60). These "other reasons," together with Descartes's reasons for (finally) disregarding them, form the subject of the belated conclusion, in which Descartes raises explicitly the question of the public nature of philosophy. Does it have such a nature, or is it not rather composed of that which naturally falls out of the way of human discourse (which, for its part, survives rhetorically on inexactness)? Descartes insists (as if in spite of his native philosophical reserve) upon its public nature, for he understands very well that method is intrinsically vernacular in character: it is precisely that which rescues philosophy from the authority of tradition and the domain of learning—from antiquity and the schools: from Latinate opinion. Hence Descartes's characterization of his audience: "And if I write in French, which is the language of my country, rather than in Latin, which is that of my teachers, it is because I hope that those who rely purely on their natural intelligence will be better judges of my views than those who believe only what they find in the writings of antiquity" (50; 78).

The *Meditations on First Philosophy,* composed in Latin and addressed to "the Dean and Doctors of the Sacred Faculty of Theology of Paris" (3), is in this respect a text that is obsolete on its own principles. For the point is that what Descartes wishes to make public is not a philosophy at all but rather principles of construction by which one might—by which *anyone* might—philosophize. Obviously Descartes has as many views or opinions as any one, but that philosophical or Cartesian portion of himself is less the source of ideas than of operations. This helps to explain the final, Baconian turn of Cartesian thought: deduction, Descartes says, is eventually a communal enterprise, because in the end it must yield to a program of experiments for the ascertaining of particular truths, whence we may learn the use of things; but since the world of particulars is so vast, and the number of experiments to be performed so many, such a program could never be the undertaking of a single person. A philosopher unable to acquire colleagues is not a philosopher, after all, but a solitary; his mind will always show large spheres of incompleteness. But notice that collegiality here is a function of administrative efficiency, not of the expression of ideas. "I still think," Descartes says, "that I should continue to write everything that I consider important as soon as I discover its truth, and do so with as much care as if I intended to publish it. In this way I will have additional opportunities to examine my ideas, for doubtless we always scrutinize more closely that which we expect to be read by others than that which we do for ourselves alone, and frequently the ideas which seemed to me true when I first conceived them have appeared false when I wished to put them on paper" (42; 65–66). One writes *as if* publicly, but only for the sake of one's thinking.

What is important is the making of philosophy—the *formation,* not the dissemination of it: one can as usefully imagine an audience as address one in fact, for an audience need not exist in response to one's thinking but only as a working principle within the course of its systematic construction.

Indeed, a real audience is likely to be of less value than an imaginary one, because the public domain of philosophy remains naturally unphilosophical: it is a versional world in which ideas flourish or die not on merits of their own (not according to principles of internal necessity, according to which truth can be systematically isolated from error) but because of the praise or blame inflicted on them by, well, by those who nourish themselves on letters—by Gysbertus Voetius, for example, the Utrecht Nemesis with whom Descartes eventually became embroiled. Nor is the problem that a real audience is likely to be hostile, without disciples; on the contrary, it is almost always the case that followers are no better than adversaries, especially in their power to complicate, distort, falsify, and sooner or later to deaden any master's thinking. Certainly for Descartes nothing could be worse than to have one's ideas degenerate into a school philosophy, which we may define in the Cartesian manner as a philosophy whose authority derives not from systematic principles but from the historical supremacy of one of its versions.

4
Systems versus Tongues; or, The New Rhetoric versus the Old

The basic operating principle of the Cartesian attitude is not that the self (or the mind) is the autonomous originator of its knowledge; it is that there is nothing that cannot be figured as a system—and why should things be figured in any other way? How else to make sense of things, since intelligibility is a function of the disposition of parts? It was Descartes's observation, however, that the mind's intelligibility—that is, not only its self-presence but, more important, its capacity for systematic operation—requires the intervention of method, for the mind is unreliable in virtue of the unpredictability of its results, but method rescues the mind from the contingency of invention by turning its history into a program (investing it, literally, with the power of writing itself down beforehand). On this point later ages would find Descartes too naive, or inattentive to his own method, and would argue that the mind's unpredictability, so far from being a defect, is an illusion—an illusion, moreover, that is systematically produced and maintained, for the mind is systematic in spite of itself: systematic, indeed, unbeknownst to itself. The hiddenness or unconsciousness of systems is the great secret of human life and assembly: everything, it turns out, is structured as a language.

Even the unmasking or theoretical disassembly of these secret structures is systematic: it is a certain way of doing things that sometimes disguises itself as, of all things, rhetoric. Here, for example, is a statement by the critic Paul de Man: "Rhetoric radically suspends logic and opens up vertiginous possibilities of referential aberration."[1] Rhetoric, of course, cannot do this by itself—what would have to happen to it for it to be capable of such a task?—but a rhetorician might have occasion to wonder what would happen if you did not arrange your thinking into the traditional polarities: as, for example, between truth and falsehood, reality and fiction, inside and outside, presence and absence, literal and figurative, signifier and signified, and so on. It is not that madness or derangement would follow, nor even that nothing would ever again make sense to you, but certainly you would have to reconsider your norms of sense and to observe (this time believing what you see) how contingent is the idea of a fixed, univocal, objective, plain, and infinitely portable meaning, that is, a meaning that is systematic rather than versional—a meaning that is never compromised by the situation in which it occurs, or by what lies next to it, or by what is hidden between its lines (or in some alien portion of history). It would be the first opinion of any ancient rhetorician that the unfixing of meanings would not mean a corresponding depletion of things to say. On the contrary, what you would have (apart from a sharp increase in mathematical desire) would be a terrific surplus of such things—a true inventory. What would not change would be the difficulty of making sense, particularly the difficulty of making sense of whatever cannot be expressed all at once, or in a single version. Rhetoric, on this view, would be the art of making sense in the face of (or in virtue of) the contingency of meanings, or their tendency to occupy the versional state.

What we find in Paul de Man is something like a Nietzschean version, or parody, of this view of rhetoric. Consider, for example, this question of questions: How do you know when you have made sense of anything? An easy answer is that making sense is an activity of practical knowledge: it is not a function of anything, rather it is something anyone can accomplish (more or less satisfactorily, depending on the situation, or the audience) so long as he practices it, as he would the piano, every day. A corollary point would be that a performance requiring practical knowledge is not the same as the operation of a method; on the contrary, one of the things to be learned from Descartes (and, rather more urgently, from de Man) is that method is what replaces practical knowledge once philosophical suspicion has been aroused as to whether anything, such as making sense, is really going on. Like Descartes, de Man is an agent of such suspicion. Like Descartes he would point out that the question is: *How do you know when* you have made sense of anything? The hard answer is that, in and of yourself (as if in Cartesian solitude), you never know. It is a major portion of de Man's teaching that "making sense" belongs, secretly, to the domain of performative and not constative "functions," which means that it is not something that can be invested with cognitive value: what we call meaning (that is, meaning something, or saying something about something: making a statement) cannot be counted as knowledge.[2] Meaning is not reference but—rhetoric.

De Man is a connoisseur of fictitious signification or, more particularly, of those forms of fictitious signification which are impossible to distinguish from the real thing. (Not to say that there is no such thing as "the real thing," because, after all, there is no saying such a thing.) For many centuries rhetoric was the routine and topical object of philosophical suspicion, as when it was figured as the art of hiding the absence of sense by intensifying the heat of performance. De Man widens the arc of suspicion dramatically by figuring everything as rhetoric; he does so, moreover, in the manner of Nietzsche, whom he quotes as follows:

> It is not difficult to demonstrate that what is called "rhetorical," as the devices of a conscious art, is present as a device of unconscious art in language and its development. We can go so far as to say that rhetoric is an extension [*Fortbildung*] of the devices embedded in language at the clear light of reason. No such thing as an unrhetorical, "natural" language exists that could be used as a point of reference: language is itself the result of purely rhetorical tricks and devices. ... Language is rhetoric, for it only intends to convey a *doxa* (opinion), not an *episteme* (truth). ... Tropes are not something that can be added or subtracted from language at will; they are its truest nature. There is no such thing as a proper meaning that can be communicated only in certain particular cases.[3]

Rhetoric in Nietzsche's mind (as, indeed, in most traditions of Western philosophy) is another name for deception, artifice, fabrication, illusion, unnatural utterance, the lie, figuration (the worst sort of contraband discourse), and so on. To this traditional characterization of rhetoric, however, Nietzsche adds a crucial note: "Language is rhetoric"—whence no utterance (nor, indeed, anything whatsoever) can be above suspicion. Nietzsche dispenses with the distinction between language and its use, or between what language is and what it can be made to do (namely, perform rhetorical "tricks"). In doing so, however, he plays a purposefully skeptical variation upon a basic Enlightenment theme, as when, in the seventeenth century, defects in the natural languages of men were regularly diagnosed as a way of authorizing the construction (or imagination) of philosophical languages, whence we obtain our concept of language as such, that is, our conception of language as a system *(langue)*. Nietzsche's terrible truth, which perhaps a Leibniz or a Bishop Wilkins could not have borne, is that these "defects" of native utterance are not able to be removed or corrected—are not accessible to rational or philosophical reform: they have not crept into language from a nearby garden of rhetorical abuses, nor are they the accidental corruptions of this or that tongue; rather, they are part of the essence of language. They are descriptive of its basic operations, its grammar, or what language must do in order to be what it is. These "defects" belong to the domain of function, not of use. For when Nietzsche speaks of language he means to say precisely that language is not a phenomenon but a system— not a tongue that one may study but a self-operating and necessarily rhetorical mechanism that one may analyze. It follows (indeed, it is part of the same point) that rhetoric for Nietzsche is not an art that one may learn in addition to the learning of a language; it is what one learns (without knowing it) when one learns a language: it is the secret that every tongue conceals.

For de Man rhetoric is the name of this secret and also (evidently by metonymy) the name of the analysis that would expose it. What he wishes principally to develop is Nietzsche's statement that "tropes are not something that can be added or subtracted from language at will; they are its truest nature. There is no such thing as a proper meaning that can be communicated only in certain particular [that is, philosophical] cases." De Man's version is that "the paradigmatic structure of language is rhetorical rather than referential or expressive of a referential, proper meaning ..." (106). "The trope," he says, "is not a derived, marginal, or aberrant form of language but the linguistic paradigm as such" (105). What is aberrant is referentiality. This is what de Man has in mind in the statement quoted above: "Rhetoric radically suspends logic and opens up vertiginous possibilities of referential aberration"—as when referentiality occurs as an operation without results. It is not that no literal (or referential) statements are possible, only that such statements are only figuratively possible, for it is figuration that makes discourse possible, whence it becomes impossible to decide, on the basis of the traditional polarities, what sort of sense any given statement is actually making. In this respect what is called rhetoric is essentially a practical hermeneutical problem, or what de Man takes to be a problem of reading:

> Since any narrative is primarily the allegory of its own reading, it is caught in a difficult double bind. As long as it treats a theme (the discourse of a subject, the vocation of a writer, the constitution of a consciousness), it will always lead to the confrontation of incompatible meanings between which it is impossible to decide in terms of truth and error. If one of the readings is declared true, it will always be possible to undo it by means of another; if it is decreed false, it will always be possible to demonstrate that it states the truth of its aberration. [76]

By "truth" de Man means (by means of subjunctive indirection) "the possibility of referential verification" (204)—which is a possibility that figuration always throws into doubt, because finally one cannot distinguish between reference and figural transference. What de Man wishes to affirm is the necessity of this readerly doubt. Accordingly his analyses are constructed to expose the deadly convergence of truth and figure, that is, the relationship in any text between a positive statement proposed in or by the text and the hidden figuration that (simultaneously and systematically) makes the statement possible and calls it into question. Traditional hermeneutics is satisfied to recover or expound (or, quite often, simply to desire) the meaning of what is said; the hermeneutics of suspicion practiced in the Nietzschean tradition tries to recover, not what is said, but what a statement does in spite of itself, or what it actually or secretly proposes, even (and especially) at the price of its own contradiction. The important point is that what is disclosed (or exposed) is not any sort of truth or revelation—nor is it, indeed, any sort of sense, even of a negative persuasion; it is rather a purely formal condition in which the mind achieves something like a perpetual transport of suspicion. One does not actually experience this transport as if it were a version of spiritual uncertainty; it cannot be said that one "experiences" anything. This state is rather to be arrived at technically, in the sense that only the operation of a method (called, famously, "deconstruction") can get you there. Imagine, in any event, a state of textual affairs in which the literal turns into the figurative, and back again; reality turns into fiction, and back again; truth into falsehood, and back again—imagine, in short, a state of pure tropology, or of perpetual turnings without ground.

Undecidability is a methodological and not a subjective condition. This helps to explain why de Man will occasionally speak of texts that spin you around as if of their own accord, or of texts that deconstruct themselves and which require, therefore, no reader—even as they are said to require no author, since they are not made what they are by any act of authorial will. Remember what is to be learned from Descartes, namely that a system is supported not so much by a foundation or a founding principle as by the strength of its inward connections. This is the strength exhibited by the Saussurean or diacritical mechanisms of language, wherein there is never any original sign from which all other signs are derived but only a totality of relations in which all signs simultaneously function, even when not in use. The part cannot precede, neither can it outshine, the whole. The value of any system depends not on what it contains, nor even on what it is for, and certainly not on who produced it, but on how it is made. The authority of any system is technical and intrinsic: once in place (or in motion), a system will appear to be self-constructing and self-operating, such that one can neither imagine that the thing never existed, nor that one could have ever been outside of it. It follows that to think systematically (or, as de Man does, in terms of systems, or as if everything were systematically composed, whether texts, minds, calculi, or cultures) is, in effect, to have your thinking done for you: one thing necessarily conducts to another, and so you are kept from going astray, or getting lost—anyhow there is no question of wandering around as if in the open. What actually happens, of course, is that you are not really conducted anywhere; you are yourself simply operating the system—or, to speak accurately, you are simply an operation within it—as when you write, or read, or complain uselessly. Systems are intrinsically hostile to transcendence: once you figure language (or a text, or a cosmos) as a system, you will be caught up within it, perhaps whirled around within it, forever.

Descartes also believed, of course, that the chief virtue of any method or system is that it will prevent you from making a mistake without knowing it. An old Scholastic saying defines logic as the achieving of truth by the discovery of error. Or, again: it is in the nature of things to go wrong; enlightenment consists in knowing when it happens. Descartes surpassed the Schoolmen by replacing school-logic with geometry and the best parts of algebra, wherein you are always informed when an error has occurred. The failure of elements to cohere or interlock signals the incursion of error, for when things are systematically combined an error anywhere will resonate everywhere. To think systematically, or on the model of mathematics (or any general theory of relations) is to possess the legendary power of self-correction—the true Philosopher's Stone, or that in which every mistake conducts to proof. Systematic thinking as Descartes envisioned it thus harbors the principle, if not actually the concrete, historical promise, of error-free knowledge, or anyhow error-free thinking, which for its part becomes the dominant Enlightenment or Modern definition of truth (as in Freud's *Future of an Illusion*): truth is the recognition and, whenever possible, freedom from error, illusion, contradiction, figuration (or licensed contradiction), and so on. Consequently the most important thing about systematic thinking is to know when you are actually performing it: obsession with certitude naturally follows, together with a fear of madness, the rigorous pursuit of epistemology, and the ravening suspicion that you cannot help being deceived.

Descartes also believed that to think systematically is to know as God knows, that is, necessarily, and without subjection to dispute. As Descartes says, "I have not only succeeded in satisfying myself in this short time on all the principal difficulties usually treated in philosophy, but have also discovered certain laws which God has so established in nature, and the notion of which he has so fixed in our minds, that after sufficient reflection we cannot doubt that they are exactly observed in all which exists or which happens in the world."[4] Preoccupation with what can be or cannot be doubted has obscured the obvious point that Descartes is not concerned with what exists but rather with *what must be the case*: the one is what men quarrel about, because they know only what is said about it (and which is amplified endlessly in a superabundance of versions); the other is what we can know, because we can construct in our minds no less than what God has constructed in his—how could God, after all, possess a mathematics different from our own? "I therefore resolved to leave this world for [people] to dispute about," Descartes says in the *Discourse,* "and to speak only of what would happen in a new one, if God should now create, somewhere in imaginary space, enough matter to make one" (27).

Thus disputation gives way to calculation, and to make this point Descartes goes on to reproduce, on paper (or in a relational and systematic space), God's creation of the world; that is, he shows God's method of doing such a thing, the principles of his calculation, for the point to be made is precisely that God creates according to principles of such inward necessity that he cannot fail (or cannot help) to produce the same sort of world over again—and over again, no matter how often he (or, for that matter, anyone else: Descartes, for example) might attempt it. Systems compromise every kind of autonomy, even God's. One can hardly fail to make the next point, which is that in Descartes's construction God, in creating the world, is not obliged to speak. He does not say, "Let there be light." Even if he did say it, no light would therefore shine. Systems are algorithmic rather than logocentric, as Leibniz knew, which is a way of explaining the Cartesian or rationalist thesis that God does not create world, he introduces procedures, in whose actual operation and results he need not maintain any loving or mythological interest—or, as John Stuart Mill thought, could not maintain an interest even if he wanted to. Hence the old schoolroom joke that Descartes proved the existence of God only to show how little God matters in the scheme of things. The God of Descartes, after all, is *only a term required by the system,* which is why his existence is so easy to prove, and so easy to forget. The same can be said of Descartes, the "I" of whose cogito is only a systematic element—not an "I" about which one has things to say but an "I" that has only a certain function to perform. As for the system itself, think of it as an undiscovered country whose center is everywhere and whose circumference is unthinkable.

One may accordingly think of de Man as a sort of fallen Cartesian—or, like Derrida, as a Nietzschean who has found, not the defects of the Cartesian attitude, but its boundless perfection: its power to take everything into account. There can be no conception of anything which does not require a prior recourse to the concept of system—neither play nor, for that matter, error, which may be said to acquire a strategic systematic function precisely to the extent that it becomes, from the enlightened point of view, not simply a wrong turn that can be systematically discovered and corrected, but that to which truth must constantly refer itself—that which truth requires in order to be recognized for what it is. As de Man says, "if truth is the recognition of a certain kind of systematic error, then it would be fully dependent on the prior existence of this error" (17)—or, more correctly, it would be dependent on the *simultaneous* operation of this error, for, where systems obtain, interdependence is the implacable rule. No less than Descartes, de Man desires enlightenment, or emancipation from error, but if error is no longer merely a fault, no longer merely the failure of something properly to occur, then emancipation from error would require emancipation from the system altogether, and this, as Derrida has remarked in a celebrated passage, is something of which one can only dream.[5] One might as well try to speak outside of language.

To be sure, this is a vexed subject. Recall, for example, the issue that divides Derrida from Heidegger. What Heidegger opposes is the systematizing of the question of being, not the question itself (Why is there something rather than nothing?), whereas Derrida opposes the question, but not systematizing, to which he maintains a relentless methodological attachment, particularly in regard to the Saussurean integrity of language, whereby meaning is always to be figured as a relation within language and not a correspondence to something outside of it.[6] For Derrida language is a system of differences whose center is, indeed, everywhere, and whose circumference is only a theoretical limit, or that beyond which, or in reference to which, it is senseless to speak. Heidegger, from this point of view, cannot refrain from desiring that which the system has already, secretly, compelled him to ask for: namely, a concept of being. Heidegger is, Derrida would say, merely "reconstituting the *same* system in another configuration."[7] Heidegger would say, however, that language (and therefore being) is irreducible to the concept of system: it is not to be understood, for example, from the standpoint of the sign, which means that it cannot be characterized simply in terms of its operations, whether of differentiation or reference, substitution or verification, displacement or conceptualization. A grammatology, among other sorts of logic, no matter how deranged, is precisely what is out of the question. Heidegger's words for language are, appropriately, not words for language: *Sprache* and, in apparent disregard of sense, *Sage:* Saying—not saying *something,* that is, not predication or assertion, but that which we listen to (and which is disclosed) when we hear language speaking.[8] Sage cannot be assimilated into any conceptual space; better to say that it belongs radically to time: anyhow it is figurable as an event but not as a structure—and it claims us as part of its occurrence, even as it resists every effort on our part to penetrate into it, to formalize it, or to appropriate it into our subjectivity as an object of knowledge. "Saying," Heidegger says, "will not let itself be captured in any statement."[9] By contrast, for Der-

rida the metaphor or figure of event on which Heidegger relies is simply
one more component of systematic thought, namely that category which is
opposed to (and produced by) the concept of system as such—as speech is
opposed to writing, presence to absence, time to space, the literal to the
figurative, the open to the closed, and so on.

Derrida complains that "the valorization of spoken language is constant
and massive in Heidegger"[10]—and he is correct, but on this point Derrida
is not always clear. He seems prepared to treat Heidegger's valorization of
the spoken as simply (once more) the expression of Western metaphysics
and its enshrinement of the Logos, that is, merely the expression of that
which universally and systematically obtains in behalf of illusions of transcendence, or in defiance of the absence of any transcendental ground, reason, or being. It would be to declare "the death of speech"—to expose the
logical fabrication of presence, meaning (as reference), truth, self, self-
evidence, and so on—that Derrida would raise a theory of language upon
a metaphorics of writing.[11] Yet Derrida knows that Heidegger's reflections
on Sage are a primary affront to system and to the whole tradition of systematic philosophy in which being is understood as the supreme signified,
the ultimate object or universal concept under which everything is to be
arranged. Heidegger is careful to establish himself outside of writing precisely in order to avoid the systematized deformation of language and being
into logical concepts. Thus he opens the domain of language as Saying in
order to preserve the temporality of language (and of his own reflections
on language as well). For Heidegger the concept of writing would be simply another way of subjecting language to the relational and objective
norms of systematic philosophy, whereas Saying is entirely uncontainable
and incomprehensible according to formal, linear, or analytic models. This
is the more true because, like being, it appears to preserve—and remain
uncontradicted by—that which it is not. Language as Saying speaks in
a "soundless voice."[12] Derrida knows that this is not the voice of logocentrism. It is language that cannot be put into words.

Derrida, for his part, takes his place squarely and actively within the domain of writing and system—*in the predicate that there is nothing else.* Here
is no doubt why the prison emerges as such a powerful metaphor in Derrida's thinking: it is a regulative metaphor and hardly needs to be made explicit. As if with nowhere else to go, Derrida seeks to pit the logic of textuality against itself in order to show that the text (even a text by
Heidegger) is always a self-operating yet self-deceiving and finally self-
destructing system, never an inscription of anything anterior or superior to
the grammar of its production—never dependent on anything that would

protect it against itself (or, much to the same point, always dependent entirely upon its own illusions). The text is the quintessence of system and the synecdoche of all that is or all that can be said to be. There is nothing that cannot be taken as a product of writing—not even sound, voice, spirit: there is nothing speakable which is not already closed up within writing. Heidegger, from this point of view, is merely attempting the unspeakable, or at all events the unwriteable, whence we ought to figure him as Orpheus, the singer who is systematically unrepresentable and entirely irrelevant to writing. At the same time, we are obliged to read Derrida as one who mirrors the great tradition of the *scripteur*, that is, the grammarian who is authorized not only to read between and around the lines of antecedent texts but to write there as well (as in *Glas*), thus to produce a discourse that, according to the logic of the closed text, is simultaneously an amplification and a defacement or undoing of all that has fallen into his hands. Derrida is our most intimate and fabulous connoisseur of systems, a fearsome and abandoned Leibniz.

In the tradition of the grammarian, Derrida provides the literacy that renders indispensable the reading of what otherwise would remain off the point—Nietzsche, for example, and, with him, de Man, who perhaps would wish to differentiate himself from Derrida as rhetoric might wish to distinguish itself from grammar—not, it turns out, a very forceful distinction, for rhetoric in this connection amounts to no more than the taxonomy of figures and the analysis of figurative writing (or the figuration of writing). That is, rhetoric in this case is identified with that most systematic and textual portion of itself.[13] It is merely a theme in the history of philosophy, endowed with a pattern of decline from Aristotle (rhetoric at its most philosophical) into tropology (rhetoric at its most rhetorical). In keeping with this pattern rhetoric's most representative text turns out to be Pierre Fontanier's *Les Figures du discours* (1830), and its most illustrious philosophical application becomes Derrida's "White Mythology."[14]

An alternative view (one not restricted to the history of rhetorical handbooks, in which the study of figures can be shown to occupy so much space) would take rhetoric to be inventive and topical rather than stylistic and analytical. I refer here to the Protagorean and Ciceronian traditions which take speech to be made up of sayings rather than of signs. Consider, by way of illustration, the complex topos of speechlessness, which includes an array of wonderful themes: the counsel of silence, the unspeakability of things, the tongue-tied philosopher (filled with truth and at a loss for words), the empty and cunning oration, and so on. The whole art of rhetoric (which, paradoxically, preserves these themes and treasures them) exists to rescue man from the fate of having nothing to say, whereas the philosopher, by contrast, is typically the solitary and silent case—witness the philosophical trance into which Socrates would sometimes fall (*Symposium,* 220c), and which seems at first so uncharacteristic of him until we remember that Socrates is the man for whom nothing can be put into words except the question. This characterization of Socrates is consistent with Plato's famous remark in the *Seventh Letter* concerning the unspeakability of contemplation—a remark that is directed not only against writing but against speech as such (342e–343a). The trouble with speech is that it is never stable: it is forever saying of something (justice, for example, or piety) that it is now one thing, now another. Nothing is ever allowed to remain the same; everything is undecidable. Speech in this wise resembles those who speak—the poet, who is never in his right mind but is characteristically in a state of transport (*Ion,* 541e); the rhapsode, who is like Proteus, turning now into one thing, now into something else (*Ion,* 541e); the Sophist, who cannot be pinned down but will dazzle you with endless stories and arguments on whatever subject you can name (*Protagoras,* 320c), and who defines a wise man as "a man who can change any one of us" (*Theaetetus,* 166d); the priest, whose utterances travel in a circle or take flight like the statues of Daedalus (*Euthyphro,* 11b–11c); and, indeed, man himself—for "man, while no mean animal, is a changeable one, with very few exceptions in a few matters" (*Thirteenth Letter,* 360d). The major and exemplary exception is Socrates, who defies every effort to turn him into something he is not: a clever speaker, a lunatic in a basket, a Wise Man, someone ready to alter his way of life for fear of death. He has always been steadfast in justice, and pointedly so during his short career in politics or as a public man: question my life, he says, and you will discover that I have always been the same (*Apology,* 33a: *kaì idía ho autòs outos*). In the *Symposium* Alcibiades, who may very well know Socrates better than anyone, complains that he was never able to get Socrates to change: the man drinks (a good deal) without getting drunk and loves without losing his self-possession. From Socrates we learn that the whole of one's life should be devoted to the stabilizing of one's opinions: "True opinions are a fine thing and do all sorts of good so long as they stay in their place, but they will not stay long. They run away from a man's mind; so they are not worth much until you tether them by working out the reason. . . . Once they are tied down, they become knowledge, and are stable. That is why knowledge is something more valuable than right opinion. What distinguishes one from the other is the tether" (*Meno,* 98a). Socrates adds at once, however, that this statement is itself merely opinion, not knowledge, for nothing can be tethered by any manner of speaking. It is in the nature of words to take wing or to fall into the wrong hands. From this point of view the history of philosophy, which begins by turning Plato's writings into positive expressions, is a terrific mistake, yet no one can pretend to have been misled. The reserve of Socrates is everywhere scrupulous and unmistakable: "to speak when one doubts himself and is seeking while he talks, as I am doing, is a fearful and slippery venture" (*Republic,* 451a). Or, again: "no reasonable man ought to insist that the facts are as I have described them" (*Phaedo,* 114d). "I will explain what my notion is," he says (of knowledge), "but there may be nothing in it" (*Theaetetus,* 146d).

Alcibiades says of Socrates that "his words are too much for the world" (*Symposium,* 213e)—a prophetic utterance—but it is also true that only within the world can his words ever make sense. Such a world will not bear any metaphysical description; metaphysically it is unspeakable, like the soul (*Phaedrus,* 246a). It is a rhetorical world in which words and things exist only in their versions. Even Socrates is versional, and in the *Apology* he must attempt to establish his own authorized version of himself. Socrates (or, more precisely, Plato's version of him) belongs to the rhetorical world as the characteristic difference that makes it intelligible. Socrates is entirely at home in this world and takes great pleasure in its company, yet the point is that his way of life presupposes such a world (as, indeed, philosophy presupposes rhetoric, which it struggles to correct or restrain). Socrates, knowing the world for what it is, merely refuses to make any positive statements in his own name. When he speaks in his own name, or in what he refers to as his customary way of speaking (*Symposium,* 199b), it is to interrogate what is said—or, much to the same point, what goes on in the world, for the world can hardly be distinguished from the speaking that composes it. When Socrates does speak rhetorically, as when he speaks on love in the *Phaedrus* and (with positive conviction) in the *Symposium,* he does so not in his own name but in the name of Stesichorus and by impersonating Diotima, as if a rhetorical utterance could never originate with the one who speaks (and, indeed, it cannot: this is the whole meaning of invention). Socrates, of course, is not transformed on these occasions; rather, his "changes" are cautionary turns that allow him to speak as the occasion requires without ceasing to be Socrates, namely, someone who is always in his right mind and who never gives speeches. Ask Socrates what justice is and he will require you to give him a definition, and soon the issue will be whether you know what you are talking about. Ask a rhetorician and he will rehearse everything that has been said about it, perhaps amplifying or embellishing as he proceeds, but always proceeding on the basis of what has already been put into words. The rhetorician knows justice not in itself (philosophically) but in its versions (rhetorically)—call him a collector of versions whose inventory encompasses the speakable, or the world. Socrates, by contrast, is *counterinventive,* as if always at a loss for words: "I like the way you take me for a sort of bag full of arguments, and imagine I can easily pull out a proof to show that our conclusion is wrong. You don't see what is happening. The arguments never come out of me; they always come from the person I am talking with" (*Theaetetus,* 161b). The rhetorician, however, knows that whatever is said (about anything whatsoever) makes sense only in relation to the situation at hand—a situation that is always in danger of getting out of hand and turning into a different state of affairs. Hence the intrinsically political nature of rhetoric, which requires the one who speaks to stabilize, not words and things, but the situation in which he finds himself and which he is called upon to take in hand by what he has to say. The rhetorician knows that what is said makes sense only in virtue of the continuity of situations, or within traditions of discourse and domains of learning—or, indeed, within a stable social, political, and cultural order. Rhetoric is thus certainly not pretty. It appears to be naturally conservative (depending on the situation), and it is always faced with the difficulty of telling the truth. As Quintilian says (with typical cunning): "Nor does rhetoric ever teach that which ought not to be said, or that which is contrary to what ought to be said, but solely what ought to be said in each individual case."[15]

This is surely why the saying of anything is regularly accompanied by the telling of a story—the singing of a tale, the writing of a history, the characterizing of an impasse with its conflicting and equally noble or ignominious allegiances. We should therefore speak perhaps not of the "relativism" of Protagoras but rather, as Werner Jaeger suggests, of his painful recognition of the historicity of meaning and truth.[16] Or put it rather that Protagoras the rhetorician is a character and a type shaped by this historicity, or by what Socrates calls "moving reality" (*Theaetetus,* 179d), which is why Protagoras is the indispensable adversary of Socrates, a figure built into the identity of Socrates as the premier character of philosophy. It is in the nature of Socrates to make the rhetorician appear by turns foolish and disreputable—a slave to time, an agent of dubious occasions, a figure of transient cunning (*Theaetetus,* 172e–173b). And Socrates is correct! There is no doubt that the rhetorician is to be understood in the midst of, if not exactly in the terms of, his philosophical defects, which derive from a world in which nothing is exactly what it is, and in which nothing can be certain to possess the sense anyone appears to make of it. Neither language nor the world is philosophical. In an essay on "Dialectic and Sophism in Plato's *Seventh Letter,*" Hans-Georg Gadamer speaks of "the multiplicity of respects in which something may be interpreted in language." Rhetoric is the art of understanding this multiplicity, mastering it and, indeed, putting it to use in making sense of things. As Gadamer says: "An unequivocal, precise coordination of the sign world with the world of facts, i.e., of the world of which we are the master with the world which we seek to master by ordering it with signs, is not language. The whole basis of language and speaking, the very thing which makes it possible, is ambiguity or 'metaphor' "[17]—that is, the changing or turning of words and expressions into one another. It is never possible to say what anything is all at once or once for all; rather, one must say it again and again, each time a little differently as each occasion requires, thus to speak the thing in all its versions, that is, in all its turnings. Thus the saying of anything requires the saying of a great deal. This is why the theme of learning became for the Romans the essence of rhetoric and the distinctive mark of the orator. "For the genuine orator," Cicero says, "must have investigated and heard and read and discussed and handled and debated the whole contents of the life of mankind, inasmuch as that is the field of the orator's activity, the subject matter of his study."[18] And Quintilian: "the material of rhetoric is composed of everything that may be placed before it as a subject of speech" (II. xxi. 4).

It thus becomes easy to understand why the powerful attraction of the unspeakable seems always to be a component of an antagonism to rhetoric. For example, one of the ways to think of Romanticism is to characterize it as that time in history when the poets began to side with the philosophers against rhetoric,[19] thus to displace the ideal of copiousness—the rhetorical ideal of the plenitude of memory and the command of things to say—with various doctrines of inward power. Romanticism in this sense would be Cartesian in its orientation or attitude, not because of any great premium that it would place upon selfhood, but because of its animosity toward received ideas. Indeed, as Robert Langbaum has shown, it is precisely the attitude of suspicion that requires in turn a high valuation of individual mental powers. Romanticism is the enlightenment of the poets.[20] That which has gone before is no longer that which requires to be treated but rather it is something to be done away with before anything can begin. Accordingly, one should say that the crucial transformation in the history of rhetoric would not be the decline from Aristotle into tropology but rather the Romantic redefinition of invention. Even as late as the Renaissance invention presupposes a history of writing, whence originality becomes an art of concealing imitation or of altering one's antecedents into unrecognizable forms;[21] but by Wordsworth's time—Wordsworth, who would no longer consider it poetic to translate Homer into heroic couplets—invention is clearly no longer an art of finding but a power of original conception. Copiousness is now a category of imagination or creativity, not a virtue of learning; knowledge is rather purchased at the cost of power. The old rhetoricians knew that there is no such thing as an original utterance purely and simply, not even when things get said in a way that diverges from tradition or established teaching: think of Philipp Melancthon's *Loci communes rerum theologicarum* (1521), the first great work of Protestant theology, which is not a system but a compendium of basic theological topics (sin, law, grace, the new man, and so on) derived from a commentary on Paul's Epistle to the Romans, which for Melanchthon is nothing less than an authorized inventory of Christian doctrine.[22] To speak is to apply what has already been said to the unforeseen situation in which you are now called upon to say something—to teach, for example, or to combat the entrenchment of error. Rhetoric in this sense is not simply a school subject but a whole life of mental training to prepare people for a moment of formal discourse, or discourse that answers to a situation. By contrast, the distinctive Romantic desire is to authorize or lay claim to an original moment of discourse, as if no one had ever spoken before, whence speech (like Wordsworth's studied literalness) is made to seem unadorned or adorned unrhetorically with signs of unpremeditated or unschooled genius. The Romantic writer desires to return to the moment before speech when poetry is allowed the prospect of its own origination—and perhaps the world's origination as well.[23] Indeed, in this case poetry is no longer expression; it is, as Robert Langbaum says, experience—something that goes on inside of you: a special way of perceiving things, a productive operation of the spirit, a vision, or that which aspires to epistemological grandeur, leaving word and world behind. Hence the great Romantic tradition of figuring poetry as that which resists utterance, or which can never be put into words, as in the pathos of Eliot's "East Coker":

> So here I am, in the middle way, having had twenty years—
> Twenty years largely wasted, the years of *l'entre deux guerre*—
> Trying to learn to use words, and every attempt
> Is a wholly new start, and a different kind of failure
> Because one has only learnt to get the better of words
> For the thing one no longer has to say, or the way in which
> One is no longer disposed to say it. And so each venture
> Is a new beginning, a raid on the inarticulate ....[24]

Indeed, not many topics can claim such an array of striking and irrepressible examples: think of the opening lines of Wordsworth's *Prelude,* in which the failure of invention doubles as a kind of self-inauguration;[25] or of Flaubert, nemesis of the received idea, who dreamed of writing a book about nothing;[26] or of Mallarmé, who, in an oddly Leibnizian fantasy, desired a "supreme language" (one accessible only to writing) and who complained against the diversity of merely natural tongues that turned every word into a lie;[27] or of Hart Crane, who imagined the sounding (somewhere) of "a single new *word,* never before spoken and impossible actually to enunciate";[28] or of Maurice Blanchot, connoisseur of the word that kills: "The ideal of literature could be this: say nothing, speak and say nothing."[29]

This inventory of examples naturally includes Derrida's proclamation of the "death of speech," his attack upon logocentrism and his critique of the sign.[30] One must add Nietzsche, and also de Man, particularly as they examine language in its weakest (or is it its strongest?) portion, namely its power of saying what cannot be said by doing so figuratively, or in a manner of speaking, or while saying something else—that is, by not quite saying it. It is the "not quite saying" of anything that inflames the hermeneutics of suspicion. For example, it is significant that, as de Man says, "Nietzsche dismisses the popular meaning of rhetoric as eloquence and concentrates instead on the complex and philosophically challenging epistemology of the tropes" (130). One can say in favor of this dismissal that it preserves the classical philosophical position vis-à-vis the popular reality of rhetoric. Aristotle, for example, repeatedly defends his decision to teach this disreputable art by saying that rhetoric would not be necessary were it not for the sorry state of the people on whom it is to be used (a philosophical audience is inaccessible to persuasion and to comedy).[31] Yet it is also true that Nietzsche could not be Nietzsche except in this wise. By "the popular meaning of rhetoric as eloquence" de Man may not have had in mind its historical meaning, yet the point is exactly that the Nietzschean attitude depends for its coherence and its authority upon a studied and romantic break with the culture of rhetoric and its ideal of the plenum of learning—*and* its artful conception of the figures.

Consider, for example, that for a writer like George Puttenham, author of *The Arte of English Poesie* (1589, but composed much earlier), the figures of speech and thought are the property of the art of rhetoric (not the whole part but a portion of its traditional lesson). But for Jean-Jacques Rousseau, author of the *Essay on the Origin of Languages* (1782, but also composed much earlier), they are the properties of language itself: that is, they are native to human speech, they originate with language as such, and are rather processes than components or adornments of discourse. The art of rhetoric as Puttenham received it does not possess a conception of language in Rousseau's sense, still less in our sense, nor can one be contrived out of his statement that "utterance also and language is given by nature to man for the perswasion of others."[32] For Puttenham, language is langage, not langue: it is made up of so many tongues of scholars and of men, and the art of rhetoric exists to instruct us, not as to their native operations, but as to their public and effective use. The figures of speech and thought do not repose in language but in art: they are not given by nature to man in the bargain of his mother tongue but require to be obtained in school, by study, and through the spectacles of books. They are meant to assist persuasion, or to produce efficacy of speech in behalf of what is being said (and why: on what occasion and for what reason). The figures have no reality for Puttenham except in relation to the situation in which they are called for, or in which someone is called upon to say something to—and to *do* something to—an audience. Their status is not logical but situational, that is, rhetorical. They are part of a reserve of memory—part of an *inventory*—and not elements in a system.

As Rousseau speaks of it, however, language is clearly making its way from langage to langue, that is, from tongue to system. Rousseau's words for language do not, of course, possess Saussurean precision. The title of his work is *Essai sur l'origine des langues,* by which he means the origin of tongues, but, as de Man has shown, what Rousseau is really attempting to accomplish is the unspeakable task of accounting for the origin of language as such. In "The Rhetoric of Blindness: Jacques Derrida's Reading of Rousseau," de Man corrects Derrida's serious (although plainly strategic) misunderstanding of Rousseau's conception of language by showing how Rousseau derives his conception, not from speech, but from music (the once and future model of non-mimetic, non-referential intelligibility):

> the avowed thesis of the *Essai* equates music with language and makes it clear that, throughout the text, Rousseau never ceased to speak about the nature of language. What is here called language, however, differs entirely from an instrumental means of communication: for that purpose, a mere gesture, a mere cry would suffice. Rousseau acknowledges the existence of language from the moment speech is structured according to a principle similar to that of music.[33]

"What is here called language ... differs entirely from an instrumental means of communication": it is no longer to be understood according to rhetorical categories of sound, voice, and spirit. What de Man makes clear is that Rousseau's concern for the origin of language masks a deeper preoccupation with how it works. Hence in the *Essai* Rousseau is quick to establish the basic and originating distinction between figurative expression and geometrical reasoning, the one being a natural (that is, original) way of speaking, the other being a plain way of speaking in which nature has been corrected by method.[34]

Not surprisingly, Rousseau's famous account of the origin of language takes the theme of correction as its regulating idea:

> Upon meeting others, a savage man will initially be frightened. Because of his fear he sees the others as bigger and stronger than himself. He calls them *giants*. After many experiences, he recognizes that these so-called giants are neither bigger nor stronger than he. Their stature does not approach the idea he had initially attached to the word giant. So he invents another name common to them and to him, such as the name *man*, for example, and leaves *giant* to the fictitious object that impressed him during his illusion. That is how the figurative word is born before the literal word, when our gaze is held in passionate fascination; and how it is that the first idea it conveys to us is not that of the truth.
>
> What I have said of words and names presents no difficulty relative to the forms of phrases. The illusory image presented by passion is the first to appear, and the language that corresponded to it was also the first invented. It subsequently became metaphorical when the enlightened spirit, recognizing its first error, used the expressions only with those passions that had produced them.[35]

What delights de Man about this passage is, of course, the notion that language originates in error, whence "the figurative word is born before the literal word." Yet in all that we read about this wonderful passage we should not forget that what Rousseau wishes chiefly to account for is the possibility of a philosophical language, that is, a language whose formal operations are susceptible to rational correction. A "correct" language in this case would be an artificial language whose "art" consists in the expression or achievement of literal statements ("these so-called giants are neither bigger nor stronger than he"). The "art" of rhetoric in this respect is turned inside out: that which is figurative is made into a description of a function, not a use; rhetoric is turned into a grammar. What is artful is henceforth literal rather than figurative. Metaphor, once a figure of speech, now becomes a figure of language and a grammar of how it actually (that is, originally) works, and also a description of what it is exactly that needs to be corrected by "the enlightened spirit." What is crucial to observe, however, is that we are now made to confront what before could never have been a problem, namely, unconscious (or systematically necessary) metaphorical utterance, such that to speak "naturally" (or without knowing or thinking about it) is always to figure one thing in the name of another. In this sense metaphor, so far from being an art of speech, becomes the premier problem of language, because we cannot help being metaphorical to the extent that we remain subject to the sedimentation of meanings, that is, their unseen, unheard literalizations or disfigurations, the so-called dying of metaphor.[36]

One can begin to see here why Rousseau is crucial to the Nietzschean tradition and the hermeneutics of suspicion, yet to make the point explicit one should say that this tradition presupposes, and indeed depends upon, an enlightened and systematic view of language. The hermeneutics of suspicion is, in effect, built into the antirhetorical motive that produced projects for a universal character or a universal writing that would transcend the babel of mother tongues. One should refer here, in addition to the well-known conceptions of Wilkins and Leibniz, to Lodwick's *A Common Writing, whereby two, although not understanding one the other's language yet by the help thereof may communicate their minds one to another* (1647) and Cave Beck's *The Universal Character, By which all the nations in the world may understand one another's Conceptions, reading out of one Common writing their own Mother Tongue* (1657).[37] The privileging of writing in these projects has not gone unnoticed, not even by Derrida.[38] Writing becomes, by virtue of its independence from speech, the principal expression of a desire for a language that is systematic rather than versional: a desire, not for a common language such as Latin, but Language as a system superior to every utterance that it makes possible. The old distinction between a vulgar and a literary or school language has been put aside in favor of a distinction between something actually spoken (whether now or whenever) and a *Lingua Philosophica* whose operations are unencumbered by such natural contingencies as living or dying. Language in this event is no longer a phenomenon of memory and speaking; it is now imagined to be a system of denotations capable of fixing the values of signs once for all in an absolute logical space—a space that resembles the clean and silent world of mathematical symbols: a refuge from the noisy and swirling world of human utterance.

In such a space man does not speak, he writes, and he does so, moreover, as if for the first time, for he does not proceed within any history of discourse but rather moves in virtue of such devices as Condillac's "analytic method," or the "connexion of ideas," whereby we may "take the materials of knowledge again in hand, and set about them as if we had never employed them before."[39] As Condillac says, "The analytic method is the only mean[s] or instrument of invention."[40] It is a way of overcoming, or of bringing to a logical standstill, the temporality of languages and, in turn, the proliferation of versions and the inevitable excursion of the mind into error. H. B. Acton tells us that Destrutt de Tracy, premier philosopher of language in revolutionary France, believed that, by itself, "a sign is only immune from misunderstanding at that moment when it is first invented and then only by the inventor himself. From that moment onwards the user cannot be sure that he 'collects under this sign exactly the same collection of ideas that he did the first time.' The possibility of differences in meaning, therefore, is all the greater when the same word is used by different people, who themselves learnt it from different people at different times and have different types of experience and expectation."[41] But methodical invention erases all of these differences by reducing the temporality of language to a systematic time in which everything is always occurring as if never before, or as if in a moment of original invention. Origin here, as in Rousseau, is a logical, not a temporal or historical category: it is not that which is recovered but that which is repeated, endlessly so, or according to the perpetual dependences of logic. The sign is rendered immune from misunderstanding by being removed from history (or usage) and figured as an element in a structure of connections (or Language) that can only operate as they did the first time, since, by necessity, or predictably, no other time can obtain.

PART THREE
ROMANTIC HERMENEUTICS

5

The Interpretation of Character in Jane Austen

The title of this chapter requires to be read in a certain way. The word "interpretation," for example, means in this case not your interpretation or mine but that which one Jane Austen character performs upon another. The difficulty is that it is never exactly possible to say what interpretation means, or what it is. Thus a subsidiary purpose of this chapter is to find out what we can learn from Jane Austen about the nature of interpretation—and also, perhaps, about the nature of character. Gradually we are accumulating things to say about interpretation, but we are no good at all at speaking about character, because quite literally we never think about it. There are only a handful of weak books on the subject, but what we really lack is a history of character, by which I mean not only a history of characterization but also a history of the theory of character, or of characterologies such as one finds in Aristotle's *Nicomachean Ethics* or in Yeats's *A Vision*.[1] If you go to your library you will find that almost all your holdings in this matter regard character as something that you build, not something that you study. Character is what unites and justifies the classroom and the playing field. Jane Austen, however, belonged to a time that still believed character to be something that requires study. Character for Jane Austen is not something that you build but rather something that you construe, like a hidden meaning.

Our text for study is from *Pride and Prejudice*, volume 3, chapter 2. At this point in the story we are at Lambton, where Elizabeth is staying with her aunt and uncle, the Gardiners. Half the chapter is devoted to the visit one morning of Darcy and his sister, Georgiana—together with Bingley, who arrives unexpectedly but, naturally, to everyone's delight. The odd thing here is that very little narrative is devoted to the visit as such: we are told nothing, or virtually nothing, of anything anyone says. What takes place takes place as if in silence or as if in secret, yet not quite silently or secretly. The real subject never reaches the level or condition of something actually spoken, but neither is this subject an inward, private, or psychological affair. Things take place beneath the surface of words and actions and explicit behavior—but the question is: What is this subsurface reality and how is it to be arrived at or recovered?

The matter may be expressed as follows: the concern here is with what is hidden and with the task of bringing it into the open or into the light. This is the task of interpretation: the so-called hermeneutical task. What is called hermeneutics occupies this middle ground between what is hidden and what is open and transparent to all. What I would like to propose is that an important part of *Pride and Prejudice*—perhaps that portion which shows us the genius of Jane Austen—occupies this middle ground of hermeneutical reality.

Actually, I do not wish to propose any sort of thesis. All I wish to do is to read a portion of *Pride and Prejudice* as a hermeneutical allegory, perhaps in the narrow appeal that the reading of anything is always a "reading-as," that is, the reading of it as something other than what it exactly happens to be. The ancients believed that the reading of any story always turns into the reading of *something more*, and that interpretation is never simply reading but rather it is getting up to say what this something more is that the story is telling us. Here let me characterize this "something more" in Jane Austen by recalling that in our modern or romantic tradition (that is, since Schleiermacher) hermeneutics is divided into three sorts: scriptural, judicial or legal, and literary. To these categories we may add a fourth—social hermeneutics or, more accurately, the hermeneutics of human social life, which is, like human character, something we think very little about, or one more thing that, in our ignorance or disregard, we have turned over to the social sciences. But human social life is not simply a province of psychology or a place of behavior; it is a domain of human understanding—and *this*, it turns out, is what Jane Austen teaches: *this* is the truth that we can learn from her.

Consider, therefore, *Pride and Prejudice*, volume 3, chapter 2, at Lambton. Elizabeth, remember, has by this time received Darcy's proposal and his no less astonishing letter; she has suffered in consequence a powerful enlightenment or disillusionment, not simply in regard to Darcy, or Wickham, or Bingley, but precisely in regard to her own powers of perception and understanding; she has visited the Darcy estate, Pemberly Woods, and encountered there what might be called a new version of Darcy; and now she sits in a drawing room with Mr. and Mrs. Gardiner, receiving as visitors Darcy and Georgiana—and Bingley, who is unspeakably agreeable and pleasing as always, expressing himself, not in words really, but in "good-humoured ease."[2] Read now the following:

> To Mr. and Mrs. Gardiner he [Bingley] was scarcely a less interesting person than to herself [Elizabeth]. They had long wished to see him. The whole party

before them, indeed, excited a lively attention. The suspicions which had just
arisen of Mr. Darcy and their niece directed their observation towards each
with an earnest, though guarded, inquiry. [261]

What I would like to know is: What is the nature of this "guarded inquiry,"
or how may it be characterized? It appears to have the character of the unspoken question which elicits the unspoken answer, as if there were taking
place here a subterranean conversation. There appears to take place, at any
rate, an exchange of meaning, because the Gardiners

> soon drew from those inquiries the full conviction that one of them [namely,
> Darcy] knew what it was to love. Of the lady's sensations they remained a little
> in doubt; but that the gentleman was overflowing with admiration was evident
> enough. [262]

If you ask, What does a Jane Austen visit entail? here you begin to get
your answer. The Gardiners are *reading* the situation, together with the
people in it, some of whom, for various interesting reasons, are more readable or legible than others. The point, however, is that such a visit as we
have here, in which nothing is happening, and nothing worth repeating is
being said, is nevertheless an urgent and busy event. The next paragraph,
for example, begins as follows:

> Elizabeth, on her side, *had much to do* [my emphasis]. She wanted to ascertain
> the feelings of each of her visitors, she wanted to compose her own, and make
> herself agreeable to all. [262]

The complications here are several. Elizabeth is perhaps not quite legible
to the Gardiners because that which they try to read is not yet fully composed—for Elizabeth's feelings in this situation are as yet ungathered and
remain therefore inaccessible even to herself. She doesn't know what she
feels and evidently she won't know until she first ascertains "the feelings of
each of her visitors." The point, of course, is that Elizabeth desires to know
that which, in this society, is almost never spoken, that which almost always
remains hidden: namely, what others are feeling, or thinking—their "intentions," or "meanings": that which would make them intelligible, but which
repeatedly leaves them inscrutable by its hiddenness. Nor, evidently, can
one really make sense of oneself except in relation to the sense one makes
of others, such that, to misconstrue others is to misconstrue oneself—as
when, earlier, after reading and rereading Darcy's letter, and thus reading
a good deal more in a new light, Elizabeth exclaims: "Till this moment I
never knew myself" (208).

By the composition of her feelings, however, Elizabeth evidently has
more in mind than simply the determination of what she feels. The composition of feelings is an essential practice of the art of manners, which re-

quires one to appear composed, self-possessed, harmonious, at ease or in repose—much like a work of art. Nothing is more painful or disagreeable than someone's loss of composure. Elizabeth's self-composition is meant for the pleasure of the company: to make or compose oneself in this situation is precisely to make oneself agreeable—

> and in the latter object, where she feared most to fail, she was most sure of success, for those to whom she endeavoured to give pleasure were prepossessed in her favour [an indispensable form of prejudice]. Bingley was ready, Georgiana was eager, and Darcy determined, to be pleased. [262]

Poor Darcy: determined, no doubt gravely or grimly, to be pleased. To be open and receptive to the artful pleasure of company is also part of the art of manners; it is clearly that portion which Darcy has had difficulty in learning.

More important, however, is the fact that the art of self-composition is also an art of concealment. For example:

> In seeing Bingley, her [Elizabeth's] thoughts naturally flew to her sister [Jane]; and oh! how ardently did she long to know, whether any of his were directed in like manner. [262]

How, in other words, to read Bingley? This shouldn't be a problem. Early in the novel an important distinction is made between two types of character, or, more accurately, between two types of human being: those who are transparent, and those who are "deep" and "intricate." Speaking of himself, for example, Bingley says: " 'Whatever I do is done in a hurry,' " for it seems true that Bingley lives as if without a second thought, as if on the surface of himself, and he is therefore easily comprehended. " 'Whatever I do is done in a hurry,' " Bingley says, to which Elizabeth immediately responds: " 'That is exactly what I should have supposed of you' " (42)—for Bingley is surely lucid and plain. There is never any question of misunderstanding him, except when others manage to obscure him, as Darcy and Miss Bingley do when they stand in Jane's way of him.

Darcy, by contrast, is too thoughtful by half: you might say that he is overcomposed. He can hardly be found anywhere in his behavior but only deep within, in a portion that he reserves only for himself. There is that in him, of course, which struggles to escape this reserve—Elizabeth is able to call him out of himself, quite in spite of himself, as when we are told, for example, that "she attracted him more than he liked. . . . He wisely resolved to be particularly careful that no sign of admiration should *now* escape him" (59–60). Thus he tries to put himself out of the way of understanding, and succeeds, or almost succeeds, but fortunately those signs of admiration are irrepressible, and—as when he proposes—they even take the form of spoken words: " 'In vain have I struggled. It will not do. My feelings will not be repressed. You must allow me to tell you how ardently I admire and love you' " (189).

Wickham, for his part, suggests a third category, in which reserve takes the form of dissimulation or dissembling, in which case what is required of interpretation is the stripping away of disguise—a demystification or un-masking of self-composition. The point, however, is that the world of *Pride and Prejudice* is a world of hidden meanings which require to be re-covered by interpretation. Nothing or no one of any interest is ever lucid or plain. Elizabeth, "studier of character" (42), presumes too much when she imagines that she can comprehend Bingley (or anyone) in a twinkling. The possibility of misunderstanding—and, above all, of a cultivated resist-ance to understanding—has always got to be presupposed. Jane Austen's contemporary, Schleiermacher, put this into the form of a hermeneutic principle: a "rigorous practice of the art of interpretation . . . is based on the assumption that misunderstanding occurs as a matter of course, and so un-derstanding must be willed and sought at every point."[3] You might say that it is precisely the possibility of misunderstanding that Elizabeth has got to learn; at all events it is what she *does* learn in consequence of her misread-ing of Darcy and Wickham—" 'I, who have prided myself on my discern-ment!—I, who have valued myself on my abilities!' " (208). Elizabeth, in-deed, is the most subtle of interpreters, but what she discovers is that discernment of native talent needs to be made rigorous by self-criticism. She discovers what, indeed, Schleiermacher had formally proposed, namely that interpretation is routinely confounded by prejudice, and that the act of interpretation is essentially an activity of self-correction, or of second, third, and progressively emended readings. There is never any understanding of anything or anyone all at once; understanding is a series of second thoughts.

And it is more: for when Elizabeth imagines that she has fathomed Bing-ley's character at a glance, or that Bingley is without intricacy, she presumes too little. We need to return to the text at hand and to the question, How does one read Bingley? Or, more exactly, How does one understand Bing-ley?—who is finally not less reserved for being so cordial and unaffected, indeed, because, he is perfectly composed and, however legible he may ap-pear (in contrast, say, to Darcy), he never gives himself away. Only buffoons like Mr. Collins and Mrs. Bennet give themselves away. Bingley must not only be read with a view toward fixing his character ("'Whatever I do is done in a hurry,'" etc.); he must also be understood in any given case, or in the midst of a given situation—and the question is, How does such an understanding take place?

Elizabeth's interpretation of Bingley is of enormous value because it gives us a glimpse of the reality of interpretation—interpretation not as an art composed of rules and methods and procedures for obtaining results but interpretation accessible in the conditions under which it actually occurs: interpretation as a form of life. Thus we learn that understanding Bingley does not require anything like getting beneath the surface, because such a thing is impossible. Interpretation is a constructive, not an investigative activity. That is, to interpret is to construe a meaning, which means to construct a version of what is meant. That which lies beneath the surface is not laid bare; rather, a version of it is built up in view of what the surface brings into appearance. Here is how Jane Austen represents it:

> In seeing Bingley, her thoughts naturally flew to her sister; and oh! how ardently did she long to know, whether any of his were directed in like manner. Sometimes she could fancy, that he talked less than on former occasions, and once or twice pleased herself with the notion that as he looked at her, he was trying to trace a resemblance. [262]

It is as if—that is, Elizabeth figures or imagines that Bingley is trying to read Jane into her, or to see her as a version of Jane. One could call this an instance of allegorical seeing, whereby one person is turned into or recomposed as another. It would be graceless and disagreeable, after all, to stare directly and unceasingly at the one you love—that is something Mr. Collins might do. Better to alternate your regard between the person herself and her facsimile or reflection: call this a mode of reserved or artful attention.

Or so Elizabeth imagines—

> But, though this might be imaginary, she could not be deceived as to his behaviour to Miss Darcy, who had been set up as a rival of Jane. No look appeared on either side that spoke particular regard. [262]

Here, by the way, is our explanatory metaphor: in this situation two kinds of speaking obtain—a speaking in words, which Jane Austen here disregards almost completely, and a speaking in looks—a speaking in behavior or in manner, a speaking that takes the form of responses to or within situations: a speaking which includes, as in the case of Bingley's apparent disregard of Georgiana Darcy, a speaking in silences and absences of attention.

> No look appeared on either side that spoke particular regard. Nothing occurred between them that could justify the hopes of his sister. On this point she was soon satisfied; and two or three little circumstances occurred ere they parted, which, in her anxious interpretation [!], denoted a recollection of Jane, not untinctured by tenderness, and a wish of saying more that might lead to the mention of her, had he dared. [262]

Bingley is alive with the will to speak, but he dare not: but never mind, because looks speak, and circumstances denote—to those able to listen and to read. Whole situations organize themselves so as to be understood, but this requires the imagining of words for them. If looks and circumstances could speak, what would they say? The answer lies in the understanding of such a one as Elizabeth, whose construction of what is hidden lends words to what is unspoken, namely, in this case, "a recollection of Jane, not untinctured by tenderness . . ."

As Jane Austen characterizes it, social behavior at its most intelligent, or when practiced by someone like Elizabeth, is an activity of interpretation, that is, a type of understanding which requires a reading between or apart from lines actually spoken. What is spoken is certain to seem beside the point: not merely a veil of words to be penetrated or drawn aside but rather a veil to be understood as a pretext or sidetext that has meaning but no significance—*talk*, as Heidegger would call it: speech that is adjacent to what is actually being said. Bingley, dared he to speak, would speak of Jane, perhaps even to her; instead, he talks with Elizabeth, saying—

> it "was a very long time since he had the pleasure of seeing her"; and, before she could reply, he added, "It is above eight months. We have not met since the 26th of November, when we were all dancing together at Netherfield." [262]

But this is more than polite tedium.

> Elizabeth was pleased to find his memory so exact; and he afterwards took occasion to ask her, when unattended to by any of the rest, whether *all* her sisters were at Longbourn. There was not much in the question, nor in the preceding remark, but there was a look and a manner which gave them meaning. [262–63]

There is a principle here which wants careful formulation, and certainly further reflection. It is not wholly accurate to say that words mean; better to say that situations mean and that words mean as they occur in them, as do looks, gestures, and concatenations of circumstances. As Wittgenstein says, to know the meaning of a word is to know how to use it—and also *when* to use it, and, above all, when *not* to use it. Rules of usage are not simply rules of grammar or semiosis but also rules of suitability and decorum. It follows that rules of decorum are not merely aesthetic; they are also hermeneutic, that is, rules of making sense.

Thus Bingley's words comprise not a speech but a figure of speech—perhaps you could call it a figure in place of speech, or a way of figuring what is unspoken and unspeakable, that is, a way of saying the unspeakable without violating its necessary and intrinsic reserve. For Bingley to announce what is on his mind or in his heart would be to obliterate it: such announcements must await their occasions to call them forth. And so Bingley speaks idly instead, trusting to Elizabeth's superior literacy in such matters to know that this idleness of conversation and regard contains exactly what Elizabeth wants to know.

What Elizabeth chiefly wants to know, of course, is what Darcy is thinking. At Pemberly the day before she had encountered Darcy by accident—

> She longed to know at that moment what was passing in his mind, in what manner he thought of her, and whether in defiance of everything she was still dear to him. [253]

—Yet how to uncover these secrets? In the characterology of *Pride and Prejudice* Darcy belongs among the deep and intricate whom it is easy to misunderstand.[4] In fact the problem of Darcy is precisely that he is unreadable, not, however, because of his depth, but rather because of his surface, which simply was not made for human social life. Late in the novel he describes his upbringing, in which, paradoxically, with great benevolence and good will, he was "allowed, encouraged, almost taught ... to be selfish and overbearing, to care for none beyond my own family circle, to think meanly of their sense and worth compared with my own" (369). In other words Darcy was raised to be wholly self-contained and, one might say, hermetic. He is someone who had never imagined that one day he would desire to address himself to someone in the world; he has never imagined that one day he would have to make himself understood without giving himself away.

Two reflections are required here concerning the problem of understanding Darcy. The first is that Darcy, not having foreseen the need or desire to make himself understood, is thrown back upon plain speaking, with disastrous results. Remember how he bursts in upon Elizabeth with his proposal of marriage. This seems to Elizabeth an even more astounding turn of events than the proposal from Mr. Collins. Darcy's behavior seems to her incomprehensible, outrageous, and presumptuous in the extreme. The point, however, is that this is a Darcy whose reserve collapses ("'In vain have I struggled ...'"), and who is therefore hurled into speech. The proposal scene is remarkable as an episode in which *everything is put into words, and nothing is understood:* more than anything else in the novel the episode shows the inadequacy of plain speaking as an agency of being understood or as an agency of social understanding. It is as if social understanding, like literary understanding, required an art for the concealment of meaning in order for there to be a meaning at all. Darcy says what is on his mind and in his heart as plainly as anyone could say it, and yet he is misconstrued. Or, rather, he is and he isn't misconstrued: the problem is that his words are forced to operate independently of any situation that could give them a meaning, or at all events give them the meaning he intends them to have. Meaning is intention—but only when one knows how to speak to the situation at hand, that is, only when one knows how and when to intend something. Meaning is intention, but only when the situation calls for it. Speech is the application and not simply the expression of meaning, as the old rhetoricians knew. In order to make sense one must first establish the situation in which it is possible to make sense, or to make the sense one wishes to make—and Darcy hasn't done this. Darcy proposes, yet the situation in which he does so hasn't called for it. In human life we are always answerable to the situations in which we speak, or else our behavior will seem uncalled for, which is what Darcy's behavior seems to Elizabeth—and, indeed, this is the way Elizabeth's response to his proposal strikes Darcy. In effect, Darcy and Elizabeth are occupying two different situations and therefore are reduced to speaking at cross-purposes. Perhaps the matter could be expressed this way: in order to make oneself understood one must first understand the situation in which one speaks. And this means that one has to know how to read the situation, together with the people in it, as Elizabeth did in the scene I have been glossing.

This helps to explain why Wickham is such a dangerous character, someone with "truth in his looks" (86) to lend authority to his words. "Whatever bears affinity to cunning is despicable," Darcy says (40); and again: "disguise of every sort is my abhorrence" (192). The difficulty is that society depends upon disguise, or the circumvention of plainness, which means that it is deeply vulnerable to wickedness that masks itself as grace. In all probability there never was a society that did not suffer (and suffer terribly) from this indispensable defect.

The second reflection concerning the problem of understanding Darcy is related to this defect. The ancients knew that *that* truth might just as well be false which cannot appear to be what it is. In a way, this proposition contains the whole meaning, as well as the basic philosophical shortcoming, of rhetoric. Rhetoric belongs to the domain of the probable, *eikos*, the world of resemblance or verisimilitude in which it is impossible to tell the difference between what is and what seems to be the case. This metaphysically intolerable world is, moreover, the world of human social life. In the human world it is never enough simply to speak the truth. Plain speaking is the natural discourse of philosophy, but in the human world it is always necessary for the truth to disguise itself—*as the truth!* It is never enough to speak the truth, you must be able to persuade others that you are doing so. It is never enough to be a good and just man, you must be able to persuade people that *that* is exactly what you are. Fail of this persuasion and the worst consequences follow.

This rhetorical state of affairs is abhorrent to Darcy, even more so than it was to Socrates, who never made the mistake of disregarding the world of appearances, for he knew that it is in this world that things make their appearance: it is in this world that Socrates was required to make *his* appearance, and no one was ever more careful than was Socrates never to appear to be anything other than a good and just man. But it is precisely this reality of appearance that Darcy disregards.

The effect of this disregard is as follows: it is to produce a plurality of Darcys, as if the man were characterless in himself and could only exist in his several versions, among which serious discrepancies are allowed to appear. It is well-known that your understanding of what is written depends on what version of it you are reading, and this in turn depends on just when and where you are reading it, and with whom. Elizabeth's problem is that she is unable to obtain consistent and uncontradicted readings of Darcy— as, indeed, she complains to him directly in one of their early conversations:

> "May I ask [Darcy asks] to what these questions tend?"
>
> "Merely to the illustration of *your* character," said she, endeavouring to shake off her gravity. "I am trying to make it out."
>
> "And what is your success?"
>
> She shook her head. "I do not get on at all. I hear such different accounts of you as puzzle me exceedingly."
>
> "I can readily believe," answered he gravely, "that report may vary greatly with respect to me; and I could wish, Miss Bennet, that you were not to sketch my character at the present moment, as there is reason to fear that the performance would reflect no credit on either."
>
> "But if I do not take your likeness now, I may never have another opportunity." [93–94]

It is as if, in order to understand Darcy at any given moment or in any given conversation, one had first to construct an authorized or authoritative version of him—one that would stand against (and ultimately dispel) various competing versions whose circulation renders him, if not actually unintelligible, at least a perpetual victim of misunderstanding.

Here, for the record, is a short checklist of the versions of Darcy:

1. There is the original Meryton Darcy: haughty, grave, reserved, fastidious, indifferent, coldly civil, etc.

2. There is the Netherfield Darcy: austere, jealous of his station—although the reader (privy to every sort of secret knowledge, or absolved of the task of interpretation) learns that Darcy is bewitched by Elizabeth and must henceforth struggle against the tendency of his affections. This is the Darcy who is repeatedly catching Elizabeth by surprise, never more so, of course, than when he proposes.

3. There is the Darcy according to Wickham: craven and disreptuable and evidently consistent with the Darcy who conspires against Jane's chances with Bingley.

4. Speaking of Bingley: there is Bingley's Darcy, who inspires in Elizabeth a crucial perplexity: "How can Mr. Bingley, who seems good humour itself, and is, I really believe, truly amiable, be in friendship with such a man? How can they suit each other?" (82).

5. There is the Darcy of the fateful explanatory letter, who undergoes considerable alteration in proportion as Elizabeth finds herself revising her understanding of Wickham. A revision in the character of Wickham requires perforce a corresponding revision in the character of Darcy.

6. There is the Pemberly Darcy: (i) first as represented by his house-keeper, who has known him since he was four and has never heard him utter a cross word; (ii) then there is the Pemberly portrait that represents, of all things, a smiling Darcy—and not smiling merely but, as it appears to Elizabeth, smiling "such a smile over the face, as she remembered to have sometimes seen, when he looked at her" (250): the lesson here is clearly that Elizabeth, like the artist, brings out of him that which is hidden—brings out the best in him, or moves him to be his best version of himself; and (iii) there is the Darcy who appears suddenly before Elizabeth leaves Pemberly, and who is inexplicably cordial and, one might say, generously civil even to her relatives.

7. There is the Darcy of the Gardiners' letter (321–25), which gives the account of how Darcy pursued Wickham and Lydia and saved the honor of all concerned. This is the Darcy who is spoken for by his actions: the Darcy of heroic narrative.

8. And this Darcy is consistent with the Darcy who speaks (at last) for himself, or who offers his own version of himself—his own self-interpretation, whose effect is to resolve the discrepancies of his character historically or autobiographically by an account of his origin, development, and critical transformation, conversion, or reform (365–71).

What we get at the end, however, is not Darcy but only an authorized version of him—his own self-characterization or rendition of his character. Who is authorized, after all, to speak for Darcy, or *of* Darcy, except Darcy himself? Socrates in the *Apology* confronted the principal difficulty of being Socrates, or of being anyone in the human social world, namely that one has to contend with various competing versions of oneself, and that in the end one must speak for oneself in order to establish the truth of one's character. No one can speak for Socrates except Socrates—not Meletus, not Aristophanes, not the citizens of Athens who have encountered him face to face, not even the Delphic oracle. "I am," Socrates says, "who am what I say I am."[5] Darcy comes round at last to this position. He had thought, he says, that it was beneath him to lay himself open to the world, and so he withheld himself from it and from its understanding, as if in fear of standing so ludicrously exposed as Mr. Collins or Mrs. Bennet.

However, there never was any question of Darcy *opening* himself, that is, revealing or exposing himself; there was only a question of being understood. And what does this mean? What does it mean, after all, to understand anyone? Of many answers to this question, let me conclude by selecting two:

1. The understanding of anything requires that you become what you know, such that the understanding of someone requires you to get inside that person or to turn yourself into him or into some sympathetic likeness of him so that you can say what it means to *be* him, as if it were possible to know him as he knows himself. The understanding of another requires that we enter into the other's self-understanding, and perhaps even that we come to understand him better than he understands himself.[6] My inclination is to characterize these formulations as identifiably "romantic," perhaps in the way that Robert Langbaum characterized *Einfühlung*, or empathy, as a "specifically Romantic way of knowing," one which finds a home in the dramatic monologue, whose characters we come to know as if by an activity of impersonation or (better) possession, since it is by lending our consciousness to these characters that we are able to experience them, not as objects of course but as subjects of consciousness whom we are able to appropriate into our own self-experience or self-possession.[7] This way of speaking leads us to what may be a peculiarly Romantic or modern desire, which is to know others as we know ourselves, or anyhow to obtain from others an intimacy which maybe no human being should be asked to give, because it is the kind of intimacy which can be exacted only from characters in a dramatic monologue, or in a novel. It has always been my impression that Freud desired to have the same kind of knowledge of other people that he could have of characters in novels. Of course the point might be that in order for Freud to know you, you would have to turn yourself into something like a character in a novel.

2. What does it mean to understand anyone? A second answer to this question presupposes a concept of character that resembles Aristotle's more than it does our own. We use the word "character" to refer to the representation of a human being purely and simply; Aristotle's word for character, however, is *ethos*, which refers not to the representation of a human being but to that which differentiates him ethically and renders him

intelligible. Character is fate, but it is also meaning. Jane Austen uses the word "character" in a way that resembles Aristotle's usage rather than our own. Here in a few words I would like to speculate that for her the understanding of anyone requires (beforehand) a determining or fixing of character, which seems like a dangerous or disagreeable business, because one's character in this context is clearly not simply an inward and private possession, not merely that which you can choose to disclose or to withhold, not exclusively something you can call your own. Character is also the kind of person you become, not simply by a natural course of development, nor even simply by upbringing or breeding, but also by inadvertence and neglect, as well as by study and choice as to how you are willing to be characterized, that is, to be understood by other people. The understanding of anyone presupposes a prior fixing or determination of character. It appears to be the case that society reserves for itself the last right or authority for the fixing of character, in the sense that what you are, or what you appear to be, slips naturally into that domain of invention: what is said about you. Woe be to you if society is mistaken in what it says—that is, if its version of you differs from the construction you would place upon yourself, or the construction you might desire for yourself or perhaps by self-reform or self-revision to achieve for yourself. Character is not only built or developed; it is also conferred, like a judgment or a meaning: this is the sense in which Jane Austen uses the word (10, 93, 243, 321, etc.). Do not underestimate the interpretive power and authority of society: you are what society says about you, whether you know it or not, or whether you even care—and this is so even when society is manifestly mistaken, as it often is. Yet who is to say? Society sometimes allows you, or at least it allowed Darcy, a voice in the matter, and it was willing, or Elizabeth was willing, to take him at his word ("'You taught me a lesson, hard indeed at first, but most advantageous'" [369]). Notice that there was hardly any arriving at Darcy otherwise except insofar as a version of him, guaranteed by testimony, is brought into being. One major question has to do with the authority of such a version. But a second and more important question concerns the limitations of human understanding, that is, whether there can be any such thing as the understanding of that which withholds itself or remains hidden. Heidegger says that the truth of the work of art occurs only in the midst of its closure or concealment, whence the paradox that our desire to understand always pursues that which is able to withhold itself from understanding, so that there is no way we can grasp or take possession of it—no hope, in other words, of knowing it from within or from the inside out as we might know an object or even as we might claim to know ourselves.

Thus there is no understanding Darcy or anyone by reaching beneath any sort of surface. There obtains in him a classic human reserve which the desire for understanding is powerless to violate. Jane Austen reminds us—or perhaps helps to teach us, as if for the first time—that understanding can never simply be willed but requires to be negotiated as a means of bringing two parties together. In this respect we might say that interpretation—that is, interpretation conceived as understanding and not merely as the decoding or deciphering of what is given once for all—can never be unilateral, as can an act of investigation or analysis, because it is a social activity, part of the historical life of man and not merely about it.

6
Energy and Interpretation in Hopkins

"The will," Hopkins wrote in the notes from the Long Retreat of 1881, "is surrounded by the objects of desire as the needle by points of the compass. . . . It has in fact, more or less, in its affections a tendency or magnetism towards every object and the *arbitrium,* the elective will, decides which: this is the needle proper."[1]

Figures of energy fall regularly from Hopkins's pen—so often, in fact, that the best way to begin to understand this writer is to think of his work in relation to the manifold and divergent imaginations of energy (energy in all its versions): (1) the metaphysical energy of Aristotle, which is the principle of activity that mediates between matter and form; (2) the mechanical force of Newtonian physics; (3) the Romantic ideas of Power, Force, Spontaneity, and Process; (4) the Vital Principle of organicism, together with its equivalent notions of metamorphosis, growth, formation, and "inner form"; (5) the energy of "Spirit" and "Life" that (as in Blake) opposes discursive reason, logical analysis, scientific empiricism, and which seeks to restore all things to an original and transcendental unity, thus to redeem reality from its mathematicization, its mechanization, its materialization, or (finally) its dismemberment into "bundles of sensation"; (6) the spiritual *energeia* of reason, language, and culture, as in the writings of Wilhelm von Humboldt; (7) the natural phenomena of heat, light, gravity, electricity, and magnetism, which form the subject matter of nineteenth-century physics; (8) Nietzschean power and Freudian energy; (9) the patterned energies of "knot" and "vortex" that are, as Hugh Kenner has shown, among the dominant explanatory metaphors of the Pound Era, when things seemed no longer to repose among essences, substances, archetypes, or fixed categories of being, but were thought instead to receive their integrity and permanence (and thus their intelligibility) from the morphology of change itself.[2]

It is within this horizon of meanings that Hopkins coined his famous word "instress": that is, the "energy of being" that shoots through the created universe and determines in each thing its distinctive form or "inscape," its singular and intelligible way of being in the world—which determines, in short, how it is to be understood.[3] But the meaning of energy for Hop-

kins cannot be contained within a definition, nor is it reducible to a statement of its correspondence to a real state of affairs—to a world, for example, in which "all things are upheld by instress and are meaningless without
it" (*JP,* 127). Instress is not reducible to a meaning because it is that which
makes meaning, or interpretability, possible, which is to say that its meaning in Hopkins's writings is to be discovered in its wide-ranging uses: for
example, in its phenomenal value as an episode of natural experience, or
as a way of speaking about (or understanding) one's perception of the external world; or, again, in its conceptual value as an explanatory model that
can be brought to bear upon a diversity of theoretical and meditative topics,
as in the early "Notes on the History of Greek Philosophy" (1868), in which
the mind is said to have "two kinds of energy," discursive and contemplative, energy by which the mind moves as in a sort of kinesis of thinking,
and energy by which the mind "is absorbed (as far as that may be), taken
up by, dwells upon, enjoys, a single thought" (*JP,* 125–26). The term "energy" is here significant for its power as a generative idea, that is, as a meaning used to generate other meanings in the development of a discourse: the
mind is figured as a capacity for "work" or activity, not as an interior space
occupied by some mental equivalent of reality, nor even as a sort of spiritual "substance" such as Descartes imagined. Mind here is consistent with
Coleridge's "intellectual energy" (a repetition in the finite mind of "divine
energy" or the Logos) and Newman's conception of "living intelligence," in
which reasoning is not a method or acquired skill but "a living spontaneous
energy within us."[4]

But the energy of Hopkins is accessible to other traditions as well. It
seems especially important to know that his life is in part coterminous with
the development of *"die energetische Weltbild,"*[5] a phrase coined by the
German chemist and Nobel Prize winner, Wilhelm Ostwald, to describe the
world-hypothesis in which nature is conceived to be neither purely mechanical nor purely organic but both—and more: namely a system of fields
whose phenomena are to be figured as so many transferences and transformations of energy. By the time Hopkins matriculated at Oxford in 1863, the
world had for a generation been witnessing the development of thermody-
namics, electromagnetism, electrochemistry, and an array of new physical
theories that took recourse to the concept of energy the way Newtonian
physics had espoused the idea of substance. Thus in 1855 William Rankine
proposed a "science of energetics" as a category of investigation for the
phenomena of matter in motion, thermometric heat, radiant heat, light,
chemical action, electric current, as well as gravity, elasticity, chemical affinity, static electricity, and magnetism.[6] As though under the pressure of these

phenomena, matter itself was becoming gradually "dematerialized"[7]—not idealized as in organicism, with its postulate of a Vital Principle in all things, but "energized," in the sense that bodies were now known to be capable of activity not only according to the old Leibnizian concept of *vis viva* (the force of matter in motion defined as the product of the mass by the square of its velocity, or mc^2), but as constant quantities persisting through successive changes in form, magnitude, and intensity.[8] The nineteenth-century physicist perceived, as did Hopkins, that each thing—even the most ponderous and inorganic body—"goes itself" (*P*, 90), and that it does so because there is more to reality than mechanical force or organic power: there is also energy, imponderable and indestructible, present everywhere but ungraspable and unthinkable except in relation to its results, and itself the medium by which things become accessible as objects of experience and knowledge. "All we know about matter," wrote James Clerk Maxwell in 1877, "relates to the series of phenomena in which energy is transferred from one portion of matter to another, till in some part of the series our bodies are affected, and we become conscious of a sensation."[9]

This shift from substance to transference reorganized the entire intelligibility of things. And if, in the end, energy fell somewhat short of being (as Ostwald thought it was) "the only real thing in the so-called outer world,"[10] it nevertheless seemed to constitute the basis for a unified-field theory of the physical sciences—"a sort of compass," Robert Mayer called it, "to guide the investigator safely forth on the sea of particulars."[11] The "humanists" of the period were, of course, more sharply attentive to Darwin, evolutionary theory, social dynamics, and the positivist pronouncements of Huxley, Tyndall, and Spencer, but in the long view the most striking scientific achievements of the century belonged to men like Maxwell, Michael Faraday, Sodi Cornot, James Joule, Rudolf Clausius, Robert Mayer, Hermann von Helmholtz—idle names[12] to most students of the nineteenth century, but not perhaps to Hopkins, who was an interested reader of Peter Guthrie Tate, the Scottish physicist who reported widely and popularly during Hopkins's adult life on current developments in physics and chemistry (he translated, for example, Helmholtz's essay on vortices and published, in 1877, his own essay on "Knots").[13] Hopkins, late in his life, momentarily entertained the idea of composing "a sort of popular account of Light and Ether" (*LL*, ii, 139), chiefly in order to rescue the subject from the technical language of Tait's book, *Light* (Edinburgh, 1884).

The work of Hopkins is not any sort of "literary" equivalent of this scientific energetics, but it cannot surprise us that figures of energy are indispensable to the way he makes sense of things—especially in the Journal,

which is in large measure a logbook of a man fascinated by displays of natural energy: electrical storms, sunsets, bursts of sharp light and color ("blue
... charged with simple instress" [*JP*, 207]), whirlwinds and northern lights,
the "spraying" or radiance of trees, flowers, and clouds, the violence of
waves hurling themselves against a shore, the power and unobstructed
sweep of a glacier—and even the sheer exuberance of a musician's fingers:
"To Madame Leupold's concert, where Madle. Mela sang in a tenor and a
girl played the violin and another, Madle. Vogt, the finger-glasses (Mattau-
phone), and certainly that instrument is chromatically more perfect than the
violin.... But 'it is the sport' to watch her fingers flying, and at the distance
the articulations vanishing, they wave like flakes or fins or leaves of white"
(*JP*, 167–68).

But these vanishing articulations are an anomaly, at least to this extent: a
sheer burst of energy will seem to Hopkins worth recording—"In taking off
my jersey of knitted wool in the dark with an accidental stroke of my finger
down the stuff I drew a flash of electric light. This explains the crackling I
heard" (*JP*, 196)—but what he is most compelled to place in his journal are
those events in which energy leaves its signature: "pencillings of purple"
(*JP*, 191), for example, which differentiate one particular sunset from other,
equally striking bursts of evening color. "In watching the sea," he writes,
"one should be alive to the oneness which all its motion receives from its
perpetual balance and falling this way and that to its own level" (*JP*, 225).
In Whitman the sea becomes for the "electric self" of the poet the transcendent power that resolves all things into an undifferentiated whole, but
what counts for Hopkins is the equilibrium of the sea's movement, not its
power purely and simply but the formal intelligibility of power—the way
power articulates itself through water. Of a Norman cathedral Hopkins says
that the "all powerfulness of instress and mode and the immediateness of
its effect are very remarkable" (*JP*, 188), but this immediateness of effect is
finally incidental to the disclosure of pattern, design, or principles of formation: incidental, in other words, to the *inscape* of energy.

The relation of energy and form in Hopkins is not esoteric, but neither
is it uncomplicated. J. Hillis Miller tells us that, "If instress is the pervasive
energy of being, upholding all things equally, inscape is the name for this
energy as it manifests itself in the distinctive structure of all things, both
outer and inner."[14] Thus Hopkins: "All the world is full of inscape and
chance left free to act falls to an order as well as a purpose" (*JP*, 230).[15] But
why should this be so? What is it in the nature of energy that should make
it expressive of order and purpose? Why are nature's improvisations so rational as to disclose always in their results a formal intelligibility, such that,

without ever expressing anything, nevertheless they make sense? A generalized answer might take its cue from the Retreat notes, in which energy is figured as "the strain of creating action as received in the creature" from God, and which "cannot cease without the creature's ceasing to be" (*S,* 137): energy can thus be expected to generate forms of harmony, in accordance with an ancient commonplace. Similarly, Hopkins explained to Patmore that "fineness, proportion, of feature comes from a moulding force which succeeds in asserting itself over the resistance of cumbersome or restraining matter; the bloom of health comes from abundance of life, the great vitality within. The moulding force, the life, is the form in the philosophic sense, and in man this is the soul" (*LL,* iii, 306–07). But what Hopkins perceives and records in his journal is finally much more specific (and much less metaphysical) than the aesthetic virtues of organic form or the cohesive power of Aristotelian soul. What he perceives are (mainly) "knots" and "whorls," "sprays" and "radiance," "branchings" and "curves," trajectories of flow, stress, tension, and compression. We know now (what Hopkins knew without generalizing the fact) that the patterns in nature are few in kind: nature plays infinite variations upon the spiral, the meandering line, the branching of lines, the explosion or radiance of lines departing from a center, and so on.[16] These shapes are determined by the energetic nature of space, which is not simply a void filled with bodies moving more or less geometrically according to Cartesian or Newtonian laws, but matrices of energy that coerce matter into certain recurrent patterns: water as it descends through a drain or flows past an eddy will always describe the energy of the vortex, rivers will always meander like snakes or branch like trees or arterial systems; strings (as everyone knows) will maddeningly loop and knot, and so will the trunks of trees; heat will radiate, as will light and the heads of dandelions. This energetic shaping of phenomena is that Hopkins calls (in the Journal) *scaping:* it is an occasion of beauty, but it is for Hopkins hermeneutic as well as aesthetic adventure. He repeatedly figures this scaping as the speech of nature, as in the instance of "a budded lime against the wall: turn, pose, and counterpoint: the *form* speaking" (*JP,* 163). To understand this speech—to discover (and formulate) the "law" by which something is shaped—is to disclose its "inscape."

However, one should not—and cannot—reduce to formula the dazzling array of senses in which Hopkins uses the terms "scape," "inscape," "stress," and "instress." For what is intriguing in its forms and versions is the relation between the "speech of nature" and the writing of the journal. In its simplest case the one is clearly the inspiration of the other: "July 11. Fine; in morning sky festooned with cobwebs; afterwards brighter; silver-bright fish-scale-bespattered sunset" (*JP*, 147)—we can call this a lyric out-burst, mimetic not in its content but in its form, because it seeks to achieve by means of figures the expressiveness of nature rather than simply the image of a scene or "scape": not the look of nature but its work. Elsewhere Hopkins will speak of "catching" an inscape, even as he speaks of "how differently quickened the ear must be to meaning and unmeaning sounds: it seemed to me very hard to think one could catch the difference between *ghali* and *ali* in quick conversation, or at a distance" (*JP*, 259). For nature, like language, is diacritical in its formations, so that a flash of lightning, in order to be intelligible, must be differentiated from "bright confusion" as though it were "uttered by a tongue of brightness" (*JP*, 212). Such an event is an instance of speech that requires the act of writing for its preservation, and this is in part a way of understanding the motive and authority of the Journal: Hopkins is nature's amanuensis. But he is more: nature will from time to time rise to a "sonnet-like inscape" (*JP*, 259), but just as often her speech will seem merely "idiomatic" (*JP*, 195) or, worse, garbled: "The trees were irregular, scarcely expressing form, and the aspens blotty" (*JP*, 147). Or (as in "quick conversation") its articulations will be so swift and interwoven that they will vanish before the mind can grasp their "meanings," as in an entry from 1872: "About all the turns of the scaping from the break and flooding of wave to its run out again I have not satisfied myself. The shores are swimming and the eyes have before them a region of milky surf but it is hard for them to unpack the huddling and gnarls of the water and law out the shapes and sequence of the running" (*JP*, 223). One cannot help thinking here of Wallace Stevens's line concerning "the maker's rage to order words of the sea."[17] This is, in effect, what Hopkins seeks to accomplish, but with this difference, that his ordering is more a matter of physics than of metaphysics or poetics. Thus, in 1874, having at last satisfied himself about the scaping of the wave, he writes: "The wave breaks in this order—the crest of the barrel 'doubling' (that, a boatman said, is the word in use) is broken into a bush of foam, which, if you search it, is a lace and tangle of jumping sprays; then, breaking down these grow to a sort of shaggy quilt tumbling up the beach; thirdly, this unfolds. ...." (*JP*, 251)—and so on: a short, improvised essay in dynamics, primitive (because metaphorical rather than mathematical) by comparison with such rigorous or anyhow more measured studies as Rankine's "On the Exact Form of Waves Near the Surface of Deep Water" (1862). Yet the point is surely that Hopkins and Rankine share a common desire to understand the morphology of motion.[18]

This concern with morphology—that is, with formal intelligibility that, in more systematic contexts, would require mathematical expression—is a matter of some importance, because it is possible to misunderstand Hopkins's use of language in his journal, and to see a given entry as, for example, Irving Massey sees it: an act of imprisonment, "the impounding of reality in words." More than this, Massey says of Hopkins's writing that "his words go out in pursuit of reality like falcons stooping to the kill: and there is a destructive effect in the contact, a bruising impact that leaves the object stunned with the force of the word."[19] Hopkins would have appreciated Massey's perceptive reading of him. For it is true that Hopkins does not always—perhaps rarely—write of nature in a plain or mimetic style: "Through such clouds anvil-shaped pink ones and up-blown fleece-of-wool flat-topped dangerous-looking pieces" (*JP*, 142): one cannot imagine here what Hopkins was looking at. Only the words remain, as in a "speech framed to be heard for its own sake and interest even over and above its interest of meaning" (*JP*, 289).

What needs to be understood, however, is that "meaning" in Hopkins's journal cannot be equated with any content which it is the writer's obligation to transmit, just as reality is not reducible to an object which it is his obligation to possess and to redistribute within the virtual space of a "speaking picture." Rather, the act of writing is an act of interpretation that brings into the open the fundamental intelligibility of nature's improvisations of form. Humphrey House tells us that "Hopkins normally made rough notes of what he saw at the time of seeing it, and wrote in the Journal sometime later from these notes" (*JP*, xxv). This suggests that the act of writing serves not simply to preserve an act of seeing but rather to complete it, as though writing were the natural outcome of seeing, not perhaps because it makes seeing possible, but because seeing is nothing apart from the interpretation of it—nothing until one has made sense of it. Of a tree, for example, Hopkins writes: "I saw how great the richness and subtlety is of the curves in the clusters, both in the forward bow . . . and in some graceful hangers on the side, but I cannot very well characterise it now" (*JP*, 152). One could say that this failure of characterization is the coordinate of a failure of perception, in the sense that it is symptomatic of a failure to see in a way that will enable language to express its version of the experience. We are talking here of a failure of understanding. One senses, in any event, Hopkins's dissatisfaction with the indefiniteness or generality of his language ("richness" and "subtlety": euphemisms, obviously, for indeterminacy). One senses dissatisfaction of this sort particularly in those cases when Hopkins is compelled to return once more to the same phenomenon. In an entry for July 10, 1866, for example, he writes: "Oaks: the organization of this tree is difficult. Speaking generally no doubt the determining planes are concentric, a system of brief contiguous and continuous tangents, whereas those of the cedar would roughly be called horizontals ..." (*JP*, 144). It is not sufficient, however, to speak "generally," for what Hopkins seeks to understand is not merely the *geometrical* form of the whole but, more specifically, the *energetic* form of its parts: "Oaks differ much, and much turns on the broadness of the leaf, the narrower giving the crisped and starry Catherine-wheel forms, the broader the flat-pieced mailed or shard-covered ones, in which it is possible to see composition in dips etc. on wider bases than the single knot or cluster. But I shall study them further. See the 19th" (*JP*, 144–45).

It is important to notice that Hopkins's concern here is not with the leaves as "things" (objects to be depicted) but with leaves as diacritical forms—differences that specify (or name) the several versions of oak. The entry from the 19th makes this concern explicit:

> I have now found the law of the oak leaves. It is of platter-shaped stars altogether; the leaves lie close like pages, packed, and as if drawn tightly to. But these old packs, which lie at the end of their twigs, throw out now long shoots alternately and slimly leaved, looking like bright keys. All the sprays but markedly these ones shape out and as it were embrace greater circles and the dip and toss of these make the wider and less organic articulations of the tree. [*JP*, 146]

"I have now found the law of the oak leaves": nor can one miss the way of speaking in which this discovery is registered. In contrast to the earlier geometrical language of "planes," "tangents," and "horizontals," Hopkins now takes recourse to the energetic language of transitive relations: the old packs of leaves "throw out ... long shoots," the sprays "shape out and as it were embrace greater circles," whose "dip and toss ... make the wider and less organic articulations of the tree." The leaves are no longer discrete objects; they have become an organization of formative activities whose dynamism appeals to Hopkins as so many acts of speech, and rather precisely so: the oak expresses its form in so many "articulations" that radiate outward in lines of decreasing ("wider and less organic") intensity, even as a human utterance will disperse its energies toward a circumference.

One may speak here of the "speech" of nature, but it is worth noticing that Hopkins is not listening, as Wordsworth might have, to what nature says; instead he is reading (the leaves, for example, are "like pages, packed, and as if drawn tightly to"). Hopkins figures himself in terms of a hermeneutic relation to the created world as to a text or Book of Nature, whose "compositions" (*JP*, 145, 155) are configurations of energy that enact, as forms of language do, events of differentiation—the "running instress," in

Hopkins's words, that "unmistakably distinguishes and individualises things" (*JP*, 215). To "read" such compositions (*JP*, 218) is an interpretive act, a naming in the human language of signs of that which inscribes itself ("distinguishes and individualises" itself) in the natural language of energy.

The interesting complication in this, however, is that the language of energy is not reducible to a metaphorics of writing but seems naturally to call for analogies of sound, voice, and spirit. The most obvious case in which this is so is in the following:

> As Kingfishers catch fire, dragonflies draw flame;
>   As tumbled over rim in roundly wells
>   Stones ring; like each tucked string tells, each hung bell's
> Bow swung finds tongue to fling out broad its name;
> Each mortal thing does one thing and the same:
>   Deals out that being indoors each one dwells;
>   Selves—goes itself: myself it speaks and spells,
> Crying *What I do is me: for that I came.*
>
> [*P*, 90]

Activity (energeia) is speech: each thing "goes itself" and, doing so, "flings out broad its name" as a distinctive presence, a "selving" of being that makes each thing accessible (because already differentiated) to human language. The language of energy in this respect bears a resemblance, not to writing, but to Heidegger's language, whose words are events of disclosure in which the being or presence of things "shines out" in a kind of primal Saying.[20] Whereas for Heidegger, however, such disclosure is incompatible with the language of signs (we cannot speak *about* or explain what is disclosed), such is not the case for Hopkins. On the contrary, for Hopkins the created world finds its completion—its fullest articulation or disclosure—in human speech. This is in part the meaning of "Ribblesdale," whose figuration of Earth's ineloquence plays dialectically against the self-disclosing energies of "As Kingfishers catch fire": "Earth, sweet Earth" appeals to heaven, but she has "no tongue to plead"; she cannot mean, "but only be": she is expressive, but lacks expression, rather like nature as it appears in one of Coleridge's Notebook entries: "We understand Nature just as if at a distance we looked at the Image of a Person in a Looking-glass, plainly and fervently discoursing—yet what he uttered, we could decypher only by the motion of the Lips, and the mien, and the expression of the muscles of the Countenance."[21] One reads, in this case, not words—not written signs—but figurations of speech that do not strike the ear. Precisely in this wise the Earth of "Ribblesdale" beckons to man for attention—for "what is Earth's eye, tongue, or heart else, where / Else but in dear and dogged man?" Man, for his part, *ought* to heed the Earth and be the medium of her appeal—ought to be Earth's advocate, speaking to heaven for her sake; but man fails of or betrays this advocacy, so turned inward is he in his concupiscence and careless of the Earth ("To his own selfbent so bound, so tied to his turn"): as though man were entropic, a bound energy (*P,* 90–91).

Again: "All things," Hopkins says in the Retreat notes, "are charged with love, charged with God and if we know how to touch them give off sparks and take fire, yield drops and flow, ring and tell of him" (*S,* 195). In such discourse all things find their fulfillment, but they need man's mediating touch, need his word as man needs the Word of God, for without such mediation the world's expressiveness would remain concealed, a latent energy—or, much to the same effect, a wasted energy in the manner of an unread, uninterpreted text:

> It was a hard thing to undo this knot.
> The rainbow shines, but only in the thought
> Of him that looks. Yet not in that alone,
> For who makes rainbows by invention?
> And many standing round a waterfall
> See one bow each, yet not the same to all,
> But each a hand's breadth further than the next.
> The sun on falling waters writes the text
> Which yet is in the eye or in the thought.
> It was a hard thing to undo this knot.
>
> [*P,* 130]

"The sun on falling waters writes the text": as the poet creates the poem, the sun's energy creates the rainbow, but the rainbow requires man's eye and thought in order to be fully actualized, even as the poet's text is not a self-contained and self-fulfilled or self-interpreting object but requires acts of reading to become fully what it was meant to be—and not acts of reading only (not merely recitals or decipherings that duplicate an original), but acts of interpretation. Here lies the central motive of Hopkins's journal: it is not simply to witness or transcribe nature's energetic forms; it is to appropriate them into his own situation and to fill them in turn with a human meaning. Bearing witness to the beauty of nature's forms is implicit in this activity, to be sure, but the activity remains preeminently hermeneutic in character—an activity of understanding in which the mind goes beyond what Hopkins calls "Simple Apprehension" and "takes the measure of things, brings word of them" (*S,* 174).

Here, then, would be the point: what is energetic in this event is not the natural form as such but rather the transference by which form is turned into meaning.

This neat formulation, however, cannot be isolated from further complications. For example, as Hopkins thinks of nature's patterned energies in terms that are accessible to human speech, so in turn he thinks of human language by analogy with natural energy. "We may," he writes in "Rhythm and the Other Structural Parts of Rhetoric—Verse" (1873–74), "think of words as heavy bodies, as indoor and out of door objects of nature and man's art." They are, that is, objects of nature that man appropriates for his art in virtue of their energetic character:

> Now every visible palpable body has a centre of gravity round which it is in balance and a centre of illumination or *highspot* or *quickspot* up to which it is shaded. The centre of gravity is like the accent of stress, the highspot like the accent of pitch, and as in some things as air and water the centre of gravity is either unnoticeable or changeable so there may be languages in a fluid state in which there is little difference of weight or stress between syllables or what there is changes and again as it is only glazed bodies that shew the highspot well so there may be languages in which the pitch is unnoticeable. [*JP*, 269]

Words are like bodies, but bodies as understood in nineteenth-century rather than in eighteenth-century physics: they are physical quantities, but not inert extensions of matter capable of change only in relation to space; rather, they possess both mass *and* energy, in the sense that they are capable of changes in form, state, equilibrium, and intensity. This way of thinking about words will perhaps make more sense if we remember that (as always) Hopkins appears to be thinking of language that is *written in order to be spoken*. Thus stress and pitch are properties of the phonetic structure of *written* language (since that which is spoken is, strictly speaking, inaccessible to the category of structure): they are accented in verse—but within the ordonnance of Hopkins's metaphor verse becomes something like an energy field in which written words behave like charged bodies: they are not ponderous particles acted upon merely by forces from without but particles that change from within. Touch them, and they undergo what physicists call "scaler" transformations (that is, transformations measured in terms of scales rather than vectors). The accent of pitch is thus a speaking that "lights up" written words according to their tonal quality (*JP*, 270), while the accent of stress is "the bringing out of the sound of the syllable, especially its vowel-sound. It is also almost necessarily a heightening of the same syllable in loudness" (*JP*, 271).

Distinctions between speaking and writing here grow difficult to maintain. What Hopkins appears to have in mind is something done to writing in the speaking of it; or, more accurately, it is something done *in* writing in the expectation that speaking will bring it into the open—bring it to fulfillment or completion. Yet (and here is the difficult point) what is brought to fulfillment or completion in speaking is something that can only be accomplished in writing. It is precisely at this tangled nexus of speaking and writing that Hopkins locates poetry, which is "speech framed to be heard for its own sake and interest even over and above its interest of meaning" (*JP,* 289), as if it were only in writing that the "inscape" of speech could be captured ("framed") in order, subsequently, to be released in speaking. Writing in this respect does not preserve a prior and superior utterance; rather, it brings out into the open that which is hidden in speech—that which is silent and reserved: the "inscape" of speech. Writing thus makes possible speech as such, that is, speech which is not merely a function in behalf of what is said but which possesses an interest of its own "over and above its interest of meaning." Poetry accents the formal features of speech—features which can only be brought forward by means of writing—as when words pass through a rhythm "like fresh water flowing through a fountain or over a waterfall, each gallon taking on the same shape as those before it" (*JP,* 280): in short, a patterning of energy.

There is here, of course, a powerful formalist bias toward language and poetry, one that is reflected in Hopkins's own verse, whose locutions regularly and deliberately subordinate meaning to "design, pattern, or what I am in the habit of calling 'inscape' " (*LL,* i, 66). But it is formalism with a difference—indeed, with several differences. We should take care, for example, not to think of this subordination of meaning in terms of the structuralist metaphors of "foregrounding" and "backgrounding," with their implication that form and meaning are discontinuous phenomena, "things" that cannot occupy the same space at the same time. Hopkins's formalism is energized rather than spatialized: he thinks of poetic writing in terms of what it has in common with nature: namely, *energetic form,* as though between speech and writing, word and world, form and meaning, poetry and reality, there were a physical continuity—physical, not in the sense of mere stuff ("cumbersome and restraining matter"), but in the sense of matter shaped by the flow of energy, or energy made articulate in something visible and tangible.

In this respect the lecture notes on verse are to poetry what the journal is to nature: an attempt to disclose the formal intelligibility of the reality in question. And as with the relation of poetry to nature, so with the (historically vexed) relation of poetry to meaning: discontinuities are mediated by the concept of energy. In a well-known letter to Bridges, for example, Hopkins remarks upon the obscurity of Bridges's sonnet, "Regret": the second quatrain, Hopkins says, is "dark," and he goes on to explain that "one of two kinds of clearness one shd. have—either the meaning to be felt without effort as fast as one reads or else, if dark at first reading, when once made out *to explode*" (*LL,* i, 90). Edward Said has written that the "ideology of most literary criticism can be plainly described as permitting the confrontation of an inquiring critic with a resisting text, that is, between a flexible subject and a completed object. All the activity derives from the critic, to whose swoops and thrusts the text offers a resisting, but in the end compliant surface."[22] This is manifestly an ideology that Hopkins did not share. For him the text is, like nature, active. Its objectivity does not consist in its graspability, still less in a surface of mere words to be penetrated by a reader in search of depths or levels of meaning; on the contrary, it is the text that penetrates the reader, even as the sound of speech will penetrate an auditor. Consider that the physicist does not think of bodies as "forms" that "possess" contents of energy; instead of figuring the object in terms of the spatial dimensions of "inner" and "outer," the physicist conceives it according to the dynamics of transformation, which is to say in terms of a "now" and a "then," as in the transformation of potential into kinetic energy—a transformation that inevitably entails the transference of energy from one body to another. Thus, for Hopkins, a text is, when read, an instance of kinesis: it is radiant with meaning, which strikes the reader as light emerging (or, indeed, exploding) from darkness.

One would, of course, like to know in more systematic fashion just how poetry is so "charged" with meaning as to be capable of such kinesis. The metaphor of energy does not resolve the problem of meaning into a theory of how meaning is possible; indeed, Hopkins does not appear to regard meaning as a problem at all—one thinks in this connection of Ernst Cassirer's opinion that meaning becomes a problem chiefly in consequence of an "inadequate metaphorical description" of language.[23] In the letters to Bridges, for example, anxiety about meaning seems to have been all on Bridges's part, especially in that first instance when Hopkins confronted him with "The Wreck of the Deutschland." Hopkins, by contrast, is all equanimity and self-possession: "Granted," he says of his poem, "that it needs study and is obscure, for indeed I was not over-desirous that the meaning of all should be quite clear." For the "problem" is not one of meaning, but of how the poem is to be read: "you might, without the effort that to make it all out would seem to have required, have nevertheless read it so that lines and stanzas should be left in the memory and superficial impressions deepened, and have liked some without exhausting all. I am sure I have read and enjoyed pages of poetry that way. Why, sometimes one enjoys and admires the very lines one cannot understand" (*LL,* i, 50).

Nor is the issue merely one of appreciation or enjoyment; rather, the point is that one should open oneself up to the poem, allow oneself to be penetrated by it, for as the poem abides in the memory it works its work of self-disclosure. Similarly nature will seem on occasion to "produce dead impressions . . . either because you cannot make them out or because they were perceived across other more engrossing thoughts," but having nevertheless penetrated the mind these impressions will eventually spring to life—"force themselves up," Hopkins says, as from the unconscious into consciousness (*JP*, 194). Or, again: "My meaning surely ought to appear of itself": the question is not *how* but *when.* "Epic and drama and ballad and many, most, things should be at once intelligible; but everything need not and cannot be" (*LL*, i, 265). The governing categories here are, notice, "at once" and "later" upon second and further readings or reflections—and even if the poem finally exceeds "explanation," its meaning does not therefore become problematical or indeterminate. "Plainly if it is possible to express a subtle and recondite thought on a subtle and recondite subject in a subtle and recondite way and with great felicity and perfection, in the end, something must be sacrificed . . . , and this may be the being at once, nay the being without explanation at all, intelligible" (*LL*, i, 265–66).

The capacity of meaning to "appear of itself," sooner or later, suggests that it is continuous, not simply with the form, but with the *presence* of the poem: it is *there,* waiting as if to explode. Just so, the idea of energy functions here as a way of situating poetry within the order of presence, wherein form and meaning are no longer isolatable components of a "structure" but have been subsumed by the categories of process, event, activity, appearance (disclosure)—and *voice.* Poetry for Hopkins presupposes voice as an agency which fulfills what is written. There is no doubt that to read a poem aloud, as Hopkins meant his poems to be read (*LL*, i, 46), is to retrieve it from writing in behalf of understanding. Concerning the "oddness" of his verse, for example, he recalls that "when, on somebody returning to me the *Eurydice,* I opened and read some lines, reading, as one commonly reads whether prose or verse, with the eyes, so to say, only, it struck me aghast with a kind of raw nakedness and unmitigated violence I was unprepared for: but take breath and read it with ears, as I always wish to be read, and my verse becomes all right" (*LL*, i, 79). The poetic text in this sense is not a document but an occasion, which means that the true medium of poetry is not language as such—not words and their diverse systematic relations—but the activity of speaking. From the standpoint of this activity, words are charged with more than linguistic meaning: they are charged with sound and, in the bargain, human presence.

Form, meaning, presence: we can think of these concepts as a series of horizons that open onto one another and constitute, in their totality, the field of poetry. Within this field there are, not discontinuities, but priorities—the priority of sound over sight, of speech over writing, and (evidently most important) of presence over all other categories, even that of meaning. How we are to understand this superior category of presence is made clear in the sonnet, "Purcell":

> Not mood in him nor meaning, proud fire or sacred fear,
> Or love or pity or all that sweet notes not his might nursle:
> It is the forged feature finds me: it is the rehearsal
> Of own, of abrupt self there so thrusts on, so throngs the ear.
>
> [*P*, 80]

In a letter to Bridges in 1883 Hopkins provided a crucial gloss to this poem, the relevant passage of which is: "So that while he [Purcell] is aiming only at impressing me his hearer with the meaning in hand I am looking out meanwhile for his specific, his individual markings and mottlings, 'the sakes of him.' It is as when a bird thinking only of soaring spreads its wings: a beholder may happen then to have his attention drawn by the act to the plumage displayed." Purcell's compositions *mean*—indeed, we are told in the poem that his "meaning motion fans fresh our wits with wonder" (*P*, 80)—but their significance for Hopkins is that, in doing so, they disclose their maker's presence: Purcell "breathes or stirs ... unmistakably in his works" (*LL*, i, 170). This is, moreover, not a psychological presence; rather, as Hopkins says in the headnote to his poem, Purcell has "uttered in notes the very make and species of man as created both in him and in all men generally" (*P*, 80). It is (as in "Kingfishers catch fire") presence of a metaphysical nature. As Purcell "flings out broad his name," he does more: the energy of his creation opens on to that "strain of creating action" received in him as in all men from God (*S*, 137), as though his utterances or compositions were centered not only in relation to their origin in the self of the artist but beyond this in relation to the transcendent origin that is God himself.

It is this dimension of energy that allows Hopkins to express both his great love for Purcell and, at the same time, his great anxiety concerning Purcell's fate. What troubles Hopkins is the possibility of Purcell's damnation (*LL*, i, 170–71)—an intolerable thought, the more so because hell consists for Hopkins precisely in the abrogation of that which makes Purcell and his works so valuable. The relevant text here is the "Meditation on Hell," from the notes for the Long Retreat of 1881, in which Hopkins seeks to comprehend "with the eyes of imagination the length, breadth, and depth of hell." Specifically, he seeks to imagine that "interior *sense of pain* which the lost suffer" (*S*, 135). (Here is that great Romantic desire to know what it is like inside others, or to understand others from the inside out.) How is the soul "so set at stress," Hopkins asks, that it can feel the pain of fire? Hopkins brings physics to bear upon metaphysics by describing the state of the damned in terms of the distinction between free and bound energy:

> The fall from heaven was for the rebel angels what death is for man. As in man all that energy or instress with which the soul animates or otherwise acts in the body is by death thrown back upon the soul itself: so in them [the rebel angels] is that greater stock of activity with which they act, intellectually and otherwise, throughout their own world or element of spirit, which is perhaps, as I have thought, flushed by every spirit living in it. This throwing back or confinement of their energy is a dreadful constraint and imprisonment and, as intellectual action is spoken of under the figure of sight, it will in this case be an imprisonment in darkness, a being in the dark; for darkness is the phenomenon of foiled action in the sense of sight. But this constraint and this blindness or darkness will be most painful when it is the main stress or energy of the whole being that is thus balked. [*S*, 137]

Hell is the imprisonment of the spirit in darkness, but in darkness felt as intellectual fire, because the spirit suffers the constraint or confinement of its energy—as though (recalling "The Windhover") the fire that would break from the spirit in the fulness of its action were turned inward to become many times more painful for being a fire that does not consume.

One is reminded here of the dynamism of repression in early psychoanalytic theory, in which normally free charges of psychic energy are bound or inhibited by consciousness. Actually, Hopkins's mode of explanation adumbrates the Blakean rather than the Freudian imagination, for Blake's several versions of the Fall are each of them dominated by figures of bound or "fibred" energy, as in the binding of Orc, the "fiery boy" and revolutionary hope of *The Four Zoas* (1797),[24] or by the dramatization of "foiled" action that generates the pain of energy turned inward or "balked"—a condition suffered by each of Blake's fallen Powers, and especially by Los, the archetypal craftsman and imaginative spirit, in whom the energy of life seems most powerfully concentrated, and who therefore endures the most intensive torment:

> Restless the immortal, inchain'd, heaving, dolorous,
> Anguish'd, unbearable; till a roof, shaggy, wild, inclos'd
> In an orb his fountain of thought.
> In a horrible dreamful slumber, like the link'd chain
> A vast spine writh'd in torment upon the wind,
> Shooting pain'd ribbs, like a bending Cavern;
> And bones of solidness froze over all his nerves of joy.
> [*The Four Zoas*, IV, 8 : 215–22]

This condition is indeed "what death is for man": for Blake it is the death-in-life of man's fallen and historical existence, as in *Jerusalem* (1800), in which Albion's archetypal fall is a fall into a chaos of the spirit: falling, he becomes "Inslav'd to the most powerful Selfhood" of Satan (49 : 30), whose laws "are death / To every energy of man" (35 : 11–12), as when the "minute particulars" of Albion (that is, all men) are "baked / In bricks" or "harden'd into grains of sand" (37 : 7, 20), or when "The open heart is shut up in integuments of frozen silence" (43 : 33).

For Hopkins, this imprisoning of energy is a metaphor for the death-in-life of hell itself, in which the straining of the soul toward God has been broken, but not its straining toward the natural plenitude of action, which is condemned to remain forever bound or constrained—a binding, moreover, of which the lost soul remains all the while horribly conscious, in a manner comparable to the nightmare recorded by Hopkins in a Journal entry from 1873:

> I thought something or someone leapt onto me and held me quite fast.... I had lost all muscular stress elsewhere but not sensitive, feeling where each limb lay and thinking that I could recover myself if I could move my finger.... The feeling is terrible: the body no longer swayed as a piece by the nervous and muscular instress seems to fall in and hang like a dead weight on the chest. I cried on the holy name and by degrees recovered myself.... It made me think that this was how souls in hell would be imprisoned in their bodies as in prisons and of what St. Theresa says of the "little press in the wall" where she felt herself to be in her vision. [*JP,* 238]

Not enervation or paralysis but the binding of energy—and a supreme horror, because the expenditure of energy is the fulfillment of being. This expenditure is the expression of the continuing "strain of creating action received in the creature" from God. This creating action "cannot cease without the creature's ceasing to be" (*S,* 37), but it were better were it so, for in hell God's creating energy is turned back upon the creature, bottled up in him as in his body, so that he experiences death, not as annihilation, but as the perpetual closure of that which maintains him in being.

We can complete this speculation by saying that the damned, therefore, are unintelligible, or beyond understanding. That which draws Hopkins to every form of composition—that by which Nature or Purcell is able to speak so powerfully to Hopkins's sympathetic understanding—is in hell put forever out of the way of experience. To understand anything, on this model, is just to stand under its power or spell. To understand in this sense would be to participate in the intelligibility of what is understood—in the creating action of what is understood—rather than to grasp it as an object or to turn it into a concept. To understand would be to find oneself subjected to an intelligibility as if to the subjectivity of another, or as if the other were able to make itself understood—able, even, to express itself—by taking over or taking possession of the one who understands. This, at any rate, would appear to be the basic hermeneutical principle at work in Hopkins's writings. It helps to explain why his characteristic posture is that of someone captivated by a presence—by Christ, Nature, or the Artist. This would be in rich contrast to the alienation in which hermeneutical life is traditionally said to begin.

PART FOUR
MODERNIST TEXTUALITY

7
De Improvisatione:
An Essay on Kora in Hell

Here's a man wants me to revise, to put in order. My God what I am doing means just the opposite from that. There is no revision, there can be no revision—
William Carlos Williams, *The Great American Novel*

From a mildly etymological point of view an improvisation is a species of unforeseen discourse. One cannot predict anything about it. It is discourse that makes no provision for its future, not in the reader's mind and certainly not in the writer's; its teleology is entirely in the present. It is discourse whose beginning is what matters, because to improvise is to begin without a second thought, thus to make do with whatever comes to hand, and under the rules there is no turning back. It is discourse governed by no provisos except that it be allowed to go on independently of results.

At the outset it will appear that its defining categories are composition and performance. Improvisation is the performance of a composition in the moment of its composition. One preserves such a moment by refusing to revise its results. To call a thing an improvisation is to say: This is as it was when originated. Or, again, an improvisation is an extemporaneous utterance, although (speaking precisely) to speak extempore is to compose in the heat of performance, and what is composed may seem less an improvisation than, say, an *Odyssey* or a song in ottava rima, wherein much is prepared for, or less than one imagines is left to chance. An improvisation that is not a public or salon event may be performed under no pressure to compose, and vice versa; it is not necessarily a thinking out loud, and perhaps it never is. It is, to be sure, speech that is allowed to stand as written; it is unrevised utterance. But mainly it is discourse that proceeds independently of reflection; it does not stop to check on itself. It is deliberate but undeliberated and unmethodical. Improvisation is thus accessible to simple definition: it is unplanned and uncorrected discourse. One cannot say beforehand how it will end, what it will say or resemble, or whether it will bear repeating. To improvise is simply to write without an end in view; it is perhaps to write with nothing in view, not even an audience. Improvisations are therefore naturally (as against rhetorically or poetically) intransitive:

they are an innocent or unfallen kind of speech, unused and unusing because undesigned and undesigning: they have designs upon no one, because they are themselves unprepared and unprepared for, uncared for and
wild in virtue of improvident authorship.

Imagine, therefore, a guileful improvisation: it would have a secret purpose and a secret history (a providence): as when Cicero advises us to write
down our Senate speeches the night before, the better to speak extempo-
raneously without misdirection. Premeditation is guilt, but it is also politics
and the better part of public wisdom. An improvisation that is repeated is
an improvisation fallen, used, sullied by intention or experience: one re-
peats it, but only by design. In this event it becomes a pensée, part of an
inventory or tradition, something found, a replenishment of memory, a sign
of copiousness, and so on.

Improvisation is a specialized form of artless discourse, an evasion of
Adam's Curse. It is unpoetic because unmade, more event than work, an
effect whose system of causes has been made to work contingently, as if to
no effect (as if: no doubt here is the contamination of art: an improvisation
is contingent, but not accidental; it is not automatic writing). An improvisation is conceived in forgetfulness or in studied ignorance; it is what happens without respect to previous statements, which is why a conversation,
although extemporaneous in its development, is not an improvisation. A
rhetoric or poetics of improvisation would never seem applicable in the
moment or situation in which one takes pen in hand. An improvisation is
arguably the most original of utterances because it is unprompted and unprecedented, impromptu and unlearned, unimitating and inimitable. It is
never the cry of its occasion, and differs therefore from the sally or the
barb, wit as riposte, because it is unprovoked as well as unpremeditated. It
is therefore doubly innocent.

Innocent, but not witless, and therein lies a true complication. Unprovoked wit is a traditional definition of genius, or of imagination: spontanei-
ties of talent, mythologies of unconscious or at all events unschooled or undisciplined generation. To such mythologies the improvisator will naturally
appeal for the sanction of his utterances: he will always claim a native or
divine authority. It is clear, however, that what we call the unconscious is,
quite as much as tradition or learning, a natural enemy of improvisational
desire. The unconscious is full of artful subterfuge; it shapes our unplanned
utterances with unforeseen forethoughts—or foreforms, if one would permit such things, for the mind is a repository of hidden and ready formations, a dark library of grammars and rhetorics whose nature it is to make
possible the inspired and the rash: dreams, talk, solemn unbreakable vows.

The unconscious is the great beforehand where everything is in rehearsal. It is made up of quotations waiting for words. It is our metaphor of awful power, the muse of sorts whose dictations produce our "unpremeditated Verse."

Here it will be good to distinguish once more between rhetorical and Romantic improvisation. Rhetorical improvisation is related to embellishment and ornamentation or adornment; it is an art of doing something to what has already been done. In music and in poetry it is a way of exceeding what is written by working between the lines or in the margin, or by using the text as a point of departure or pretext or as a program of intervals. Improvisation in this case is not an art of free origination; it begins instead with what is received, which it then proceeds to color, amplify, alter, or fulfill, never to abolish or forget. Rhetorical improvisation presupposes invention as an art of finding or figuring, whereas, for the Romantic, invention is unschooled and autonomous creation, antiplagiary, a studied freedom from readable antecedents. Romantic improvisation begins with a blank sheet of paper; rhetorical improvisation begins with a sheet of paper on which a poem or score is written but which contains to the knowing or the artful eye large and indeterminate areas of something left unsaid, unsung, or tacitly unfinished (as even the *Aeneid* remains unfinished). It would in practice be hard to distinguish Romantic improvisation from a spontaneous overflow of powerful feelings, or indeed origination of any kind. Romantically, to poetize is as much as to improvise; the rest is the business of reason, the agency of recognition and revision, reminder of the better or the proven way.

Improvisation is gameless play: gameless, because what improvisation requires is a type of disruption. Imagine an improvised chess game, and you get something the Marx brothers would play. Chess is heavy with rules, but what matters is the concentration of foresight and decision that attaches to each sequence of moves. Chess is more plot than character (no move has meaning by itself). It is a game from which improvisation has been systematically abolished (like chance), nor can improvisation return even as a last or desperate gamble (it would be present only as a symptom of the game's disintegration, or at best as outcry of someone's defeat). Thus openings and secondary deployments and strategies in unforeseen circumstances are capable not only of being repeated but of acquiring fame and bearing names, as though the true antagonists in chess were forms of practice rather than of action or agency. Chess is the victory of method. In chess improvisation is indistinguishable from the blunder or mere ignorance; it is a departure from that which has a determinable and conceivably fortunate end. What is not foreseeable or provident in chess is always a form of undoing, and what is undone is someone's participation in the game. Thus an improvisation would become parody or anarchy or buffoonery (or satire): it would require the disruption not only of moves but of rules and usages and even of the principles of mental order on which such a thing as chess (art, the state, culture) is based: and not mental order only, but the order of intentions and transactions by which players are brought into systematic and sometimes affectionate kinship. Moves in chess speak: they communicate intentions and compel answers. Improvisations are by contrast inscrutable and unanswerable and presuppose the operations of a solitary singer.

To say that writing is intransitive is to say that it is meant chiefly to be made, not read. A certain unreadability is built into every intransitive utterance, and in improvisations this unreadability is writ large by the natural invisibility of improvisational results. Certainly one function of improvisation is to outwit the reader; it is to disrupt readerly or systematic expectations and the consequent ability to recognize what is taking place. The unpredictability of improvisational discourse means exactly that the improvisator is hard or impossible to follow: we cannot get a line on him, because his lines do not proceed or follow one another in linear or generic fashion: we cannot see where he is going, cannot anticipate his turns, and are literally left standing there, unreading, not knowing what to say, as he disappears into the page. At such moments we do not know where we stand, yet we have not exactly lost our way because there is no way to lose: the improvisation is meant to send us off in false directions, but only in the appeal that no directions are true because none exist. Improvisation confounds in principle every Cartesian ambition or value. The improvisation is ungeneric precisely to the extent that it confounds those signals that we normally use to complete a text we have not finished reading; it dismantles the virtual or heuristic whole that we need to construct in order to guide us through the parts of what we read. And even when we have finished reading we cannot say exactly what it is that we have read: it impresses us mainly by being familiar, perhaps, but not quite the thing we had in mind.

From a formalist point of view it would follow that an improvisation is a kind of negative discourse: intransitive, yet not formal or aesthetic, or so intransitive as to be in general disregard of beauty. A formalist would say that formal relations of the kind one looks for in poetic or artful speech (or in any conventional discourse whatsoever) do not always occupy the foreground of the improvisational utterance, neither are they absorbed into something uttered. What is unaccountable is the seeming care with which form is averted without being abolished. Relations appear to exist, but only to disappear the moment we try to comprehend them according to familiar models of intelligibility. No other form of discourse appears to possess this elusiveness of form: elusiveness, for what the improvisation achieves is not formlessness but transience and namelessness of form, its ghostly and in-substantial presence or behavior. Form is contingent. The formalist would say that the improvisation achieves an aversion rather than a subversion (and certainly not a version) of form, which is why the improvisation that declines into babble is usually rejected as (simply) a failed utterance. And this is also why improvisations are always incitements to interpretation, with mixed and unimpressive results, the more so as interpretation naturally de-forms the improvisation into the sort of discourse it most nearly resembles. Perhaps one could speculate that it is not in the nature of improvisations to make sense, which is why they naturally intoxicate human understanding.

Accordingly, the first improvisation of William Carlos Williams's *Kora in Hell* traps us into an inadvertent reading: "Fools have big wombs. . . ." The sentence seems indistinguishable from a quotation: we have heard (some-thing like) it before. It is a saying, an adage or proverb, and it contains a moral appropriate to its form: fools indeed have big wombs, for they are fertile and prolific and their progeny have spread to every human culture, each of which maintains a vast literature on the subject. But Williams's first improvisation is not consummated in this commonplace. In its entirety, the improvisation reads as follows:

> Fools have big wombs. For the rest?—here is pennyroyal if one knows to use it. But time is only another liar, so go along the wall a little further: if black-berries prove bitter there'll be mushrooms, fairy-ring mushrooms, in the grass, sweetest of all the fungi.[1]

One may as well know that pennyroyal is a medicinal herb ("small leaves and a prostrate habit"—*OED*), thought once to be effective against common hysteria, and somewhat bitter to the taste, which is perhaps why the voice of the improvisation, after warning us against the false promises of time, guides us further along the wall (where the pennyroyal doubtless grows), past the also-bitter blackberries, to the fairy-ring mushrooms *(Marasmius orcades),* "sweetest of all the fungi." Surely one could go further still, thus perhaps to assemble different categories of folk wisdom—for example: (1) adages concerning fools (and those who count on time for something bet-ter); (2) treatment of nervous disorders; (3) the superiority of the fairy-ring mushroom. Interpretation is as resourceful as improvisation—but to what end? In this case the end of interpretation cannot be the recovery of any-thing like an intention. What we have above sounds like an excerpt from a longer speech: *sounds like,* which is roughly the sort of illusion that improvisations are gifted to sustain—illusions of interpretable discourse which, however, seem in the end to fall between recognizable categories of utterance. Connections are missing that presumably a context could supply, which is where interpretation comes in (no doubt desperately) to imagine now this context, now that one, in order to build among the parts of the improvisation a congruence that is plainly absent—a congruence unavoidably unwritten and which the text seems actively to resist.

A minor lesson to be drawn from this is that improvisations tend to occur at the level of the discourse, not at the level of the sentence. Improvisations at the level of the sentence would be indistinguishable from what any competent speaker of a language could produce for any reason whatsoever (or for no reason at all), and without really trying. "Colorless green ideas sleep furiously" might be figured as a sort of improvisation at the level of the sentence, chiefly because it has sustained a disruption of linguistic rule without dispersing into babble: it still sounds like a sentence, and can even be made to read like one when transposed to a provident context. A similar analysis can be brought to bear upon Williams's justly admired "When beldams dig clams their fat hams . . . "—which is, however, only part of an utterance that illustrates nicely the theory of gameless play:

> When beldams dig clams their fat hams (it's always beldams) balanced near Tellus's hide, this rhinoceros pelt, these lumped stones, buffoonery of midges on a bull's thigh—invoke,—what you will: birth's glut, awe at God's craft, youth's poverty, evolution of a child's caper, man's poor inconsequence. Eclipse of all things; sun's self turned hen's rump. [55]

(Tellus's hide is the earth's skin and is consonant with the improvisation's anatomical bias.) The body of this improvisation is motored by three substantives: "this rhinoceros pelt, these lumped stones, buffoonery of midges," which (taken together) "invoke,—what you will," that is, almost anything at all, or whatever can be fitted into the sound of an epithet: "birth's glut, awe at God's craft, youth's poverty," etc. No need to stop at "man's poor inconsequence": the list could go on—for the list as a mode of utterance is one of the more powerful mechanisms by which any discourse can amplify itself. The list, in contrast to the game, is more character than plot—is episodic, one damn thing after another, or containing no internal demands for a conclusion. A list is something that one can introduce into a sentence as a way of making it perpetually unfold, which theoretically it can do because a list does not end, it stops, often owing to weariness, or because a well of invention has run dry. A list is a way of exceeding the limits of the sentence without actually abolishing them.

When old women dig clams they get down on their haunches, which hover therefore near the sand. Students of Williams will recognize in this information a characteristically treasured fact, an observation released from its reasons: simply one of those things Williams tends to notice. A more complicated attention to fact is contained in this improvisation:

> There's the bathtub. Look at it, caustically rejecting its smug proposal. Ponder removedly the herculean task of a bath. There's much camaraderie in filth but it's no' that. And change is lightsome but it's not that either. Fresh linen with a dab here, there of the wet paw serves me better. Take a stripling stroking chin-fuzz, match his heart against that of grandpa watching his silver wane. When these two are compatible I'll plunge in. But where's the edge lifted between sunlight and moonlight. Where does lamplight cease to nick it? Here's hot water. [74]

There's the bathtub: when you look at it you will see not simply an object but a whole society of meanings—a world of reasons. Thus you will recognize a bathtub by its superior attitude: it belongs to (or among) the better sort of people. As for camaraderie, the better sort of people do not engage in it. Camaraderie exists among soldiers, ballplayers, young boys, grandfathers and grandsons: camaraderie is not a bathtub word, and for much the same reason it is not a female word. One naturally prefers filth to cleanliness as one prefers company to solitude. Most often one bathes alone and acquires thereby a self-satisfaction not possible to share: one feels better, perhaps one is better for having bathed (although Dr. Williams does not think so). Naturally a bathtub would propose a bath: propose is a bathtub word. Comrades, for example, do not propose; colleagues propose, as do superiors, associates, junior partners seeking ready advancement. One does not go unbathed into the world of proposals, no more than one enters the company of women so, nor certainly does one go filthy into a single woman's company, where a proposal is apt to occur, sooner or later: whence the comradely world is lost. What is gained is access to the world kept by the better sort, a world of solitude, where one is required to tolerate endlessly the smugness of junior partners who probably bathe twice a day. So you see one has to decide carefully whether to bathe, for every bath taken or rejected is a statement of allegiance and profession of value, unless one is dead tired, in which case bathing becomes a herculean labor: the time and effort required simply to climb into a tub of water must be weighed against how good it would surely feel. Reasons. Go ahead. Here's hot water.

An improvisation is an unwashed utterance.

Is there a law peculiar to an improvisation by William Carlos Williams? An eighteenth-century *improvissatore* would seek to improvise an utterance that would show none of the effects of its production; it would be his desire to produce the illusion of orderly composition spontaneously achieved (a song in ottava rima, with not a syllable out of place). Notice that this is a variation on the classical dream of an artfulness that can produce artless or natural perfection, whence it becomes the obligation of the artist to conceal his art, or to hide the effort that his artifice naturally requires (even, as Castiglione suggested, by producing the semblance of unrevision). The improvissatore does not disregard the perfection of art: his performance is governed by the same ideal of the homogeneous work that governs all art: it is his desire to seem to accomplish at first try what other singers require planning and revision to produce. Pope, who originally lisped in numbers, desired no less, but understood more: namely, that planning and revision are the activities that make effortless art possible. Romantic improvisation (or what is called "creativity") is not inconsistent with this classical view, for it rests upon a belief in the trustworthiness of imagination, which is said to be able to produce on its own (without the intervention of conscious will, or simply by following the native laws of its development) a whole work, a homogeneous text figurable as an organism, something whose parts are integrated into a superior unity and which can compete against (perhaps is even greater than) the great works of art produced by the ancient masters.

But Williams's improvisations are dependably heterogeneous. The improvisation of the bathtub, for example, contains these lines: "But where's the edge lifted between sunlight and moonlight. Where does lamplight cease to nick it?" The question readers are trained to ask is: How do these lines fit in with the whole? In order to answer this question we would have to imagine reasons why the improvisator would compose them—not an impossible job, but one that would be difficult to bring off without seeming absurd, because Williams's purpose (the whole point of writing improvisations) is to avoid the reasons of art. It is to resist composition of a discourse whose parts are accessible to uniform accounting. Indeed, in an improvisation by Williams the privileged line is no longer the line that seems to condense and confirm the whole; equally welcome now is the incongruous line, such that a uniform reading of an improvisation may have to leave one or more lines out of account—hence the fate of "But where's the edge lifted between sunlight and moonlight": one reads by pretending the line isn't there. As always, interpretation performs the duty that revision declines: namely, the silent removal of incongruities.

For Williams, the imagination will not naturally produce an utterance that contains in itself the reasons why it is so and not otherwise; it does not aspire to the condition or illusion of art. We are thus on the verge of affirming still one more time the doctrine of anti- or counterpoetry, and no doubt we can plead sufficient reason for doing so; yet such a doctrine no more gives the law of Williams's improvisations than would a theory of esemplastic power. The imagination does not aspire to—but neither does it flee from art. A poem can be made out of anything, including a familiar amble of Tennysonian decorum: "there's many a good backroad among clean raked fields" (77). An improvisation by Williams is likely to be heterogeneous in its assembly, but it is not therefore anaesthetic. When assembling the parts of *Kora in Hell* Williams left out those improvisations which were merely failed utterances; he did not hesitate to include many unaccountable lapses into art. One of Williams's improvisations is a story of the Good Physician. It begins: "After thirty years staring at one true phrase he discovered that its opposite was true also" (68). The story is an illustration of this opening statement as of a moral: the doctor is indeed an embodiment of the Good Physician (he answers calls in the middle of the night, etc.). But every act or event that confirms him in his nobility becomes transparent to him: he sees through every confirming moment to that which contradicts it— contradicts it without, however, falsifying it: "Summoned to his door by a tinkling bell he looked into a white face, the face of a man convulsed with dread, at the laughter back of its drawn alertness" (69). Or, again: "He plunges up the dark steps on his grotesque deed of mercy. In his warped brain an owl of irony fixes on the immediate object of his care as if it were the thing to be destroyed, guffaws at the impossibility of putting any kind of value on the object inside [an unborn child] or of even reversing or making less by any other means than induced sleep—which is no solution—the methodical gripe of the sufferer" (69). The "owl of irony" is a phrase worth having, although one suspects that a more deliberate, revisionary, and therefore less figurative Williams would not have written it. It is an allegorical phrase, and so well does it summarize the story that one could imagine it as the title—which is one way of saying that in this improvisation part and whole are combined in an entirely traditional way.

And this suggests in turn that the law peculiar to an improvisation by Williams is not the law of formal violation pure and simple but the law of unpredictability (as in Cicero, for whom *improvisum* is the figure by which an expression takes an unexpected but forgivable turn). One imagines that if anomalies had crept prominently into the improvisation of the Good Physician, Williams would have allowed them to stand and would have relished their prominence; but the art of writing improvisations does not stipulate (how could it?) that nothing but anomalies shall be composed. Perhaps it is this that makes *Kora in Hell* different from the continental affronteries with which it is still sometimes associated: there is in Williams no active principle of derangement, no unsparing abuse of sense. There is, for example, very little that can be called anomalous in the following:

> Something to grow used to; a stone too big for ox haul, too near for blasting. Take the road round it or—scrape away, scrape away: a mountain's buried in the dirt! Go yourself down along the lit pastures. Down, down. The whole family take shovels, babies and all! Down, down! Here's Tenochtitlan! here's a strange Darien where worms are princes. [57]

Country Life in America. Chapter 1. The Rock. Once every farm in America had its rock story. (Great-grandpa Kirsch tried to raise it when he cleared this field. So did pa. Finally pa said: Holds the land together. Once when we brought home our first tractor I took the plow over it and got me such a whipping. No one can tell how deep it goes. China. South America. Stella says it's probably down as far as Uncle Ben.) The rock is quintessential, as Thoreau and Stevens knew: it is that which remains intractable; it is the instance of our circumventions and, accordingly, that to which our attention repeatedly returns as to the truth or origin of things. Every unmoved rock is piece and principle of the frontier, unsettled by illusions.

Scholia: Tenochtitlán was the ancient capital of the Aztecs, since replaced by Mexico City. It is where Cortes was instead of the peak on which Keats placed him. The real and perhaps unfamiliar Darién is in Panama; or perhaps it is whatever lies across a frontier, or beneath it, where worms are princes because if you dig deep enough you come to a place where things are upside down. No anomalies here.

Still, one's attention returns to the story of the Good Physician and its opening statement ("After thirty years staring at one true phrase he discovered that its opposite was true also"); there is something representative about it. The natural inclination of criticism is to read this principle of mutual contradiction as a testament not only of Williams the physician but also of Williams the writer—but this is so only in a special sense. Contradiction is the privileged and indispensable category of skepticism (skepticism is perhaps impossible except by recourse to contradiction as an authorizing principle). Yet this is not quite so for Williams, who regards contradiction less as a sign of unreason or a failure of logic than as a frequent state of affairs: the simple consequence, for example, of real events, which, lacking providence, contrive to interfere with one another, as do on occasion the several parts of an improvisation. Improvisation is history. Whereas contradiction is traditionally the occasion of despair or of superior attitudes toward credulity, for Williams it is simply great good fun, and, what is more, a condition of plenitude or the completeness of things, as if that which could not be contradicted could therefore not be whole. Accordingly, when one of the improvisations of *Kora in Hell* fails of itself to produce a whole waywardness—

> This is a slight stiff dance to a waking baby whose arms have been lying curled back above his head upon the pillow, making a flower—the eyes closed. Dead to the world! Waking is a little hand brushing away dreams. Eyes open. Here's a new world.

—Williams felt compelled to add these lines:

> *There is nothing the sky-serpent will not eat. Sometimes it stoops to gnaw Fuji-yama, sometimes to slip its long and softly clasping tongue about the body of a sleeping child who smiles thinking its mother is lifting it.* [76]

The improvisation here is an episode of uncontaminated domestic warmth, such as one would expect a Good Physician to affirm; the "interpretation" which Williams placed after it is a countervailing macabre fantasy composed by (who else?) the "owl of irony." So far from being a sign of unreason or something not working, the contradiction is a construction, the work of a later, ordering and editorial hand: the "owl of irony" is self-consciously dialectical, but rhetorically rather than logically so. Rhetoric (like history) provides for the expression of opposite and inseparable truths, whereas logic requires that we choose between them or seek their assimilation into a superior and resolving order. For rhetoric (like history) is eventual in its proceedings and copious (rather than systematic) in its results: it declaims now one truth, now another, in the interest of leaving nothing unspoken, whereas logic aspires to the simultaneity and cleanliness of system, into which nothing incongruous may proceed without transformation or, failing that, without doing damage to the before and after of every thought. It may be for this reason that philosophers regularly give us an implausible estimate of the world; it is certainly why there is no one more hateful to the philosopher than the rhetorician, who has his eye fixed not on systems but on the plenum of his inventory, because he knows that you must be ready to take everything into account in a world where nothing is predictable and anything can happen. Hence the sophistry of history: that which is true is simply that which occurs, as everything does, sooner or later. Mind or philosophy, the content or method of your thinking, have nothing to do with it.

An improvisation by Williams is essentially a private utterance, but only in odd and complicated ways. By his time the improvisation had ceased to be a public form or type of public verbal performance (extempore lyricism to musical accompaniment: an Enlightenment pastime). As written discourse an improvisation by Williams is by its very nature privately performed, but it is therefore publishable in a way that an eighteenth-century improvisation is not. As a mode of extempore utterance an improvisation by, say, Metastasio is naturally fleeting: it is speech whose most compelling feature (how does he do it?) cannot be preserved by writing. The improvisation belongs in this case to the world of sound, voice, and spirit, which written records always betray. One does not write improvisations of this sort, one writes them down, as an improvissatore sometimes did, to the disappointment of many. An improvisation by Metastasio is first spoken (or sung), then written, which means that it is never an instance of original but only of secondary or documentary writing—and confirmation of the principle that to write down one's improvisations is to turn them into bad writing. Hence, by contrast, the originality of an improvisation by Williams, which is never anything but written: not written speech but writing pure and simple, which imitates the spoken utterance chiefly by not getting revised. Improvised writing imitates the most unwanted feature of spoken discourse (waywardness), which writing was invented to get rid of, since writing makes the correction of discourse possible. It is because it is unrevised that an improvisation by Williams is essentially private: it is writing in a form which the public almost never sees, the original form, which only the writer sees and which it is ordinarily his profession to remove from view by a variety of secondary operations of the pen. In this respect a chief property of improvisational discourse will be its difference from published (and therefore professional) forms of writing. The dynamics of publication provide especially for revision, and not revision only but repeated application of correctional arts designed to produce a fair or finished copy: an edition. But an improvisation by Williams is writing deliberately left in draft, as though not meant for publication: relentlessly original, private and unreadied writing incompletely composed in defiance of the decorum of print culture. An improvisation by Williams pleads the decorum of unbookish or unlettered writing, as in the work of a talented but undisciplined amateur, the unschooled or untrammeled poet whom no one (unless Shakespeare) has imitated so perfectly as our Good Physician.

The mild irony is that *Kora in Hell: Improvisations* (1920) is a book, and one that swells with many bookish devices: its making required that private writings be mediated by certain editorial or explanatory alternatives to revision: a prologue, ancillary commentaries, intervening "interpretations" and short statements of principle—varieties of self-exegesis that gather the improvisations into a state of legitimacy (an authorized version). Hugh Kenner once made the happy observation that bad writing is writing that gets published by mistake. One function of the editorial and hermeneutic machinery in *Kora in Hell* is to make sure no one supposes that a mistake has been made: we are meant to understand that whoever put this book together knew very well what he was doing (for example, risking himself against the assumption, widely held, that no one gets it right the first time). The improvisations are uncontrolled, but not out of control. They may fail (they may fail to please), but they are not failed versions of that in which others have succeeded: not inadvertent failures published by mistake: not bad writing. They are (let us speculate) experimental, like so many lyrical ballads, and so have a provision for failure built into their originating motive: he who experiments may fail, but in unprecedented ways apt to be more savored than scorned. Experiments resemble improvisations insofar as one cannot know how they will turn out: they may successfully disclose only what we cannot hope to achieve. To disclose a saving motive the improvisator takes recourse to self-exegesis, which since ancient times has been a primary form of authorizing discourse, especially when the "unschooled" or vernacular writer desired to free his lines from the trammels of Latin. We know how Williams aspired to vernacular eloquence, and how he redoubled his effort when confronted by the literariness of Eliot, Pound, and Stevens. Of more direct interest is his offhand or comic desire for a museum of vernacular art:

> I wish Arensberg had my opportunity for prying into jaded households where the paintings of Mama's and Papa's flowertime still hang on the walls. I propose that Arensberg be commissioned by the Independent Artists to scour the country for the abortive paintings of those men and women who without master or method have evolved perhaps two or three unusual creations in their early years. . . . Carefully selected, these queer products might be housed to good effect in some unpretentious exhibition chamber across the city from the Metropolitan Museum of Art. [11–12]

One wonders what it would be like actually to visit the kind of exhibition Williams has in mind. Fortunately, one need not specify in detail what such an exhibition would contain, because "abortive paintings"—no doubt everywhere to be found—would be worth gathering into one place only in behalf of a mainly satiric principle, or principle of divergence and ridicule: a museum of "unusual creations" and "queer products" ("The pure products of America"?) would make sense *only* if it were placed in opposition to ("across the city from") the Metropolitan Museum of Art. By "across the city" Williams means precisely on the wrong side of the tracks, for the hangings of such an exhibition would be intelligible or valuable chiefly in terms of what is missing among them: high art, canonized art, art worth preserving for its own sake—authoritative art. One would therefore visit such a gallery as one would profess a new allegiance, or renounce an old authority.

Such testimony is related to the way vernacular utterances make their claim upon literary or trained attention: they are divergences from the better sort of speech, lapses from Latin or Literature into vulgarity—failed utterances, to be sure, but unmistakenly so, in the mad conviction that failure of a vulgar or divergent kind is a mode of violence and therefore of refreshment: that is, originality. Originality is, among other things, a failure to preserve what everyone had thought valuable. To speak in Latin is to speak the language of preservation—the language of writing and museums, of poetry and tradition, of philosophy and truth—but to speak a vernacular is to strike out on one's own, "without master or method," improvising decorum, not knowing where one will end up because no one has gone this way before.

What authorizes vulgarity? On the wrong side of the tracks anything goes: it is where poetry may be made out of anything (so long as it is not other poems). For example, "One day Duchamp decided that his composition for that day would be the first thing that struck his eye in the first hardware store he should enter. It turned out to be a pickax which he bought and set up in his studio. This was his composition" (12). (To improvise is to make do with whatever comes to hand.) A hardware store is not a museum, not by itself it isn't, but it contains everything requisite to the making of one— a museum of modern art or, as Duchamp would have it, a museum of American art: a vernacular museum which to the unschooled (academic) eye would be indistinguishable from a hardware store. How does one become schooled to see such a hardware store as a museum? One does so by consideration of such gestures as Duchamp's: the decision to compose a pickax (or whatever) by picking one up at the nearest hardware store was an authorizing decision, as much an act of interpretation as of creation, and an individual appropriation of the cultural procedures by which many brute and transient things get institutionalized as things worth preserving. Whence comes Duchamp's authority to render such a decision? For an answer we may turn to *Kora in Hell,* which requires us to consider how on earth we can regard these makeshift utterances as art, that is, as something worth preserving. By what right did Williams collect his improvisations into a book when these improvisations are (to the unschooled eye, of which early reviewers had many) indistinguishable from bad writing?

It could be said that what is modern is always unauthorized from the standpoint of what precedes it. It is at least true that modernism is always a vernacular phenomenon. Any reasonable definition of modernism—one which could be applied to Dante or Chaucer as well as to Williams—would provide for the corollary that in a modern state of affairs we have only the artist's word for what he is doing. Williams once remarked that the modern writer must be his own interpreter, because he alone is sufficiently schooled in his labors to be able to speak with authority concerning them. When two or more self-interpreters understand one another you have the beginnings of a school; if disciples appear you may have a movement; when critics replace the masters as voices of instruction you have a tradition, and the end of modernism, and a need to improvise.

8

Error and Figure in Ulysses

If we were all suddenly somebody else. (*U*110)

She could see at once by his dark eyes and pale intellectual face that he was a foreigner, the image of the photo she had of Martin Harvey, the matinée idol. ... (*U*357)

She must have been thinking of someone else all the time. (*U*371)

When Gerty McDowell looks (or peeks) at Bloom she regards him as someone else. It is now widely understood that this misperception or misconstruction illustrates a basic principle of Joyce's fiction. The principle, however, has a complicated interpretive life; it is possible to be of (at least) two minds concerning its formulation. Hugh Kenner, for example, would say that the principle is essentially Pyrrhonist in character: in Joyce's fiction people are relentless in getting things wrong. For Fritz Senn, however, the principle is metaphorical: in Joyce's fiction everyone gets turned into somebody else.[1]

Kenner's view emphasizes Joyce's naturalism and its consequent irony.[2] The girl whom Stephen encounters at the end of part 4 of the *Portrait* is almost certainly a common whore. Stephen, in transport on the matter of his identity, misidentifies her as a figure of innocence. Senn, by contrast, would emphasize precisely the figuration by which the girl makes her appearance.[3] "She seemed like one whom magic had changed into the likeness of a strange and beautiful seabird" (*P*171). The scene is an episode of poetic transformation; it is what goes on in an epiphany. Kenner would say, however, that what is going on is a transcendent piece of self-delusion. It is characteristic of Joyce to forbear mention of the girl's most salient aspect: her reality.[4] It is unmentioned because it is what Stephen at this moment is powerless to experience. The girl's reality, once acknowledged by the careful or untransported reader, spreads across the scene like a deep stain: the irony is indelible. What Stephen does not or cannot know is exactly the point on which Joyce instructs the reader: namely, that the vision Stephen imagines himself to be having could only occur in a book. Against this Senn would say that the girl's reality, such as it may be, is simply Joyce's point of departure; it is that which a mind like Stephen's naturally transmutes into strangeness and beauty. The girl is not what she is but what she becomes, or comes to mean, for meaning requires the turning of one thing into another; it is a figural transformation or substitution by which reality grows intelligible, that is, accessible to predication. It is the girl's *change* that Stephen experiences; it is her state of likeness that he values. And, what is more, all of this is a parable or model of how things make sense in Joyce's fiction. To which Kenner (playing Sextus Empiricus) might reply: Just so, things make sense Pyrrhonistically, by sleights and cunning correspondences. Things are never what they mean to us. One wonders what the girl would make of all this ("O rocks!").

The natural desire of the congenial mind would be to collapse these two positions into one another, thus to encourage the view that behind or above them a Higher Synthesis is waiting to be born. Alas, the Jesuits taught me that the truth always lies side by side, never in between. It is in this spirit that I would like to hold Senn and Kenner at odds for a while, no doubt against their better interests and desires, if only to regard the Joycean symmetry of their opposition. It may be that Joyce's fiction makes sense not once but twice—now in one way (Kenner's), now in another (Senn's)—owing to the systematic nature of its construction.

Senn's position is ancient and rhetorical; it derives, appropriately, from the art of reading Homer and, later, Scripture: when what is said cannot be the case, it must be taken in another sense, or in a manner of speaking appropriate to another context. The letter killeth, etc., and so it requires to be turned into a figure. Kenner's position is modern and historical-critical; it derives from the Enlightenment hermeneutic that whatever cannot be taken literally ought not to be taken at all, for, as we know from experience, darkness is regularly the occasion of deceit. The figure killeth, the letter giveth life; or, much to the same point, that which is plain conduces not to error.

Consider, for example, that the basic unit of Joyce's fiction is the encounter. In most cases, however, the encounter does not, on the whole, amount to very much; that is, Joyce's encounters are intrinsically ironic, because our expectations of dramatic confrontation are almost never fulfilled, and when they are fulfilled, as (presumably) in "The Dead," it is because the encounter has turned inward to assume psychological and—Senn would say—metaphorical importance. Thus Senn tells us that in "Nausicaa" both Gerty and Bloom "are emotionally and psychologically exalted. 'Nausicaa' is a chapter of culminations, of aspirations and high expectations, of sky-gazing and firework-gazing, of ecstatic flights and raised limbs."[5] It is true, of course—in fact, it is the whole point—that these ascents are chiefly figurative. "In

Gerty's and Bloom's brief coming together, there is no coition (they do not go together, *co-ire*); both merely linger in relative proximity, within visual range, and then continue on their lonely ways. . . . There is no consummation, no verbal contact"[6]—in short, nothing. It is a *Dubliners* story, "An Encounter" with different characters but with a strikingly similar turn of events. The major difference lies in the figuration, which transforms the naturalistic base into a network of metaphorical connections (whereby, for example, we get a prefiguration of Bloom's encounter with Stephen, or a version of Bloom's relation with Martha Clifford or, for that matter, his relation with Molly). Each of these connections no doubt reflects ironically on the narrative—but remember that irony is itself a figure of speech, whence we may observe that to figure Gerty as, say, the Blessed Virgin, or even as Molly (who knows that only "silly women believe love is sighing I am dying" [*U*758]), is to locate her within a system of differences that renders her character more exactly or, rather, more significantly than naturalism could ever manage. No one can be mistaken about Gerty. "Gerty's outlook," Senn says, "is characterized by self-inflated infatuations beyond critical questioning, by hyperbole, self-deception, and a basically timid selectivity"[7] (a true Dubliner!). The real irony, however, is that precisely these defects make her perfect for Joyce's art. Everywhere in *Ulysses* identities are mistaken, and therefore multiplied, nowhere more typically than in consequence of Gerty's fantasies, for she imagines better than she knows: her error in romanticizing Bloom as "her dreamhusband" (*U*358) corresponds to other, similar "errors," as when Bloom is figured, by his own hand, as Henry Flower, or as Don Poldo de la Flora by Molly (*U*759, 778). Moreover, Gerty's error forms an instance of a major theme of *Ulysses*: What do people see in one another, and in themselves? This question occupies Stephen and Bloom all day long; in "Nausicaa" Bloom broods on it. "Saw something in me" (*U*369), he says as Gerty hobbles off, and he is right.

Just so, error is unstable, and can turn quickly into meaning—and figures exist to facilitate (or conceal) this turning. "As figures be the instruments of ornament in euery language," George Puttenham says, "so be they also in a sorte abuses in speach, because they passe the ordinary limits of common vtterance, and be occupied of a purpose to deceiue the eare and also the minde, drawing it from plainnesse and simplicitie to a certain doubleness, whereby our talke is the more guilefull and abusing, for what els is your *Metaphor* but an inuersion of sence by transport . . . ?[8] Thus poetry is, traditionally, a species of error, a form of incorrect discourse: it is not authorized, as are philosophical utterances, but licensed, as are madmen, fools, lovers, and other creatures of wise delusion. Kenner would locate Joyce adjacently to this way of thinking, which is roughly where the history of the novel is to be found. The novel, after all, emerges at about that time when writers begin to side with philosophers against rhetoric, thus to insist (as certain readers of Scripture had already come to insist) on the virtues of the literal attitude. The novel is a form of narrative fiction which tries to hide or escape its fictional nature by asking to be taken literally. As Kenner says, the novel is not original invention, but forgery,[9] the subtlest form of parody (which some in turn call the most artful, because most invisible, rhetorical figure of them all). Geoffrey Hartman once tried to account for Wordsworth's literalness by saying that he was the first poet to be afraid of his own imagination.[10] This is as much as to say that Wordsworth desired a poetry that would be free of error. In a way, this is how Kenner regards Joyce, whom he figures as a writer of documents,[11] that is, one who composes not by imagination but by parody and transcription—by writing down, not by thinking up. Joyce is not a naturalist in the manner of Zola but a renegade or left-footed rhetorician, a literalist: a writer who takes recourse to documentation as the surest way to literal (antifigurative, or error-free) composition.

Critics have never been able to enjoy the knowledge that the quotient of fiction in Joyce's work is actually very small. Senn, for example, finds it hard to conceal his dismay that Joyce may have contrived his affair with Martha Fleischman in order to have something to transcribe into *Ulysses*. Joyce's letters to Martha, Senn says, "allow us some rare glimpses into that mysterious process of distillation which turns living experience into distanced art. The situation already has about it an air of laboratory experiment arranged with a view to literary exploitation."[12] In other words, as Bloom might have expressed it, ten to one there's no mystery in it at all. To forge something in the smithy of your soul, after all, is to proceed only upon the knowledge you acquire firsthand. The Romantics learned by painful experience (as Stephen appears to be learning in *Ulysses:* "See this. Remember." [*U*192]) what the Augustans arrived at by philosophical persuasion: you cannot rely on "the mysteries of literary creation"[13] to get you through; you've got to know what you're doing, and above all you've got to get your facts straight. Homer nodded by not knowing any better when he put a rudder on the bow of a ship.[14] Joycean fiction reposes with Johnsonian certainty on this principle of documentation, which, however, Joyce happily confounds by composing a book whose characters are mistaken about nearly everything. And he does this because he is an Augustan in the manner of Swift, not Johnson.

Kenner, at all events, reads Joyce as the last of the great Augustan satirists, whose genius was for parody, and whose theme was epistemological failure.[15] Specifically, Joyce shares with Swift and the Swift-like Pope of *The Dunciad* a common point of departure: What would happen if things actually were as our Modern Philosophers represent them to be? Consider Lockean psychology, which from an Augustan point of view resembles an inventory of satirical premises: *A Tale of a Tub* is a sort of gloss on the idea that the mind knows not things but only its ideas, which had better accord with things, else "our most serious thoughts will be of little more use than the reveries of a crazy brain."[16] Or, again: the mind is composed chiefly of what enters it in experience. This premise is of great interest because it implies a principle of characterization, that is, character-formation, wherein etiology is determined by antecedent conditions: for example, heredity (whence follows a natural obsession with fatherhood, ancestry, national character, etc.), and environment. Dublin as a source and occasion of shaping experiences is anything but a dead city, as even Kenner once figured it to be;[17] on the contrary, it is dangerously alive, an active agent that forges in the smithy of its soul endless human versions of itself: Dubliners, who decline almost without variation from early dreams of adventure and escape ("wild, untrammeled, free") into types and fixities of bitter disenchantment ("Tell no more of enchanted days"). If one desires to glimpse "the mysteries of literary creation," Joyce shows where they are to be found: not in the fervid soul of a minor dedalian figure but in Dublin Major, the true Daedalus, whose amanuensis is simply a Dubliner who figured out what was happening to him.

Not quite. If all of this sounds like a parody of Zola, it should, because it is. The documentary mode allowed Joyce to take literally what in fact could only exist on paper: What would happen if things actually were as naturalism represents them to be? Answer: they would be as they are in *Dubliners*, which gives us our first glimpse of Joyce's two-edged sword. Swift was no Lockean, but he understood how by parodying Locke one could produce Gulliver, whose mental failures are so many descriptions of how the Lockean mind is supposed to work.[18] Nor was Pope a Lockean, but he understood how by a parody of Lockean principles one could produce a Cibber, that is, one whose mind was shaped not by the reading of Homer but by empirical forces innocent of any classical *paideia*. Imagine now a mind shaped not by Homer but by Cibber. Or by *The Count of Monte Cristo*, followed by Byron, followed by a distinctly Pre-Raphaelite version of Thomas Aquinas. Or by the *Princess Novelette*,[19] whose idiom shaped Gerty McDowell as truly as if she had been a character in its pages: "It was Madame Vera Verity, directress of the Woman Beautiful page of the Princess novelette, who had first advised her to try eyebrowleine which gave that haunting

expression to the eyes ..." (*U*349). And who was Gerty? Why, someone for
Bloom to read, as if, no doubt, in a masterpiece by Paul de Kock: "Yes, it
was her he was looking at and there was meaning in his look. His eyes
burned into her as though they would search her through and through,
read her very soul" (*U*357). And Bloom? Someone for Gerty to read, of
course: "He was in deep mourning, she could see that, and the story of a
haunting sorrow was written on his face" (*U*357). This is hermeneutic comedy, and so is the whole of *Ulysses*, whose characters occupy themselves by
seeking in the real world unsubstantial images which their souls constantly
behold. What do people see in one another, and in themselves? Bloom
knows: "When you feel like that you often meet what you feel" (*U*369). Recall the famous line, "Think you're escaping and run into yourself" (*U*377).
Or Stephen's more artful version: "We walk through ourselves, meeting
robbers, ghosts, giants, old men, young wives, widows, brothers-in-love. But
always meeting ourselves" (*U*213). From an Augustan point of view this is
madness. Locke, however, believed that understanding reduces to a process
of reflection, whereby the mind turns inward to study its operations and
results, whose truth it must seek in turn to verify in further consultation
with experience, until by repeated and methodical adjustments certitude is
achieved. And certitude is recognition, or the mind's encounter with what
it knows.

Someone has surely counted the instances of self-encounter in *Ulysses*,
starting with Stephen's famous glance into the cracked looking glass ("As he
and others see me" [*U*6]) and arriving at a corresponding moment recalled
by Molly as she wonders how Boylan regards her: "I looked a bit washy of
course when I looked close in the handglass powdering a mirror never
gives you the expression ... " (*U*749). My favorite among these instances
occurs in "Nausicaa" when Bloom sniffs himself: "Mr Bloom inserted his
nose. Hm. Into the. Hm. Opening of his waistcoat" (*U*375). Pyrrhonistically,
alas, the smell of the lemon soap he has been carrying all day intervenes,
isolating himself from himself (which is just as well: Bloom is as down on
himself right now as he has even been: doesn't want to be himself); or, to
shape the matter in more Senn-like and metaphorical fashion, the soap
turns Bloom into a likeness of itself, which means that now the two of them
share the likeness of a lemon. It is as he sniffs himself that Bloom encounters the "nobleman" (*U*375)—a routine misnomer—whom "Cissy Caffrey
called the man that was so like himself" (*U*354),[20] and what does Bloom do
but turn the man into a version of himself, even as he turns himself into a
version of someone else?—"Sure he has a small bank balance somewhere,
government sit. Walk after him now make him awkward like those news-

boys me today. Still you learn something. See ourselves as others see us. So long as women don't mock what matter? That's the way to find out. Ask yourself who is he now. *The Mystery Man on the Beach*. Prize titbit story by Mr. Leopold Bloom. Payment at the rate of one guinea per column. And that fellow today at the graveside in the brown macintosh" (*U*375–76). Now think of Bloom's face, with "the story of haunting sorrow" written on it; and think of the moment in "Circe" when The Man in the Macintosh rises to accuse Bloom of being an imposter (that is, one who turns himself into someone else):

> Don't you believe a word he says. That man is Leopold M'Intosh, the notorious fireraiser. His real name is Higgins. [*U*485]

(Anent "the story of haunting sorrow": the real name of The Man in the Macintosh is, in all probability, Mr. James Duffy of "A Painful Case.")

"Nausicaa" (and, by an elaborate combination of metaphorical turnings, *Ulysses*) is a cunning assembly of self-encounters, each one a comic diversion from the venerable and Augustan ideal of self-knowledge. (Recall Mulligan's wonderful "Know thyself." [*U*216]) Thus for Bloom self-consciousness is simply what occurs to you when someone looks at you: a form of awkwardness that can grow intolerable when that someone is your wife's lover (*U*183). Bloom, on the whole, would prefer invisibility: "See, not be seen" (*U*265) is his watchword, as when he is careful to deprive Gerty of his profile (*U*369). His more complex self-effacement in "Nausicaa" tells the tale: he resolves upon the uselessness of self-predication ("I ... AM. A ... Let it go" [*U*381]), and, more telling still, he dispels his reflection in a tidepool: "Bend, see my face there, dark mirror, breathe on it, stirs" (*U*381). When Bloom looks at himself in a mirror in "Ithaca," he is reminded of a riddle whose theme is anonymity, or the concealed subject:

> *Brothers and sisters had he none,*
> *Yet that man's father was his grandfather's son.* [*U*708]

Self-knowledge is something Bloom can live without—but then we remember that for the Augustans self-knowledge is chiefly a function of being undeceived, and Bloom is remarkable for his undeceptibility, as in "Eumaeus." He has his fantasies, to be sure, and he is mistaken or oblivious to many things within him and without, and then there are his plans ("he ought to get a leather medal with a putty rim for all the plans he invents" [*U*765]), but as Dubliners go he is unusually free of illusions, and (like Ibsen or O'Neill, or a true naturalist) he seems to know better than anyone the indispensable role illusions play in human life: "See her as she is spoil all" (*U*370). And, after all, who is Gerty apart from her self-reflections, self-projections, and momentary occupation in Bloom's regard? No one. A Dubliner. Someone with "dreams that no-one knew of" (*U*363–64), and little else: an allegory of pathos ("Poor girl!" [*U*367]).

As Bloom concludes in "Lestrygonians" with sad philosophical grace: "No one is anything" (*U*164)—but actually this conclusion is less melancholy, less Pyrrhonistic, than Bloom may intend, for (as the Augustans knew) the self does not exist apart from the ways in which it makes its appearance in the world. Identity is conferred from the outside in, not (as Cartesians suppose) from the inside out. Character is that which is enroled according to known ethical dispositions; it is not that which is found by introspection but that which is acquired by study and choice. As Aristotle explained, drama occurs because choices take place in the world, which tends to have a mind of its own, and among people who are similarly self-disposed: politics is the alternative to tragedy, which is why tragic heroes, whose characters are fixed by fate, make terrible kings. What do people see in one another, and in themselves? Part of Stephen's problem surely is that everyone keeps trying to turn him into something he doesn't want to be.[21] Simon wants him to be another Dedalus to raise up the family's wretched fortunes ("You're your father's son" [*U*43]); Mulligan wants him to be Daedalus the Greek in a joint Hellenization of Ireland (*U*7), never mind that Mulligan's name is Malachi ("But it has a Hellenic ring, hasn't it?" [*U*4]), or that he wants Stephen to play the Irish bard in a fleecing of Haines (*U*7); Bloom sees in Stephen Stephen's mother and father (and, indeed, very nearly the whole Dedalus family), but more important he suspects that Stephen has "his father's voice" (*U*659), and so he imagines for the young man a fine career as an artiste, with himself in charge; and Molly?—"Im sure itll be grand if I can only get in with a handsome young poet at my age" (*U*776). Interestingly, Molly associates Stephen with Bloom's statue of Narcissus (*U*775), the young man undone by unchecked self-regard, or, depending on how you look at it, self-ignorance in the face of his own image: anyhow he was turned into a flower. Dublin for its part wants to turn Stephen into a Dubliner, and appears to be succeeding against Stephen's own efforts to turn himself into an artist. Stephen, of course, is at odds with himself ("I, a changeling" [*U*45]), brooding upon possibility, unable (Hamlet-like) to choose, preoccupied with the problem of character and role: "What's in a name? That is what we ask ourselves in childhood when we write the name we are told is ours" (*U*210). And who is Stephen?

I pull the wheezy bell of their shuttered cottage: and wait. They take me for a dun, peer out from coign of vantage.
—It's Stephen, sir.

—Let him in. Let Stephen in.
A bolt drawn back and Walter welcomes me.
—We thought you were someone else. [*U*38–39]

Here is a recognition scene, whose secret point is that Stephen is, of course, someone else, or wants to be. To know oneself is to know what one has become; it is the ability to tell one's story. We may speculate that what Stephen desires is to be remembered for that which, at present, he has yet to become. "I'll show you my likeness one day" (*U*43), he says, as if he had no likeness yet to show.

What's in a name? It depends on how interpretable it is, or what you can say about it. Most names leave you with nothing to say ("Shakespeares were as common as Murphies" [*U*622]). In a heroic age every name has a story behind it, in fact several, each one able to be triggered by an epithet, which is a sort of mnemonic link between a name and its meaning, or its moral: its ethos or character (that which identifies a person). Part of Stephen's problem is that his name has already got a story behind it, only he is not part of the story: in his case a name that became, by metonymy, an epithet (The Daedalus) has become, no one knows how, a surname (Dedalus), and Stephen's job is to turn it back into an epithet, his own: he has got to make a story for himself. (Puttenham, by the way, called metonymy "The Misnamer," a form of catachresis.)²² A name has something in it if you can account for its use: "Wily Odysseus." Why is he called that? Well, let me tell you. . . . This Homeric mode of intelligibility is parodied everywhere in *Ulysses*, most abundantly in "Eumaeus," as when the narrator tells a long and useless anecdote to account for the misnomer, "Lord John Corley" (*U*616–17), or when Murphy identifies Simon Dedalus not as Stephen's father but as someone else: a sharpshooter in Hengler's Royal Circus (*U*624). What's in a name? Nothing: "two identical names," as Bloom says in a similar connection, with nothing between them but "a striking coincidence" (*U*662). Actually, there is only one name but two different people, and it is in the nature of "Eumaeus" (and in the nature of *Ulysses*) to efface this sort of difference, thus to produce a case of mistaken identity:

—You know Simon Dedalus? he asked at length.
—I've heard of him, Stephen said. [*U*623]

What's in a name? Everything: there's not really a mistake here, only (as Wittgenstein would say) a difference between two situations, one which contains Stephen's father, and one which does not. We who know who Stephen's father is naturally on hearing his name transfer him from one situation to another, thus momentarily to suppose, as does Stephen, that Murphy is talking about a Simon Dedalus who, on second thought (Bloom's), could not be the one Murphy is talking about. This is a quintessential hermeneutic situation. The point, however, is that there is no *formal* difference between mistaken identity and metaphor: both are produced by a transfer of meaning from one situation to another, that is, by a substitution or equivalence that is literally false—the two Simons in question are not the same man—but figuratively true: the two men are combined in a single name. It is a textbook case of double meaning, or figurative error (philosophers in a benign mood call it "semantic innovation"): metaphor works by producing a momentary mistake, which the mind then corrects by construing the difference between literal and figurative utterance, that is, by discovering what is coincident between two situations. This is what Bloom does in the case of the two Simons, and he has proved to be quicker than many readers to read the situation: "Curious coincidence," he says (*U*624), and he is right. What is curious, however, is the relationship between the literal and the figurative that the coincidence forms. Murphy's Simon is not literally the Simon whom we know, yet he is (we assume, perhaps generously) literally named "Simon," as is Stephen's father. The lesson here in the operations of human language is a good one: the two Simons are figures (or versions) of one another, yet literal in themselves.

Here we discover one of the principles on which *Ulysses* is built: a coincidence of situations allows a transference of meaning, as in "Sirens," when Bloom's situation sufficiently coincides with Lionel's in *Martha* ("All is lost now" [*U*272]) to turn him into "Lionelleopold" (*U*288), even as Simon Dedalus's rendition of "Lionel's Song" so transports Bloom as to turn him into "Siopold" (*U*276), quite apart from the fact that both men have lost their wives and their sons, death and alienation intervening differently but symmetrically. The same principle turns Bloom into Odysseus, God the Father, King Hamlet, Shakespeare, Daedalus, Moses and Elijah, and so on. It is on this principle that the relationship between Stephen and Bloom is normally arranged:

Stephen	*Bloom*
Artist (imagination)	Scientist (observation)
Signs and Symbols (Realist)	Facts and objects (Nominalist)
Faces the past (death)	Faces the future (life)
Irish (Gaelic): Ireland	Jewish (Hebrew): Israel
Rejects Ireland	Rejected by Ireland
Imprisoned (fugitive): escape	Exiled (outcast): return
Ascetic (intellect)	Sensual (appetite)

Stephen	*Bloom*
Fasts	Eats
Drunk	Disgustingly Sober
Unbathed (hydrophobe)	Bathed (hydrophile)
Mother-Son	Father-Daughter
Cold (antipathy): pride	Warm (sympathy): humility
Rebellion (thin-skinned)	Acceptance (thick-skinned)
Heroic (hyperbolic)	Naturalistic (ironic)
Tragic (Hamlet): rigid	Comic (cuckold): resilient
Introspective (self-conscious)	Extrospective (repressed)
Imprudent (romantic)	Prudent (domestic)
Schooled (theoretical)	Unschooled (practical)
Philosophical/theological	Empirical/materialist
Religion: mystery = power	Religion: organization = power
Heretical	Skeptical
Idea (soul)	Experience (body)
Shakespeare (artist-begetter)	Shakespeare (father-begetter)
Unable to produce a work	Unable to produce a son

And so on: most readers of *Ulysses* could amplify and correct this arrangement in a hundred ways. The point is that Bloom and Stephen become figures of one another almost without reason: they were meant for each other in ways impossible for them to understand. Put them in separate novels and they will hardly make sense; put them in the same novel and you get a sense of providence and design, metaphysical plenitude and repose:

> Both then were silent?
>
> Silent, each contemplating the other in both mirrors of the reciprocal flesh of theirhisnothis fellowfaces. [*U*702]

What do people see in one another, and in themselves? Less (or more) than meets the eye—which is perhaps the whole meaning of figuration.

The problem with all of this is that metaphor is not intrinsically benign. On the contrary, it has regularly been the contention of philosophers that metaphor is simply a two-faced or two-edged version of catachresis and that it upholds the world of the lie, where illusion and deceit obtain in behalf of those who know what's going on (Bloom) as against those who do not (Martha Clifford). *Ulysses,* on this view, is a book of aliases wherein, indeed, "No one is anything" (*U*164), because false names are used in the universal absence of true ones (the state of catachresis). This is true Pyrrhonism: Bloom is not Henry Flower, but neither is he Bloom ("Our name was changed too" [*U*623]), nor is he Virag, which is the name of something else, and so on in an infinite regression of name-changing: "all kinds of words changing colour" (*U*644) to produce the primary illusions of substance and identity. Bloom is hardly Odysseus, God the Father, King Hamlet, or anyone except as he wanders (as do we all) through a world of words where any-one can become anything: sons their own fathers, husbands their own wives, bawds their own cuckolds, and everyman his own seducer.

Who, then, is Bloom? Here is how he represents himself in "Circe":

BLOOM

Gentleman of the jury, let me explain. A pure mare's nest. I am a man misun-derstood. I am being made a scapegoat of. I am a respectable married man, without a stain on my character. I live in Eccles street. My wife, I am the daugh-ter of a most distinguished commander, a gallant upstanding gentleman, who do you call him, Majorgeneral Brian Tweedy ... [*U*457]

Bloom is Bloom, and also Molly: he who imagines this may imagine more, as "Circe" requires us to do with its "stage directions" that maintain Bloom in a state of running transformation.[23] The theme of "Circe" is misrepresen-tation, or the multiplication and distortion of images, yet in each distortion there is some correct metaphorical application, this being the screw that turns *Ulysses*. Bloom's first appearance in "Circe," for example, is an in-stance of self-encounter wherein that which is false is also, in a manner of speaking, true:

(*... From Gillen's hairdresser's window a composite portrait shows him gallant Nelson's image. A concave mirror at the side presents to him lovelorn longlost lugubru Booloohoom. Grave Gladstone sees him level, Bloom for Bloom. He passes, struck by the stare of truculent Wellington but in the convex mirror grin unstruck the bonham eyes and fatchuck cheekchops of Jollypoldy the rixdixdoldy.*) [*U*433–34]

Here is "Circe's" first version of Bloom's complex inwardness, or, to speak correctly, his manysidedness, for Bloom does not divide into inward and outward dimensions but rather has aspects or features that array themselves side by side, that is, adjacently, one thing turning into another, on the prin-ciple that no one is anything all at once but given (as in metaphor, or in life) world enough and time a composite may be produced showing how anyone can become anything, as when Gladstone, for example, is made to see in Bloom what Bloom sees in Gladstone: namely, another Bloom, who, in this exchange of glances ("Bloom for Bloom"), sees his reflection in the window superimpose itself momentarily on Gladstone's portrait (a coinci-dence, or passing fancy). "Circe" is really nothing more than this: an epi-sode of contrivances—funny mirrors, magical transformations, possession by spirits of one sort or another, repressions in gaudy and expressionist return, and (above all) rhetoric, which is the art of making anything appear to be the case:

> *(Bloom walks on a net, covers his left eye with his left ear, passes through several walls, climbs Nelson's pillar, hangs from the top ledge by his eyelids, eats twelve dozen oysters (shells included), heals several sufferers from kings' evil, contracts his face so as to resemble many historical personages, Lord Beaconsfield* [if Gladstone, why not Disraeli?], *Lord Byron, Wat Tyler, Moses of Egypt, Moses Maimonides, Moses Mendelssohn, Henry Irving, Rip Van Winkle, Kossuth, Jean Jacques Rousseau, Baron Leopold Rothschild, Robinson Crusoe, Sherlock Holmes, Pasteur, turns each foot simultaneously in different directions, bids the tide turn back* [does it?], *eclipses the sun by extending his little finger.)* [U495]

We know that most of what occurs in "Circe" isn't really happening, and by "really" we mean "literally," on the assumption that things are taking place figuratively, that is, in some manner of speaking—unconsciously ("What you longed for has come to pass" [U535]), but also in a way that allows for any sort of matter to be represented, even that which cannot be thought, since there is no manner of speaking in which nothing is not expressible: there is nothing, for example, which Bloom (*thaumaturgos*, or he who can make anything happen or otherwise appear to be the case) cannot do—he has, after all, while yet a virgin, just given birth to "eight male yellow and white children," and *"All are handsome, with valuable metallic faces, wellmade, respectably dressed and wellconducted, speaking five modern languages fluently and interested in various arts and sciences. Each has his name printed in legible letters on his shirtfront: Nasodoro, Goldfinger, Chrysostomos, Maindorée, Silversmile, Silberselber, Vifargent, Panargyros"* (U494). What's in a name? Everything, because that which can exist nowhere else, not even in the unconscious, can occur in words—even the unspeakable can become speakable, if nothing else, not only in Bloom's debasement at the hands of Bella or Bello Cohen (U530–45), but elsewhere in such things as "the quadrature of the circle" (U699), to the attainment of which Bloom (less thaumaturgic than young and undaunted) devoted part of 1886.

The lesson here is not difficult, although it wants careful wording: a basic principle of Joycean composition is that the meaning of the word "literal" has been altered sufficiently to make us take the word "literally" *literally*, that is, not as an equivalent or metaphor of "really" (no, nor even as a metaphor of "mentally") but literally as in *letters on the page*, for apart from the inner world and the outer there is that other world of the letter where "anything goes," or where rhetoric is unrestrained by philosophy—a kingdom of misrule where we may take things literally (where, indeed, we may even take figures literally) without reprisal.

Even lies, after all, have to be plausible: as if to acknowledge this thought "Circe" fades into "Eumaeus." In the one episode we can take everything literally because anything goes, everything is the case; in the other we can take nothing literally because nothing is the case, everything is bogus: not even the figures of speech can be trusted to produce anything, because the dominant figure of "Eumaeus" is periphrasis or circumlocution, which regularly takes the parodied form of saying nothing in so many words—that, in any case, is how the narrator is required to proceed, "Eumaeus" being, as everyone knows, the episode in which nothing happens. Not quite nothing, perhaps, but "Eumaeus" raises (in so many words) the question of what's in a name if one's name is Murphy: there's evidently nothing for it but to make a name for oneself by inventing stories out of nothing, the only requisite being that one has got to be good at it, for, as Murphy learns (probably not for the first time in his life), nothing is more deadly than to be transparent before one's audience, against whom, in a last gesture of romance, Murphy draws a knife (*U*628). Or, again, how do you make a Dublin cabman's shelter interesting? By imagining that its keeper has a name ("the once famous Skin-the-Goat, Fitzharris, the invincible") with a story behind it (the Phoenix Park Murders), "though [Bloom] wouldn't vouch for the actual facts, which quite possibly there was not vestige of truth in it" (*U*621). The saving figure in "Eumaeus" is Bloom, the outsider who is not about to be taken in by anything anyone says ("being of a sceptical bias" [*U*655]), nor by whatever is reputed or appears to be the case, not even the asseverations of Holy Writ concerning, for example, the immortality of the soul: "My belief is, to tell you the candid truth, that those bits were genuine forgeries all of them put in by monks most probably ..." (*U*634). The damnéd figure is, of course, Stephen, parody of the Pyrrhonist, not simply because Dublin seems at last to have reduced this reader of signatures to skepticism ("Sounds are impostures" [*U*622]), but because he has lapsed into a burlesque of Pyrrhonean *ataraxia:* not equanimity or quietude in the face of confounding appearances, but *anaisthesia:* not the suspension of judgment, but its obliteration.[24]

Almost any philosopher will tell you, however, that Stephen will be destroyed, not by Dublin (nor by its avatar: drink), but by metaphor: by turning reality into something else he leaves himself defenseless against its contrary ways, as when he encounters an old woman, turns her into a "messenger from the secret morning" (*U*14), then suffers the cold truth that she has nothing to say to him: "me she slights" (*U*14). Bloom, of course—

is Bloom: "Born with a silver knife in his mouth. That's witty, I think. Or no. Silver means born rich. Born with a knife. But then the allusion is lost" (*U*170).[25] Bloom's errors are errors of fact, not of figure (figures are beyond him, like the hundreds of roles he plays), and if his world seems accordingly narrow in comparison with the ones Stephen is inclined to imagine for himself, it remains a world that is generally powerless to deceive him. To which the rhetorician will respond, almost as if to agree, that Bloom's world is narrow only in comparison with the book in which he literally exists. Or no. Figuratively.

Conclusion:
Representation and Understanding

What does it mean to understand the representation of anything? The oddity of this question makes it a good one, that is, a question not able to be answered and therefore a source of reflection—and understanding. Normally we do not speak of the *understanding* of a representation; instead we tend to figure representation as we do reality, namely, as an object of experience—usually a visual experience, although (curiously) when we speak of a "misrepresentation" we are likely to have in mind, not what we see, but what we hear, or what we have been told. Sight, not sound, is the medium of enlightenment. As Thucydides says, writing gives you the facts, whence you may see for yourself what happened, but singing gives you hearsay and is not to be trusted.[1] We are trained to believe our eyes and doubt our ears.

Representations are things to look at as we look at scenes or landscapes, whether painted or real. In one sense, at any rate, it is surely enough to say that to understand a representation is to know what is represented. "A picture of a human face," Wittgenstein says, "is a no less familiar object than the human face itself."[2] Understanding in this sense can be assimilated into a copy- or correspondence-theory of knowledge; or it can be made part of a general theory of recognition, wherein there is never any understanding of anything the first time around. You know what you are looking at only when you see it again, or when you have seen it before. Interestingly, to recognize something is very often to know what it is called, or perhaps *how* it is called, as if to recognize something were not far removed from the ability to recall it or to summon it into view—but perhaps one need not actually have seen the thing, only to have heard about it, or to know how to talk about it. A representation in this respect could be figured not only as a shadowing of reality but a foreshadowing of it, whence remembrance might be figured in turn as a representation of experience *before* the fact, or perhaps as the natural companion of experience (as of Vergil to Dante): that which allows you to know what you are seeing, or what to look for. To know something is to know what it looks like. Consider what we mean by the familiar expression, "I've never seen anything like it!" What must a thing resemble in order to be recognizable? Answer: something seen before, as if the present, in order to be recognizable, had to resemble—or to make its appearance—as a representation of the past.

One of the things that you understand when you understand a representation is the simple fact that one has occurred. A little reflection, however, will spoil this idea, because representations do not always simply take place. Recall the story that William Carlos Williams tells of Marcel Duchamp: "One day Duchamp decided that his composition for that day would be the first thing that struck his eye in the first hardware store he should enter. It turned out to be a pickax which he bought and set up in his studio. This was his composition."[3] One of the things we are to understand here is that representation has not taken place. Anyhow Duchamp's composition of the pickax is not a representation of a pickax; it is the thing itself: the unmediated reality. What has happened is that the pickax has been made to occupy a representational situation: it takes place right where we might expect a representation of something to occur, but somehow the occasion of representation has been subverted or interrupted (or, more accurately, parodied) by the unexpected appearance of reality. Thus what we have here is an instance of non-representation, or, if you like, non-representational art, which is also what we have in Duchamp's "Nude Descending the Staircase": namely, the non-representation of a nude, etc. We know what a nude descending the staircase would look like if we saw one: that is, we would recognize it at once, or we would know it for what it is.

This last is an interesting expression—knowing something for what it is. What does it mean to know something for what it is? Plato would say that in this event we would know what it stands for: namely, itself—or, more accurately, we would see it *as* itself, on the principle, which both Plato and Heidegger would affirm, that the seeing of anything is always a *seeing-as*.[4] For Plato this means that in seeing we recognize a version of something that, in fact, we cannot see except in virtue of a difficult philosophical elevation.[5] From the Platonic point of view nothing exists except in its versions, not even me, who is present here and now (as I write) in only one of my versions, whence you may know me for what I am: namely, a representation of something not otherwise accessible: me.

For the understanding of a representation, however, we may need to go beyond resemblance and recognition, if only momentarily. To understand a representation is not merely to know what is or is not represented. I recognize a pickax when I see one and this goes for representations of a pickax as well, but it is not certain that understanding has yet been brought into play. It is not that there is nothing mimetic, or knowledgeable, in the understanding of a representation, but consider what happens when you allow the distinction between understanding and knowing. This distinction is basic to Heidegger's thinking and to the hermeneutics of Hans-Georg Gadamer.[6] The point is that knowledge is always of objects, whereas, in the understanding of something, that *something* is not present (or represented) as an object. It has a different sort of being from that of an objective entity that I can take possession of, thus to examine it or to analyze it into its constituent forms and ingredients. In this context the understanding of a representation would be different from a formal study of it: to understand a representation would not be simply to know how it is made, how it got produced, or how it works (or claims to work). It might not even be to know what it is. Among certain philosophers, understanding might not even count as knowledge. Heidegger would say that to understand something is to know what it means to stand in its presence.[7] This is quite different from grasping that thing as an object of knowledge; on the contrary, we should think of it rather as a reversal of power whereby that which is present takes possession of *us* or overtakes us and subjects us to *its* power. This brings us on to difficult ground, however, for if representation is what is at issue here we must ask: What does it mean to stand in the presence of a representation? For Heidegger, this is as much as to ask: What does it mean to understand the *truth* of a representation?[8]

In this context the understanding of a representation would be inseparable from the understanding of the situation in which it occurs. From Heidegger's point of view, representations, like works of art, do *not* occur in places like museums; that is, they are not to be taken out of time and figured as timeless portrayals.[9] This means at once that a representation cannot be figured in terms of a vehicle and its contents or, again, in terms of anything portable or transportable as from one age to another or from one level of generality to another. It cannot be made the theme of dissemination. It is not the embodiment of anything nor is it accessible to the various categories of human or artistic expression. Rather, representation as a Heideggerian topic would have to be figured according to the dynamics of concealment and disclosure.[10] Representation in this case would not be any sort of signification: a representation of something would not "stand for" it; rather, it would be one of the ways in which that thing makes its appearance. In such an event something would always be held back or in reserve, that is, concealed or dissembled. Think of legal representation: when your attorney speaks in your defense he represents you, not in the sense that he stands for you, but in the sense that he stands in your place and articulates your position. The relationship between you and your attorney is not a relationship of signification; it is entirely situational in character. He does not stand for you but takes over for you and acts in your behalf, doing what you are called upon to do by the situation that now obtains: having murdered, say one of your wife's lovers, you must now defend yourself before the law. There is no question here of any resemblance between you and your attorney; there may not be any agreement or correspondence between the two of you—you may, feeling entirely self-justified, wish not to be defended at all; but that does not alter the situation. Your intention is of no matter: intentionality in this case is built into the state of affairs in which you find yourself. Thus, for example, it is the task of your attorney, quite apart from what you may wish or what he may believe, to bring into the open or to place in view some applicable portion of you that, saving his representation, would remain hidden, or perhaps have no legal bearing. Likewise, of course, he must conceal some portion, or again he must construe the situation in a certain way in order to place you in it in the best possible light. To understand his representation would thus be to understand your side of the situation or your side of the case at hand. Your side of the case no doubt contains falsehoods of one sort or another—misrepresentation may be a native component of every representation—but these falsehoods are quite beside the point: the point is that your side of the case, whatever its metaphysical defects, is called for by the situation and is, indeed, required by it if it is to be what it is, that is, something that legally takes place.

The virtue of this analogy is that it allows us to consider an instance of representation at some remove from the usual questions of what is real and what isn't. It also helps to complicate the thoughtless connection people sometimes make between representation and reference. Finally, it prepares the way for this reflection: to understand a representation means to understand (not an object of any sort, nor a sign or reference but) a representational situation, none of whose components is required to be illusory or, for that matter, real: the question of appearance and reality may not be altogether worth raising. In a wonderful essay on "Pretending," J. L. Austin observes that unreality may not enter into a situation of pretense at all, or at least not in a way that matters. "We must not," he says, "allow ourselves to be too much obsessed by the opposition ... between pretending and really being."[11] Take the example of the crook who cases the house he intends to rob by pretending (or while pretending) to wash its windows; as it happens, he actually *does* wash the windows. He is not doing anything mimetic. The actual doing of one thing merely disguises, Austin says, the intention to do something else—but nothing is done in either case which cannot be called "real." "The essence of the situation in pretending," Austin says, "is (not so much that my public behaviour must be non-genuine behaviour, as rather) that my public behaviour is meant to disguise some reality, often some real behaviour."[12] Pretending is, let us say, a species of misrepresentation, but what is being misrepresented is not an action (the crook, in pretending to wash the windows, actually washes them); what is being misrepresented is the situation in which the washing of windows occurs: there is more to the situation than meets the eye, or the eye is not privy to the whole of what is going on—a situation is not being understood, and pretending, one might say, is precisely a way of preventing the understanding of what is taking place.

Pretending, Austin says, belongs to the category of *not exactly doing something*.[13] The crook represents himself as a man washing windows, that is, *merely* washing them, which is what he happens to be doing, although not exactly. To understand this representation would, presumably, be to understand that it is, however, a misrepresentation of what is taking place—but how is one to understand this? No doubt we may imagine understanding here as a type of unmasking. The situation is being disguised by one of the actions really being performed in it. It is, therefore, up to the one who would understand to penetrate or to strip away the disguise. It may be, however, that the metaphor of unmasking cannot be applied to understanding but only to what one does afterward—after, as Wittgenstein would say, one has studied the situation. The crook intends to rob the house, but you will not ever recognize this if you simply consult the crook or his actions, because neither is, strictly speaking, any sort of veil to be penetrated; you must consult the situation, which is, in this case as in every other, all that anyone can ever understand. It is not, after all, an intention that is being concealed—not exactly, and anyway intentions are never anything else but concealed; what is being concealed is some considerable portion of the situation itself. Wittgenstein, by the way, says that "an intention is embedded in its situation,"[14] which means that the understanding of an intention requires the understanding of the situation in which it occurs; and this, it turns out, is true of representations as well. To understand a situation requires an investigation to find out what is going on. As Wittgenstein says, you must always look and see what is the case.[15]

The difficulty, of course, is that most investigations do not and cannot get under way until it is too late. In all likelihood you will not have understood that the crook was casing the house for its valuables until after the robbery has occurred, at which point the truth of his representation or misrepresentation—his washing of the windows—will shine out at you. There is perhaps no way that an investigation could have disclosed anything beforehand, saving that the crook would give himself away—situations, as

Heidegger would say, have that way about them: they are self-disguising, naturally reserved or secretive. They close themselves up before every effort to penetrate to their nature, which is why they are finally more accessible to reflection than to investigation—and sometimes they are not accessible at all, as in the situation that surrounds, or rather fails to surround, the celebrated Nietzschean enigma, " 'I have forgotten my umbrella.' "[16] To understand a sentence is to understand the situation in which it occurs, which time provides, and also takes away; and, when time has done its work, scholarship or imagination must be brought into play, often to no effect. To understand anything is to understand a situation. but the understanding of any situation requires that you enter it in order to become part of what you would understand. This is a basic hermeneutic principle, whose corollary is that only outsiders know things, but insiders understand them. A situation cannot be understood except by one who is already contained in it, which is why it is difficult for us to understand Nietzsche's " 'I have forgotten my umbrella.' " A situation that withholds itself or conceals its truth is one that is closed off to the one who desires to know what is going on. This is why the understanding of anything is analogous to one's entry into a secret, or into a conspiracy, which would have been one of the ways (no doubt the only way) to have understood before the robbery that the windowwasher was a crook. The crook, after all, is the one who understood the situation: no one, we may surmise, understood it better than he, whence he could have conceivably taken you into his confidence, or let you in on the situation, which would have been the same as letting you in on the secret. One perhaps should add that the crook alone is in a position to understand, since he is (not creating it exactly, but) shaping the situation to his own ends, or conforming it to his intentions.

Here we may begin to understand more forcefully Heidegger's hostility toward museums. Understanding requires that you find a place for whatever it is you wish to understand, but from Heidegger's point of view museums are no place for works of art, even as, from Paul Ricoeur's point of view, libraries are perhaps no place for texts:[17] or, alternatively, one could say that texts are no place for utterances like " 'I have forgotten my umbrella.' " " 'I have forgotten my umbrella' " does, to be sure, occupy a situation of sorts, one so commonplace that, as even Derrida admits, it is impossible not to know what happened: somebody forgot his umbrella, if only in a manner of speaking (the manner represented perhaps by the quotation marks: somebody forgot his umbrella—but not exactly).[18] The enigma here lies not in the text but in the occasion of it. What is *not* mysterious (or "undecidable") is the reason why we know so much and understand so little: there's a story here that, so far as one can tell, never got told, which means, among other things, that what you have here is once more a non-representational situation, that is, a situation in which a representation such as we might have wished for does not take place, whence we are left in the dark. From Heidegger's point of view, a work of art in a museum is a bit like Nietzsche's " 'I have forgotten my umbrella' ": it has the worldless character of a stone: it is merely an aesthetic object, or an object of interest, something analogous to an object of knowledge, which in its turn has about it the character of a brute object.[19] Heidegger's position would be that we have got to understand more than meets the eye if we are to understand what we are looking at: for example, if we are thinking of works of art, we have surely got to understand the history of art—only we have got to understand this history in a certain way. We have got to understand it, not as art history, that is, not as a *theatrum mundi* or *speculum mentis*—not simply art as a totality of special objects that we may view or know or own; rather, it would mean understanding a work as it makes its appearance within what Gadamer calls "effective-history": history that catches up the one who would understand and places him in some portion of itself, whence he becomes a part of that which he would understand.[20]

In this respect—and this will be my final point—the understanding of a representation will always implicate us in the task of self-understanding, which means in this case not anything like the understanding of a mind or ego but rather refers to the situation of understanding itself, that is, the conditions under which it is actually occurring: there is no understanding of anything unless this situation is understood first. We speak as if the world and ourselves as part of it belonged to a realm of knowledge, whereas it were better to say that all of this belongs to history, and this is principally true of ourselves, namely those who wish to know. No doubt knowledge of a certain kind requires that we overcome the contingencies of every historical situation, but it might be that precisely this achievement would remove us from the possibility of understanding anything, which means that that which we would know would always be something other than the reality of it, some "mere representation," as they used to say—some Kantian or logical specter not quite able to live and move among us.

Notes

INTRODUCTION

1 *La Divina Commedia,* XXX. 76–77, ed. Maria Dazzi Vasta (Torino: G. B. Paravia, 1960), p. 418.
2 Persius, *Satire* I. 114–15: "And yet Lucilius flayed our city: he flayed you Lupus, and you Mucius, and broke his jaw over you" (Loeb trans.).
3 Juvenal, *Satire* I. 153–54: " 'What man is there that I dare not name? What matters it whether Mucius forgives my words or no?' " (Loeb trans.). Juvenal is thought here to be quoting from Lucilius.

CHAPTER 1

1 *Poetry, Language, Thought,* trans. Albert Hofstadter (New York: Harper & Row, 1971), p. 54: "We believe we are at home in the immediate circle of beings. That which is, is familiar, reliable, ordinary. Nevertheless, the clearing is pervaded by a constant concealment in the double form of refusal and dissembling. . . . The nature of truth, that is, of unconcealedness, is dominated throughout by a denial. Yet this denial is not a defect or a fault, as though truth were an unalloyed unconcealedness that has rid itself of everything concealed. If truth could accomplish this it would no longer be itself. This denial, in the form of a double concealment, belongs to the nature of truth as unconcealedness."
2 *The Genesis of Secrecy: The Charles Eliot Norton Lectures, 1977–78* (Cambridge: Harvard University Press, 1979), esp. pp. 124–45.
3 *On First Principles,* trans. G. W. Butterworth (New York: Harper & Row, 1966), p. 272.
4 See *The Holy Qur'ān: Arabic Text, Translation, and Commentary* by Maulānā Muhammad 'Alī, 4th ed. (Lahore, Pakistan: Ahmadiyyah Anjuman Ishā'at Islām, 1951), Sūra 3:6: "He it is Who has revealed the Book to thee; some of its verses are decisive [i.e., clear]—they are the basis of the Book—and others are allegorical [i.e., ambiguous]. Then those in whose hearts is perversity follow the part of it which is allegorical, and seeking to give it (their own) interpretation. And none knows its interpretation save Allāh, and those firmly rooted in knowledge. They say: We believe in it, it is from our Lord. And none mind [i.e., remember] except men of understanding."
5 See Labib al-Said, *The Recited Koran* (Princeton, N.J.: Darwin Press, 1975), pp. 15–60; Helmut Gätje, *The Qur'ān and Its Exegesis,* trans. Alford T. Welch (Berkeley: California University Press, 1976), pp. 23–30, and also pp. 55–57; John Wansbrough, *Qur'ānic Studies: Sources and Methods of Scriptural Interpretation* (Oxford University Press), pp. 1–31. See also Mas'ud Ibn Umar Sa'd al-Dīn al-Taftāzānī, *A Commentary of the Creed of Islam,* trans. Earl Edgar Elder (New York: Columbia University Press, 1950), p. 58: "The Qur'ān, the speech of Allah, is uncreated. . . . "
6 "The Origin of the Work of Art," *Poetry, Language, Thought,* pp. 46–49.
7 As in Plato, *Phaedo* 102d, where Socrates says that he is beginning to sound like something written down (*suggraphikos*).
8 Trans. Shlomo Pines (Chicago: University of Chicago Press, 1963), I, p. 16: "God, may he be exalted, knows that I have never ceased to be exceedingly apprehensive about setting down those things that I wish to set down in this Treatise. For they are concealed things; none of

them has been set down in any book—written in the religious community in these times of *Exile*—the books composed in these times being in our hands. How can I now innovate and set them down?"

9 See the *Guide of the Perplexed*, I, pp. 17–20.

10 See Aristotle, *On Interpretation*, IV. 16b–17a; and Ammonius: "By these arguments Aristotle teaches what the things principally and immediately signified by sounds are, and these are thoughts. Through these means we signify things; and it is not necessary to consider anything else as intermediate between the thought and the thing, as the Stoics do, who assume what they name to be the meaning [lektòn]." Trans. Jason L. Saunders, *Greek and Roman Philosophy after Aristotle* (New York: Free Press, 1966), p. 77. See also Andreas Graeser, "The Stoic Theory of Meaning," in *The Stoics*, ed. John M. Rist (Berkeley: University of California Press, 1978), pp. 77–100.

11 As in the *Cratylus*, for example, and in Aristotle's *Categories*.

12 Trans. D. W. Robertson, Jr. (Indianapolis, Ind.: Bobbs-Merrill, 1958), pp. 43–48.

13 Ibid., pp. 87–88: "Therefore a method of determining whether a locution is literal or figurative must be established. And generally this method consists in this: that whatever appears in the divine Word that does not literally pertain to virtuous behavior or to the truth of faith you must take to be figurative."

14 See the *Letter of Aristeas*, trans. Moses Hadas (New York: Harper & Brothers, 1951), 161 (p. 163). See also D. W. Gooding, "Aristeas and Septuagint Origins: A Review of Recent Studies," *Novum Testamentum* 13 (1963): 357–79. The *Letter of Aristeas* is usually dated around 100 B.C.

15 Cf. the *Ihya 'ulum ad-din* of al-Ghazzali (d. 1111): "According to the opinion of some scholars, every verse [of the Qur'ān] can be understood in sixty thousand ways, and what then still remains unexhausted (in its meaning) is still more numerous (akthar)." Helmut Gatje, *The Qur'ān and Its Exegesis*, ed. and trans. Alford T. Welch (Berkeley: University of California Press, 1977), p. 229.

16 Philo, *De Vita Mosis*, II. 37–40 (Loeb trans.).

17 See the *Letter of Aristeas*, 310–11: "When the rolls had been read the priests and the elders of the translators and some of the corporate body and the leaders of the people rose up and said, 'Inasmuch as the translation has been well and piously made and is in every respect accurate, it is right that it should remain in its present form and that no revision of any sort take place.' When all had assented to what had been said, they bade that an imprecation be pronounced, according to their custom, upon any who should revise the text by adding or transposing anything whatever in what they had written down, or by making any excision; and in this they did well, so that the work might be preserved imperishable and unchanged always." Cf. Philo, *De Vita Mosis*, II. 34: " . . . they could not add or take away or transfer anything, but must keep the original form and shape."

18 *Introduction to the Massoretico-Critical Edition of the Hebrew Bible* (New York: KTAV, 1966), pp. 305–06. This book, one of the great works of textual scholarship, was first published in 1896.

19 *The Cambridge History of the Bible*, ed. Peter Ackroyd and C. F. Evans (Cambridge: Cambridge University Press, 1970), I, p. 112. See also, in this same volume, Shemaryahu Talmon, "The Old Testament Text" (pp. 159–99), and C. F. Evans, "The New Testament in the Making" (pp. 232–84).

20 See G. W. Anderson, "Canonical and Non-canonical," in *The Cambridge History of the Bible*, pp. 113–59.

21 Pesaḥim 112a, *The Babylonian Talmud*, trans. I. Epstein (London: Soncino Press, 1938), X, p. 577.

22 See J. Weingreen, *From Bible to Mishna: The Continuity of Tradition* (New York: Holmes & Meier; Manchester: Manchester University Press, 1976), pp. 1–33.

23 Quoted by Moshe Greenberg, "The Stabilization of the Text of the Hebrew Bible, Reviewed in the Light of the Biblical Materials from the Judean Desert," *Journal of the American Oriental Society* 76 (1956): 305. See also Shemaryahu Talmon, "The Three Scrolls of the Law That Were Found in the Temple Court," *Textus* 2 (1962): 14–27.

24 *From Bible to Mishna*, pp. 14–15. See also H. M. Orlinsky, "The Origin of the Kethib-Qere System: A New Approach," *Supplements to Vetus Testamentum* 7 (1959): 184–92.

25 See W. Emery Barner, "Ancient Corrections in the Text of the Old Testament," *Journal of Theological Studies* 1 (1900): 387–414.

26 Trans. William G. Braude (New Haven: Yale University Press, 1968), I, p. 92 (Piska 5).

27 *Scripture and Tradition in Judaism: Haggadic Studies* (Leiden: E. J. Brill, 1961), p. 68.

28 *Exodus Rabbah*, V. 1, trans. S. M. Lehrman, *Midrash Rabbah*, ed. H. Freeman and Maurice Simon (London: Soncino Press, 1939), III, pp. 103–04.

29 *Song of Songs Rabbah*, I. 1. 8, trans. Maurice Simon, *Midrash Rabbah*, IX, pp. 9–10.

30 *Exodus Rabbah*, XV. 7, *Midrash Rabbah*, III, pp. 169–70.

31 *Numbers Rabbah*, XIV. 10, trans. Judah J. Slotki *Midrash Rabbah*, VI, p. 613.

32 See J. A. Emerton, "The Purpose of the Second Column of the Hexapla," *Journal of Theological Studies*, S. S. 7 (1956): 79–87.

33 S. P. Brock, "Origen's Aims as a Textual Critic of the Old Testament," *Studia Patristica* 10 (1970): 216–18. See Origen's "Letter to Africanus," in *The Ante-Nicene Fathers*, ed. Alexander Roberts and James Donaldson (New York: Scribner's, 1926), IV, pp. 386–92.

34 As Origen complained to Africanus, ibid., p. 387: "What needs there to speak of Exodus, where there is such diversity in what is said about the tabernacle and its court, and the ark, and the garments of the high priests, that sometimes the meaning does not even seem to be akin?"

35 *A Select Library of the Nicene and Post-Nicene Fathers*, ed. Philip Schaff (New York: Scribner's, 1907), I, p. 327.

36 See Jerome's "Preface to Job," in *A Select Library of Nicene and Post-Nicene Fathers of the Church*, Second Series, ed. Philip Schaff and Henry Wace (Grand Rapids, Mich.: William B. Eerdman's, 1890), VI, p. 488.

37 "Preface to the Book of Hebrew Questions," ibid., p. 486.

38 *City of God*, XVIII. 43, trans. Gerald Walsh et al. (Garden City, N.Y.: Image Books, 1958), pp. 414–15.

39 *Confessions*, XII. 18, trans. Rex Warner (New York: New American Library, 1963), p. 300.

40 *On First Principles*, p. 259.

41 *Confessions*, XII. 24, p. 305.

42 Trans. R. B. Tollinton, *Selections from the Commentaries and Homilies of Origen* (London: Macmillan, 1929), p. 54.

43 "On the Birth of Abel and the Sacrifices Offered by Him and by His Brother Cain," 163. I. 2 (Loeb trans.).

44 The treatise has been translated by G. F. Hourani, *Averroës and the Harmony of Religion and Philosophy* (London: Luzac, 1961), and is available in *Philosophy in the Middle Ages: The Christian, Islamic, and Jewish Traditions*, ed. Arthur Hyman and James J. Walsh (Indianapolis, Ind.: Hackett, 1973), pp. 287–306. See p. 293: "The reason why we have received in Scripture texts whose apparent meanings contradict one another is in order to draw the attention of those who are well grounded in science to the interpretation which reconciles them." Cf. Maimonides, *Guide of the Perplexed*, I, pp. 17–20.

45 *Philosophy in the Middle Ages*, p. 300. See also p. 293: "The Reason why we have received a Scripture with both an apparent meaning and a hidden meaning lies in the diversity of people's natural capacities and the difference of their innate dispositions with regard to assent."

46 *Guide of the Perplexed*, I, pp. 6–7.

47 *A Compend of Luther's Theology*, ed. Hugh Thomas Kerr (Philadelphia: Westminster Press, 1943), p. 4.

48 *Luther's Works*, II: *Lectures on Genesis*, 6–14, ed. Jaroslav Pelikan and Daniel E. Poellot (St. Louis: Concordia, 1970), pp. 150–65 ("Concerning Allegories").

49 *The Anti-Nicene Fathers*, IV, p. 399.

50 Quoted by Basil Hall, "Biblical Scholarship: Editions and Commentaries," in *The Cambridge History of the Bible*, ed. S. L. Greenslade (Cambridge: Cambridge University Press, 1963), III, p. 51.

51 *Luther's Works*, XXXIX, ed. Eric W. Gritsch (Philadelphia: Fortress Press, 1970), p. 178 ("Answer to the Hyperchristian, Hyperspiritual, and Hyperlearned Book by Goat Emser in Leipzig—Including Some Thoughts Regarding His Companion, the Fool Murner" [1521]). An earlier edition gives this more lucid translation: "The Holy Spirit is the plainest writer and speaker, and therefore His words cannot have more than one, and that the very simplest, sense, which we call the literal, ordinary, natural sense. That the things indicated by the simple sense of His simple words should signify something further and different, and therefore one thing should always signify another, is more than a question of words or of language." See *Works of Martin Luther* (Philadelphia: A. J. Holman, 1930), III, p. 350.

52 *Werke* (Weimar Edition, 1897), VII, p. 97 ("Assertio omnium articulorum M. Lutheri per bullam Leonis X novissimam damnatorum" [1520]).

53 *Works of Martin Luther*, III, p. 347. See also *Luther's Works*, XXXIX, p. 176: "What kind of glosses do I add?"

54 See Beryl Smalley, *The Study of the Bible in the Middle Ages* (Oxford: Basil Blackwood, 1952), pp. 44–66. See esp. p. 56. See also Beryl Smalley, "The Bible in Medieval Schools," in *The Cambridge History of the Bible*, ed. G. W. H. Lampe (Cambridge: Cambridge University Press, 1969), II, pp. 197–220.

55 See Rosamond Tuve, *Elizabethan and Metaphysical Imagery* (Chicago: University of Chicago Press, 1947), pp. 30–32.

56 *Luther's Works*, II, pp. 151–52.

57 Ibid., XXXIX, p. 355.

CHAPTER 2

1 *Letters from Petrarch*, trans. Morris Bishop (Bloomington: Indiana University Press, 1966), p. 198. The quotation is from a letter to Boccaccio dated October 28, 1366.

2 *Institutio oratoria*, 10.2. 8, 10–13, trans. Michael Winterbottom, *Ancient Literary Criticism: The Principal Texts in New Translations*, ed. D. A. Russell and Michael Winterbottom (Oxford: Clarendon Press, 1972), p. 401.

3 *Works of Geoffrey Chaucer*, ed. F. N. Robinson (Boston: Houghton Mifflin, 1957), p. 479.

4 Erich Auerbach, *Literary Language and Its Public in Late Antiquity and in the Middle Ages*, trans. Ralph Mannheim (New York: Pantheon Books, 1965), p. 65.

5 *Petrarch: The First Modern Scholar and Man of Letters*, trans. James Harvey Robinson (1898; reprinted ed., New York: Putnam, 1970), p. 193.

6 *An Essay of Dramatic Poesy and Other Critical Writings*, ed. John J. Mahoney (Indianapolis, Ind.: Bobbs-Merrill, 1965), p. 96. Further references to this preface and also references below to the *Essay of Dramatic Poesy* will be to this edition.

7 *Works*, ed. H. T. Swedenberg, Jr. (Berkeley: University of California Press, 1972), II, p. 59 (lines 183–86).

8 See Plutarch, *Theseus*, 20. 1–2. See also J. A. Davison, "The Transmission of the Text," in *A Companion to Homer*, ed. Alan J. B. Wace and Frank H. Stubbings (London: Macmillan, 1963), pp. 215–33. See esp. p. 221: "There is no reason to suppose that the reading public in the late fifth century (or for two centuries after that) had any feeling that such a thing as

a 'correct' text of the poems was desirable, much less attainable, or that it was the book-sellers' business to provide it."

9 Witness the *Glossa Ordinaria*, among endless examples. See Beryl Smalley, *The Study of the Bible in the Middle Ages* (Oxford: Basil Blackwood, 1952), pp. 44–66. The problem of writing and textuality that is raised here is treated in detail in the next chapter.

10 Trans. Eugene Vinaver, who quotes the passage in *The Rise of Romance* (Oxford: Clarendon Press, 1971), p. 16. See *Les Lais de Marie de France*, ed. Jean Rychner (Paris: H. Champion, 1966), p. 2:

> Custume fu as ancïens,
> Ceo testimoine Precïens,
> Es livres ke jadis feseient,
> Assez oscurement diseient
> Pur ceus ki a venir esteient
> E ki aprendre les deveient,
> K'i peüssent gloser la lettre
> E de lur sen le surplus mettre. [lines 9–16]

This passage has drawn the attention of many scholars. See especially Leo Spitzer, "The Prologue to the *Lais* of Marie de France and Medieval Poetics," *Modern Philology* 41 (1943): 96–102, but esp. pp. 101–02 on Priscian as the type of grammarian or *'homo literatus.'* See also D. W. Robertson, Jr., "Marie de France, *Lais*, Prologue, 13–16," *MLN* 64 (1949): 336–38, and Mortimer J. Donovan, "Priscian and the Obscurity of the Ancients," *Speculum* 36 (1961): 75–80.

11 *Literary Language and Its Public*, p. 190.

12 *Arthurian Romances*, trans. W. W. Comfort (London and New York: Everyman's Library, 1914), p. 1. The French text is from Chrétien, *Sämtliche Werke*, ed. Wendelin Foerster (Halle: M. Niemeyer, 1884), III, p. 1. See also Michelle Freeman, *The Poetics of translatio studii and conjointure* (Lexington, Ky.: French Forum, 1979).

13 *The Rise of Romance*, p. 30. See also pp. 33–52 for a discussion of *conte* and *conjointure*, and esp. p. 37: "It is, then, the art of *composition* in the etymological sense of the term that [Chrétien] seems to regard as the proper means of turning a mere tale of adventure into a romance, and it is upon this delicate art, which only a learned man can practise properly, that he wants the reader to focus his attention. At the same time, however, he does not want us to forget that conjointure is merely a method of dealing with the material; it is not a substitute for the conte, but something which a skilful poet can and must superimpose upon it. One element is to be added to the other, and the poet would defeat his purpose if he tried to suppress one in favour of the other."

14 *Arthurian Romances*, p. 91; *Werke*, I, p. 1 (lines 17–44).

15 *Parzival*, trans. Helen M. Mustard and Charles E. Passage (New York: Vintage Books, 1961), p. 65. See Wolfram, *Parzival*, ed. Gottfried Weber (Darmstadt: Wissenschaftliche Buchge-sellschaft, 1967), p. 97 (115.21–116.4).

16 *Italian Literature: Roots and Branches*, ed. Giose Rimanelli and Kenneth John Atchity (New Haven: Yale University Press, 1976), p. 211.

17 My indebtedness here is to Douglas Kelly, *"Translatio Studii*: Translation, Adaptation, and Allegory in Medieval French Literature," *Philological Quarterly* 57 (1978): 287–310.

18 *Truth and Method* (New York: Seabury Press, 1975), p. 454.

CHAPTER 3

1 René Descartes, *Meditations,* trans. Norman Kemp Smith, *Descartes' Philosophical Writings* (London: Macmillan, 1952), p. 209.

2 *Discourse on Method,* trans. Laurence LaFleur (Indianapolis, Ind.: Bobbs-Merrill, 1950), p. 2. It is hard to choose among English translations of the *Discourse.* I have used LaFleur's translation for two mildly arbitrary reasons: it is the most widely available and it is the most vernacular, particularly in contrast to the translation by Haldane and Ross (London: Cambridge University Press, 1911), whose Victorian locutions seem almost Latinate to American ears. I will not say (but who could not make the argument?) that LaFleur's translation is more faithful than any other English version to Descartes's vernacular purposes. Hereafter LaFleur's translation will be cited first in the text, followed by references to the French text, *Discours de la méthode,* ed. Etienne Gilson (Paris: Librarie Philosophique: J. Vrin, 1930), p. 2.

3 *Meditations,* trans. Laurence LaFleur (Indianapolis, Ind.: Bobbs-Merrill, 1960), p. 17, hereafter cited as *M.* This translation amalgamates three texts: "the second Latin edition of 1642 . . . , the first French translation of 1647 . . . , and the second French translation" of 1673 (p. vi).

4 Descartes loved these grottoed fountains, whose automata could not only move but could sing and dance as well. In his *Treatise on Man* (1633), trans. Thomas Steele Hall (Cambridge: Harvard University Press, 1972), Descartes wrote:

> And truly one can well compare the nerves of the machine I am describing to the tubes of the mechanisms of these fountains, its muscles and tendons to divers other engines and springs which serve to move these mechanisms, its animal spirits to the water which drives them, of which the heart is the source and the brain's cavities the water main. Moreover, breathing and other such actions which are ordinary and natural to it, and which depend on the flow of the spirits, are like the movements of a clock or mill which the ordinary flow of water can render continuous. External objects which merely by their presence act on the organs of sense and by this means force them to move in several different ways, depending on how the parts of the brain are arranged, are like strangers who, entering some of the grottoes of these fountains, unwittingly cause the movements that then occur, since they cannot enter without stepping on certain tiles so arranged that, for example, if they approach Diana bathing they will cause her to hide in the reeds; and if they pass farther to pursue her they will cause a Neptune to advance and menace them with his trident; or if they go in another direction they will make a marine monster come out and spew water into their faces, or other such things according to the whims of the engineers who made them. And finally when there shall be a rational soul in this machine, it will have its chief seat in the brain and will there reside like the turncock who must be in the main to which all the tubes of these mechanisms repair when he wishes to excite, prevent, or in some manner alter their movements. [22]

5 *Descartes: Philosophical Letters,* trans. Anthony Kenny (Oxford: Clarendon Press, 1970), p. 244.

6 In a letter to Lazare Meysonnier, January 29, 1640, Descartes gave this brief explanation:

> My view is that this gland is the principal seat of the soul, and the place in which all our thoughts are formed. The reason I believe this is that I cannot find any part of the brain, except this, which is not double. Since we see only one thing with two eyes, and hear only one voice with two ears, and altogether have only one thought at a time, it must necessarily be the case that the impressions which enter by the two eyes or by the two ears, and so on, unite with each other in some part of the body before being considered by the soul. Now it is impossible to find any such place, in the whole head, except in this gland; moreover, it is the middle of all the concavities; and it is supported and surrounded by the little branches of the carotid arteries which bring the spirits into the brain." [ibid., 258]

CHAPTER 4

1 "Semiology and Rhetoric," *Allegories of Reading: Figural Language in Rousseau, Nietzsche, Rilke, and Proust* (New Haven: Yale University Press, 1979), p. 10.

2 See Paul de Man, "Rhetoric of Persuasion (Nietzsche)," *Allegories of Reading*, pp. 119–31. These pages are a constant allusion to J. L. Austin. See Austin, "Performative-Constative," trans. G. J. Warnock, in *Philosophy and Ordinary Language*, ed. Charles E. Caton (Urbana: University of Illinois Press, 1970), pp. 22–54. See also Austin, "Performative Utterances," *Philosophical Papers*, ed. J. O. Urmson and G. J. Warnock (Oxford: Oxford University Press, 1979), pp. 233–52.

3 Trans. Paul de Man, who quotes the passage in "Rhetoric of Tropes (Nietzsche)," *Allegories of Reading*, pp. 105–06. See also Nietzsche, "On Truth and Lies in a Nonmoral Sense," *Philosophy and Truth: Selections from Nietzsche's Notebooks of the Early 1870's*, trans. Daniel Breazeale (Atlantic Highlands, N.J.: Humanities Press, 1979), pp. 84–89. See J. P. Stern, "Nietzsche and the Idea of Metaphor," in *Nietzsche: Imagery and Thought*, ed. Malcolm Pasley (Berkeley: University of California Press, 1978), pp. 64–82.

4 *Discourse on Method*, pp. 26–27. See above, chapter 3, note 2.

5 "Force and Signification," *Writing and Difference*, trans. Alan Bass (Chicago: University of Chicago Press, 1976), p. 28.

6 See, principally, "Differance," *Speech and Phenomena*, trans. David B. Allison (Evanston, Ill.: Northwestern University Press, 1973), pp. 129–60.

7 " 'Ousía' and 'Grammé': A Note to a Footnote in *Being and Time*," *Perspectives in Phenomenology*, ed. F. Joseph Smith (The Hague: Martinus Nijhoff, 1978), p. 86.

8 See "The Way to Language," *On the Way to Language*, trans. Peter D. Hertz (New York: Harper & Row, 1971), pp. 111–36.

9 *On the Way to Language*, p. 134. CF. *Being on Time*, trans. John Macquarrie and Edward Robinson (New York: Harper & Row, 1962), p. 209.

10 "The Ends of Man," trans. by several hands, *Philosophy and Phenomenological Research* 30 (1969): 53.

11 As explained in *Of Grammatology*, trans. Gayatri Chakravorty Spivak (Baltimore: The Johns Hopkins University Press, 1976), pp. 6–10ff.

12 *On the Way to Language*, p. 124.

13 Hence the alliance of rhetoric and semiology in de Man, who writes as follows:

> One of the most striking characteristics of literary semiology as it is practiced today, in France and elsewhere, is the use of grammatical (especially syntactical) structures conjointly with rhetorical structures, without apparent awareness of a possible discrepancy between them. In their literary analyses, Barthes, Genette, Todorov, Greimas, and their disciples all simplify and regress from Jakobson in letting grammar and rhetoric function in perfect continuity, and in passing from grammatical to rhetorical structures without difficulty or interruption. Indeed, as the study of grammatical structures is refined in contemporary theories of generative, transformational, and distributive grammar, the study of tropes and figures (which is how the term *rhetoric* is used here, and not in the derived sense of comment or of eloquence or of persuasion) becomes a mere extension of grammatical models, a particular subset of syntactical relations. [6]

14 "White Mythology: Metaphor in the Text of Philosophy," trans. F. C. T. Moore, *New Literary History* 6 (1974): 5–74, and esp. 56–60.

15 *Instituto oratoria*, II. xvii. 35–36 (Loeb trans.).

16 *Paideia: The Ideals of Greek Culture*, trans. Gilbert Highet, 2d ed. (New York: Oxford University Press, 1945), I, pp. 291–321.

17 *Dialogue and Dialectic: Eight Hermeneutical Studies on Plato,* trans. Christopher Smith (New Haven: Yale University Press 1980), p. 111.

18 *De Oratore,* III. xiv. 54 (Loeb trans.).

19 See Jerrold E. Seigel, "Ideals of Eloquence and Silence in Petrarch," *Journal of the History of Ideas* 26 (1965): 147–74; reprinted in Seigel, *Rhetoric and Philosophy in Renaissance Humanism* (Princeton, N.J.: Princeton University Press, 1968), pp. 31–62.

20 *The Poetry of Experience: The Dramatic Monologue in Modern Literary Tradition* (New York: W. W. Norton, 1957), pp. 9–37.

21 See G. W. Pigman III, "Versions of Imitation in the Renaissance," *Renaissance Quarterly* 33 (1980): 1–32.

22 In the dedicatory letter to the *Loci communes* Melanchthon says that he is "merely stating a list of the topics to which a person roaming through Scripture should be directed. Further, I am setting forth in only a few words the elements on which the main points of Christian doctrine are based. I do this not to call students away from the Scriptures to obscure and complicated arguments but, rather, to summon them to the Scriptures if I can." Trans. Wilhelm Pauck (Philadelphia: Westminster Press, 1969), p. 19. The point here is to draw the contrast between what is open and topical and that which is closed or systematically self-contained.

23 See Gerald L. Bruns, *Modern Poetry and the Idea of Language* (New Haven: Yale University Press, 1974), pp. 6–7, and passim.

24 *The Complete Poems and Plays, 1909–1950* (New York: Harcourt, Brace, 1958), p. 128.

25 See Geoffrey Hartman's discussion of this failure in *Wordsworth's Poetry, 1787–1814* (New Haven: Yale University Press, 1964), pp. 33–69.

26 *Selected Letters of Gustave Flaubert,* trans. Francis Steegmuller (New York: Harcourt, Brace, 1953), pp. 127–28.

27 "Crise de verse," *Oeuvres complètes* (Pléiade Edition), ed. Henri Mondor and G. Jean-Aubrey (Paris: Gallimard, 1945), p. 364.

28 "General Aims and Theories," *The Complete Poems and Selected Letters and Prose of Hart Crane,* ed. Brom Weber (Garden City, N.Y.: Anchor Books, 1966), p. 221.

29 "La Littérature et la droit à la mort," *La Part du feu* (Paris: Gallimard, 1949), p. 327: "L'idéal de la littérature à pu etre celui-ci: ne rien dire, parler pour ne rien dire." See *Modern Poetry and the Idea of Language,* pp. 189–205 ("Negative Discourse and the Moment before Speech").

30 *Of Grammatology,* p. 8. See also Derrida, "Violence and Metaphysics: An Essay on the Thought of Emmanuel Levinas," *Writing and Difference,* pp. 79–153, and esp. p. 147: "A speech produced without the least violence would determine nothing, would say nothing, would offer nothing to the other; it would not be *history,* and it would *show* nothing: in every sense of the word, and first of all the Greek sense, it would be speech without phrase." Violent speech, interestingly, is in this context rhetorical, whence Derrida is led to ask, "Is a language free from all rhetoric possible?"

31 *Rhetoric,* III. 1. 1404a: "as we have said, external matters do count for much, because of the sorry nature of an audience." Trans. Lane Cooper (Englewood Cliffs, N.J.: Prentice-Hall, 1932), p. 184. The characterization of the audience in the *Rhetoric* contrasts sharply with its characterization in the *Poetics,* where Aristotle speaks as if he were a member of the audience (*Poetics,* XIII. 1453a).

32 Ed. Edward Arber (London: A. Constable, 1906), p. 24.

33 *Blindness and Insight: Essays in the Rhetoric of Contemporary Criticism* (New York: Oxford University Press, 1971), p. 131. See Derrida, *Of Grammatology,* pp. 206–16.

34 *On the Origin of Language,* trans. John H. Moran and Alexander Gode (New York: Frederick Ungar, 1966), p. 11.

35 Ibid., pp. 13–15. De Man comments on this passage in "Metaphor (Second Discourse)," *Allegories of Reading*, pp. 151–52:

Rousseau's example of a man encountering another man is textually ambiguous, as all situations involving categorical relationships between man and language have to be. What happens in such an encounter is complex: the empirical situation, which is open and hypothetical, is given a consistency that can only exist in a text. This is done by means of a metaphor (calling the other man a giant), a substitutive figure of speech (*"he* is a giant" substituting for *"I* am afraid") that changes a referential situation suspended between fiction and fact (the hypothesis of fear) into a literal fact. Paradoxically, the figure literalizes its referent and deprives it of its para-figural status. The figure dis-figures, that is, it makes fear, itself a para-figural fiction, into a reality that is as inescapable as the reality of the original encounter between the two men. Metaphor overlooks the fictional, textual element in the nature of the entity it connotes. It assumes a world in which intra- and extra-textual events, literal and figural forms of language, can be distinguished, a world in which the literal and the figural are properties that can be isolated and, consequently, exchanged and substituted for each other. This is an error, although it can be said that no language would be possible without this error.

36 See Derrida, "White Mythology," and *Of Grammatology*, pp. 270–80. See also Heidegger, *Der Satz vom Grund* (Tübingen: Verlag Günther Neske, 1957), pp. 88–89: "Only within metaphysics is there the metaphorical." See Ronald Bruzina, "Heidegger on the Metaphor and Philosophy," *Cultural Hermeneutics* 1 (1973): 305–24.

37 See Jonathan Cohen, "On the Project of a Universal Character," *Mind* 63 (1954): 49–63.

38 *Of Grammatology*, pp. 24–25.

39 *An Essay on the Origin of Human Knowledge* (1756), trans. Thomas Nugent (Gainesville, Fla.: Scholars' Facsimiles, 1971), p. 313. See also pp. 319–20:

If God were to create an adult person, with organs so perfect, that the very first moment of his existence he enjoyed the full use of reason, this man would not meet with the same difficulties as we in the investigation of truth. He would invent no signs but in proportion as he experienced new sensations, and made new reflexions. His first ideas he would combine according to the circumstances in which he found himself; he would determine each collection of particular names; and when he wanted to compare two complex notions, he might easily analyze them, because he would meet with no difficulty in reducing them to the simple ideas of which he himself had framed them. Thus as he invented words only after he had framed his ideas, these would be always exactly determined, so that his language would not be subject to the obscurity and ambiguity which prevails in ours.

40 Ibid., p. 327. The point here is that the conception of invention as unprecedented or original discovery is a distinctive feature of the Enlightenment attitude.

41 "The Philosophy of Language in Revolutionary France," *Studies in Philosophy: British Academy Lectures,* ed. J. N. Findlay (London: Oxford University Press, 1966), p. 166.

CHAPTER 5

1 Among the stronger attempts at a study of character are W. J. Harvey, *Character and the Novel* (Ithaca, N.Y.: Cornell University Press, 1965); Charles C. Walcutt, *Man's Changing Masks: Modes and Methods of Characterization in Fiction* (Minneapolis: University of Minnesota Press, 1966); Martin Price, "The Other Self: Thoughts about Character in the Novel," *Imagined Worlds,* ed. Maynard Mack and Ian Gregor (London: Methuen, 1968), pp. 279–99;

Robert Scholes and Robert Kellogg, "Character in Narrative," *The Nature of Narrative* (New York: Oxford University Press, 1966), pp. 160–206.

2 *The Novels of Jane Austen,* ed. R. W. Chapman, 3d ed. (London: Oxford University Press, 1932), II, p. 261.

3 "The Compendium of 1819," *Hermeneutics: The Handwritten Manuscripts,* ed. Heinz Kimmerle, trans. James Duke and Jack Forstman (Missoula, Mont.: Scholars Press, 1977), p. 110.

4 I am grateful to Frances Ferguson for pointing out to me that it is no doubt Darcy's reserve that attracts Elizabeth's interest. Precisely because he is so difficult to understand, he challenges her conception of her abilities.

5 *Apology,* 30c.

6 See Schleiermacher, "The Compendium of 1819," *Hermeneutics,* p. 112. For Schleiermacher there is not only an objective and historical but also a subjective and "divinatory" component of hermeneutics, such that, "Before the art of hermeneutics can be practiced, the interpreter must put himself both objectively and subjectively in the position of the author" (p. 113). See Edgar Allan Poe's "The Purloined Letter," which turns upon precisely this hermeneutic principle: that which is secret or hidden is uncovered in virtue of "an identification of the reasoner's intellect with that of his opponent." See *The Complete Tales and Poems of Edgar Allan Poe* (New York: Vintage Books, 1975), p. 215. This is the story that contains the famous anecdote of the hermeneutic schoolboy, who says: " 'When I wish to find out how wise, or how stupid, or how good, or how wicked is any one, or what are his thoughts at the moment, I fashion the expression of my face, as accurately as possible, in accordance with the expression of his, and then wait to see what thoughts or sentiments arise in my mind or heart, as if to match or correspond with the expression' " (pp. 215–16). In other words, in order to understand another you must turn yourself into a version of him.

7 *The Poetry of Experience: The Dramatic Monologue in Modern Literary Tradition* (New York: W. W. Norton, 1957), p. 79.

CHAPTER 6

1 *The Sermons and Devotional Writings of Gerard Manley Hopkins,* ed. Christopher Devlin, S. J. (London: Oxford University Press, 1969), p. 157; cited hereafter as *S*. References to Hopkins's writing will be to this volume, and to the following: *The Poems of Gerard Manley Hopkins,* 4th ed., ed. W. H. Gardner and N. H. McKenzie (London: Oxford University Press, 1967), cited as *P; The Journals and Papers of Gerard Manley Hopkins,* ed. Humphrey House and Graham Storey (London: Oxford University Press, 1959), cited as *JP; The Letters of Gerard Manley Hopkins,* ed. Claude Colleer Abbott (London: Oxford University Press, 1935), cited as *LL,* i; *The Correspondence of Gerard Manley Hopkins with Richard Watson Dixon,* ed. Claude Colleer Abbott (London: Oxford University Press, 1935), cited as *LL,* ii; *Further Letters of Gerard Manley Hopkins Including His Correspondence with Coventry Patmore,* ed. Claude Colleer Abbott (London: Oxford University Press, 1956), cited as *LL,* iii.

2 See Hugh Kenner, *The Pound Era* (Berkeley: University of California Press, 1971), pp. 145–72.

3 The term "energy of being" has been used by a number of commentators—for example, by W. H. Gardner in his Introduction to *Poems and Prose of Gerard Manley Hopkins* (Baltimore: Penguin Books, 1953), p. xx; and J. Hillis Miller, *The Disappearance of God: Five Nineteenth-Century Writers* (New York: Schocken Books, 1965), p. 289.

4 See *The Notebooks of Samuel Taylor Coleridge,* ed. Kathleen Coburn (New York: Bollingen, 1961), II, 1145, 17.19; and Newman, "Implicit and Explicit Reason," in *Philosophical Readings in Newman,* ed. James Collins (Chicago: Henry Regnery, 1961), p. 110.

5 *Vorlesungen über Naturphilosophie* (Leipzig: Veit, 1902), p. 163.

6 *Miscellaneous Scientific Papers,* ed. W. J. Millar (London: Charles Griffin, 1881), pp. 208–09.

7 See N. R. Hanson, "The Dematerialization of Matter," in *The Concept of Matter,* ed. Ernan McMullin (Notre Dame, Ind.: Notre Dame University Press, 1963), pp. 549–61.

8 See Charles Coulston Gillipsie, *The Edge of Objectivity: An Essay in the History of Scientific Ideas* (Princeton: Princeton University Press, 1960), pp. 352–405; Ernst Cassirer, *The Problem of Knowledge: Philosophy, Science, and History since Hegel* (New Haven: Yale University Press, 1950), pp. 95–117; and William P. D. Wightman, *The Growth of Scientific Ideas* (New Haven: Yale University Press, 1951), pp. 268–317. D. W. Theobald, in *The Concept of Energy* (London: E. & F. N. Spon, 1966), gives an account of energy as a concept in physical science that is more or less accessible to the layman.

9 *Matter and Motion* (New York: Macmillan, 1920), p. 89.

10 *Allgemeine Chemie,* 2d ed. (Leipzig: Veit, 1893), II, p. 1014.

11 *Die Mechanik der Wärme* (Leipzig: W. Engelmann, 1911), p. 9. Quoted by Cassirer, p. 96.

12 Maxwell (1831–79) developed the electromagnetic theory of light and revolutionized physics with his concept of the electromagnetic field; Faraday (1791–1867) was perhaps the greatest experimental scientist of his day in electricity and magnetism (perhaps the last great scientist not to know mathematics: his experiments are recorded in prose); Cornot (1796–1832), Joule (1818–89), Mayer (1814–78), and Helmholtz (1821–94) all developed, independently of one another, a version of the law of conservation of energy. See Thomas S. Kuhn, "Energy Conservation as an Example of Simultaneous Discovery," in *Critical Problems in the History of Science,* ed. Marshall Clagett (Madison: University of Wisconsin Press, 1959), pp. 321–56. Clausius (1822–88) developed the concept of entropy.

13 See, for example, Tait's lectures on *Some Recent Advances in Physical Science, with a Special Lecture on Force* (London: Macmillan, 1885). The lectures were given, Tait says, "in the spring of 1874, at the desire of a number of my friends,—mainly professional men—who wished to obtain in this way a notion of the chief advances in Natural Philosophy since their student days." He adds: "The only specific requests made to me were that I should treat fully the modern history of Energy" (p. xxi).

14 *The Disappearance of God,* p. 289.

15 In his notes for the Long Retreat of 1880, Hopkins defined "Chance" as "the *energeia,* the stress, of the intrinsic possibility which things have" (*S,* 123).

16 See Peter S. Stevens, *Patterns in Nature* (Boston: Little, Brown, 1974), esp. pp. 3–16, 37–48, 79–131.

17 *The Collected Poems of Wallace Stevens* (New York: Alfred A. Knopf, 1964), p. 130.

18 *Miscellaneous Scientific Papers,* pp. 481–94. In this same entry on waves Hopkins writes: "The laps of running foam striking the sea-wall double on themselves and return in nearly the same order and shape in which they came. This is mechanical reflection and is the same as optical: indeed all nature is mechanical, but then it is not seen that mechanics contain that which is beyond mechanics"—namely, "instress" (*JP,* 252).

19 *The Uncreating Word: Romanticism and the Object* (Bloomington, Ind.: Indiana University Press, 1970), p. 92.

20 See "The Nature of Language," *On the Way to Language,* trans. Peter D. Hertz (New York: Harper & Row, 1971), pp. 57–108.

21 *Notebooks* (Princeton: Princeton University Press, 1973), III, 3401.34.

22 "Notes on the Characterization of a Literary Text," *MLN* 85 (1970): 768.

23 " 'Spirit' and 'Life' in Contemporary Philosophy," *The Philosophy of Ernst Cassirer,* ed. Paul Arthur Schilpp, trans. Robert Walter Bretall and Paul Arthur Schilpp (Evanston, Ill.: Northwestern University Press, 1949), p. 878.

24 References are to *The Prophetic Writings of William Blake,* I, ed. D. J. Sloss and J. P. R. Wallis (Oxford: Clarendon Press, 1926).

CHAPTER 7

1 I have used the first edition of *Kora in Hell: Improvisations* (Boston: The Four Seas Company, 1920), which seems to contain fewer errors and omissions than do subsequent editions. The first edition is a beautiful book; it would be good to have a facsimile of it.

CHAPTER 8

1 Hugh Kenner, "Joyce and Pyrrhonism," *Boston University Journal* 25, no. 1 (1977): 12–21, which becomes "Myth and Pyrrhonism" in *Joyce's Voices* (Berkeley: University of California Press, 1978), pp. 39–63; and Fritz Senn, "Book of Many Turns," *James Joyce Quarterly* 10, no. 1 (1972): 29–46, reprinted in *Ulysses: Fifty Years,* ed. Thomas F. Staley (Bloomington: Indiana University Press, 1974), pp. 29–46.

2 Thus Kenner: "That naturalistic core, precisely that, we have taken too much for granted." See "Molly's Masterstroke," *James Joyce Quarterly* 10, no. 1 (1972): 19–28, reprinted in *Ulysses: Fifty Years,* pp. 19–28. See also Kenner's review of Richard Ellmann's *Ulysses on the Liffey* (New York: Oxford University Press, 1972) in *James Joyce Quarterly* 10, no. 2 (1973): 279: It's not that Ellmann's is a bad book, Kenner says. "It's rather that just the dimension of *Ulysses* he most frequently seems on the point of opening up for us—precisely the natural substrate, real people in a real city—is constantly being thwarted by the schematic need to turn the people instantly into terms in a massive allegory."

3 I have no idea, of course, what either Kenner or Senn actually would say. What I'm saying is a construction (side by side) of the positions they appear to occupy, by no means rigidly. These positions seem to me the two most coherent and satisfying positions on *Ulysses* that Joyce criticism has given us.

4 Kenner, "The Rhetoric of Silence," *James Joyce Quarterly* 14, no. 4 (1977): 382–93.

5 "Nausicaa," in *James Joyce's Ulysses: Critical Essays,* ed. Clive Hart and David Hayman (Berkeley: University of California Press, 1974), p. 277.

6 Ibid., p. 278.

7 Ibid., pp. 301–02.

8 *The Arte of English Poesie* (Kent, OH: Kent State University Press, 1970; facsimile reprint of the London, 1906, edition), p. 166.

9 *The Counterfeiters: An Historical Comedy* (Garden City, N.Y.: Anchor Books, 1973), esp. p. 52.

10 *Wordsworth's Poetry, 1787–1814* (New Haven: Yale University Press, 1964), p. 39.

11 *The Stoic Comedians: Flaubert, Joyce, and Beckett* (Berkeley: University of California Press, 1962; 1974), pp. 30–66.

12 *James Joyce's Ulysses: Critical Essays,* p. 287.

13 Ibid., p. 290.

14 *The Pound Era* (Berkeley: University of California Press, 1971), p. 47.

15 Already in *Dublin's Joyce* (Boston: Beacon Press, 1962), p. 200, it is said that Stephen and Bloom possess "modes of consciousness comparable in their inadequacy"; and that "Bloom is a parody of the Enlightenment" (p. 217). This theme is continued in *The Stoic Comedians, The Counterfeiters, Joyce's Voices,* and so on. See also Kenner, "In the Wake of the Anarch," *Gnomon: Essays on Contemporary Literature* (New York: McDowell, Obolensky, 1958), pp. 171–88.

16 *An Essay Concerning Human Understanding,* ed. A. D. Woozley (New York: New American Library, 1964), p. 348.

17 *Dublin's Joyce,* pp. 2ff.

18 As explained in *The Counterfeiters,* esp. pp. 91–132 ("The Gulliver Game").

19 Senn, in *James Joyce's Ulysses: Critical Essays,* pp. 309–10, following Kenner, *The Stoic Co-*

medians, pp. 1–29, esp. p. 15: "The hack writer . . . is the supreme realist." See Kenner, *Joyce's Voices,* pp. 15–38.
20 This is, of course, a pun: "himself" refers to Gerty's father.
21 See Kenner, "The Cubist Portrait," in *Approaches to Joyce's Portrait: Ten Essays,* ed. Thomas Staley and Bernard Benstock (Pittsburgh: Pittsburgh University Press, 1976), pp. 171–84.
22 *The Arte of English Poesie,* p. 318.
23 See Kenner, "Circe," *James Joyce's Ulysses: Critical Essays,* pp. 341–62.
24 The ethical goal of skepticism is explained by Sextus Empiricus in *Outlines of Pyrrhonism,* I, pp. 7–10.
25 Bloom inadvertently (or by coincidence) alludes to "Chrysostomos" (*U*3) and "Kinch, the knife-blade" (*U*4), thus illustrating the principle that everyone in *Ulysses* is golden-mouthed, or silver-tongued, or speaks sharply to some point, since no one is able to say anything without producing a metaphor.

CONCLUSION

1 *Historia,* I, xx.1–xxii.4.
2 *Philosophical Grammar,* trans. Anthony Kenny (Berkeley: University of California Press, 1974), p. 167
3 *Kora in Hell: Improvisations* (Boston: The Four Seas Company, 1920), p. 12.
4 See *Being and Time,* trans. Peter D. Hertz (New York: Harper & Row, 1971), pp. 188–91.
5 Thus the philosopher is he whose *dianoia* is sufficient to carry him high enough so as to be able to see justice or temperance face to face (*Phaedrus,* 249c–250d).
6 See *Being and Time,* pp. 182–203, and especially p. 198; and *Truth and Method* (New York: Seabury Press, 1975), pp. 235–74.
7 In this sense the end of understanding would be, not knowledge as a mental possession, but truth as aletheia. In "The Origin of the Work of Art" (*Poetry, Language, Thought,* trans. Albert Hofstadter [New York: Harper & Row, 1971], p. 51) Heidegger writes:

> the hidden history of Greek philosophy consists in this, that it does not remain in conformity with the nature of truth that flashes out in the word *aletheia,* and has to misdirect its knowing and its speaking about the nature of truth more and more into the discussion of a derivative nature of truth. The nature of truth as *aletheia* was not thought out in the thinking of the Greeks nor since then, and least of all in the philosophy that followed after. Unconcealedness is, for thought, the most concealed thing in Greek existence, although from early times it determines the presence of everything present.

8 Here one should consult Heidegger's discussion of Van Gogh's painting of a pair of shoes in "The Origin of the Work of Art." See *Poetry, Language, Thought,* pp. 32–37, and esp. p. 36: "What happens here? What is at work in the work? Van Gogh's painting is the disclosure of what the equipment, the pair of peasant shoes, *is* in truth. This entity emerges into the unconcealedness of its being. The Greeks called the unconcealedness of beings aletheia. We say "truth" and think little enough in using this word. If there occurs in the work a disclosure of a particular being, disclosing what and how it is, then there is here an occurring, a happening of truth at work." In other words, what is disclosed in the work is not the image but the truth of what is represented, that is, the truth of the entity, namely the peasant shoes.
9 "The Origin of the Work of Art," p. 40: works in museums are "torn out of their own native sphere." And again:

> Well, then, the works themselves stand and hang in collections and exhibitions. But are they here in themselves as the works they themselves are, or are they not rather here as objects of the art industry? Works are made available for public and private art apprecia-

tion. Official agencies assume the care and maintenance of works. Connoisseurs and critics busy themselves with them. Art dealers supply the market. Art-historical study makes the works the objects of a science. Yet in all this busy activity do we encounter the work itself?

William Carlos Williams would have loved this paragraph. See *Kora in Hell,* pp. 11–12.

10 "The Origin of the Work of Art," p. 54, but esp. pp. 45–50 on the "earthly" nature of the work of art, which is, not the source, but the occasion or reason of the natural reserve of everything that is made of stone, color, language, and so on. It is this reserve—this ability of the work of art to withhold itself from understanding—that makes it possible for us to understand the nature of truth as aletheia or unconcealedness.

11 *Philosophical Papers,* ed. J. O. Urmson and G. J. Warnock, 3rd ed. (Oxford: Oxford University Press, 1979), p. 257.

12 Ibid., pp. 262–63. One can affirm a deep kinship between Austin (and Wittgenstein) and Heidegger on the primacy of situation in the task of understanding an expression, representation, or, indeed, anything at all. See Derrida, "Signature, Event, Context," in *Glyph,* Johns Hopkins Textual Studies, ed. Samuel Weber and Henry Sussman (Baltimore: The Johns Hopkins University Press, 1977), pp. 172–97. One can see in this remarkable essay how much Derrida remains a logician who is trying to undo the restraints of logic, and who is so concentrated in his attention—so impassioned or obsessed in this task—that he misses the genuine freedom that Austin offers him, which is to say the freedom that Derrida claims to desire.

13 Ibid., p. 271. See also pp. 267–68: "in a pretence there is preference for an element of the extempore, and in the situation that prompts it an element of emergency—there is at least something that has to be hidden. True, there are 'elaborate' pretences: but if there is too much of this, with making-up and dressing-up like an actor rather than a mimic or a diseuse, we begin to prefer to speak of, say, impersonation or imposture or disguise. To pretend to be a bear is one thing, to roam the mountain valleys inside a bearskin rather another."

14 *Philosophical Investigations,* trans. G. E. M. Anscombe (New York: Macmillan, 1958), p. 108 (337).

15 Ibid., p. 31 (66): "don't think, but look!"

16 See Jacques Derrida, *Spurs: Nietzsche's Styles,* trans. Barbara Harlow (Chicago: University of Chicago Press, 1979), p. 123.

17 "What Is a Text? Explanation and Interpretation," in David Rasmussen, *Mythico-Symbolic Language and Philosophic Anthropology* (The Hague: Martinus Nijhoff, 1971), p. 138.

18 *Spurs,* p. 129: "Everyone knows what 'I have forgotten my umbrella' means." See Wittgenstein, *Philosophical Investigations,* p. 142 (525): " 'After he had said this, he left her as he did the day before.'—Do I understand this sentence? Do I understand it just as I should if I heard it in the course of a narrative? If it were set down in isolation I should say, I don't know what it's about. But all the same I should know how this sentence might perhaps be used; I could myself invent a context for it." To which Wittgenstein adds: "(A multitude of familiar paths lead off from these words in every direction.)"

19 Hence Heidegger's distinction between thing and work in "The Origin of the Work of Art." See *Poetry, Language, Thought,* pp. 20–39. Of course, it should be added that, for Heidegger, a thing is not a brute object either.

20 *Truth and Method,* pp. 268–69.

NAME INDEX

Ackroyd, Peter, 26
Acton, H. B., 106
Akiba, R., 27
Alcibiades, 98–99
Ammonius, 184n10
Aquila, 33
Aristotle, 21, 83, 101, 111, 122, 125, 129, 190n31
Auerbach, Erich, 51
Augustine, 22, 34–38, 43, 184n13
Austen, Jane, 111–23
Austin, J. L., 178–79, 196n13
Averroës, 39–40

Bacon, Francis, 63–64, 68
Beck, Cave, 106
Blake, William, 125
Blanchot, Maurice, 103
Boccaccio, Giovanni, 47–48, 58–59
Borges, Jorge Luis, 45
Bridges, Robert, 136, 137

Cassirer, Ernst, ix, 137
Castiglione, Baldassare, 152
Chaucer, Geoffrey, 47–49, 57–59, 158
Chrétien de Troyes, 51–52
Cicero, 101, 146, 153
Clausius, Rudolf, 127
Coleridge, Samuel Taylor, 126, 133
Condillac, Etienne Bonnot de, 106, 191n39
Cornot, Sodi, 127
Crane, Hart, 103

Dante, 9–11, 54, 158, 175
Darwin, Charles, 127
Davison, J. A., 186–87n8
De Man, Paul, 88–107, 189n13, 191n35
Derrida, Jacques, 41, 94–97, 180, 190n30
Descartes, René, 1, 19, 63–87, 88–89, 92–95, 126, 188n4, 188n6
Dronke, Peter, 53
Dryden, 49–50, 53
Duchamp, Marcel, 158, 176

Eliot, T. S., 102, 157
Erasmus, Desiderius, 33
Ezra, 26

Faraday, Michael, 127
Ferguson, Frances, 192n4
Fontanier, Pierre, 97
Foucault, Michel, ix
Freud, Sigmund, 93, 140

Gadamer, Hans-Georg, 56, 101, 177, 181
Galileo, Galilei, 19, 74, 85
Ginzburg, Christian, 25
Gottfried von Strassburg, 51
Greene, Thomas, 55

Hartman, Geoffrey, 163
Heidegger, Martin, xiv, 17–18, 19–20, 45, 53, 95–97, 117, 123, 133, 177, 180–81, 813n1, 191n36, 195n7, 195n8, 195n9
Helmholtz, Hermann von, 127
Hesiod, 53
Hildegard of Bingen, 54
Homer, 53
Hopkins, Gerard Manley, 125–42, 193n15, 193n18
Horace, 10
House, Humphrey, 131
Humboldt, Wilhelm von, 125
Huxley, Thomas, 127

Ibsen, Henrik, 166

Jerome, 34–38, 43
Johnson, Samuel, 68, 163
Jonson, Ben, 49–50
Joule, James, 127
Joyce, James, 20, 160–74
Juvenal, 11

Kelly, Douglas, 186n17
Kenner, Hugh, 124, 156, 160–64, 194n2, 194n15
Kermode, Frank, 18

Langbaum, Robert, 101–02, 122
Leibniz, Gottfried Wilhelm von, 90, 94, 106
Locke, John, 164–65
Lodwick, Francis, 106
Lowell, Robert, 45
Lucilius, 11

197

SUBJECT INDEX